PRAISE FOR *HIDDEN GEOPO*

"*Hidden Geopolitics* rejects simplistic dichotomie.
state actors, between geopolitics and globalization. It is a nuanced and helpful exploration of ways to analyze and grapple with an ever more complex world."
—Anne-Marie Slaughter, Bert G. Kerstetter '66 University Professor Emerita of Politics and International Affairs, Princeton University

"I have been a strong proponent of taking territory seriously in the contemporary world. But that does not mean that we should ignore the ways in which territorial arrangements and the networks, flows, and assemblages associated with globalization are intertwined. *Hidden Geopolitics* makes a compelling case for their interpenetration. Drawing on different facets of his rich scholarly oeuvre, John Agnew has developed an account of remarkable historical and geographical depth that offers telling insights into how often-underappreciated geographical extensions of power have shaped, and continue to shape, the world in which we live."
—Alexander B. Murphy, University of Oregon

"At the moment the news is simultaneously filled with both the Great Power ambitions of Russia to regain a sphere of influence lost since the Cold War, as well as the importance of the SWIFT banking transfer network in the West's subsequent choking off of the Russian economy. Agnew's treatise on hidden geopolitics, existing between the national and the global, could not be more timely in thinking through contemporary geopolitics."
—Jason Dittmer, University College London

"Timely and incisive, Agnew once again rethinks the field of geopolitics by turning attention away from analyzing traditional actors—such as the territorial nation state—to consider instead the wealth of agents and processes involved in global capital flows. *Hidden Geopolitics* provides a conceptual toolkit to understand the geographical implications of offshore financing and associated illicit and licit flows of money. It will be an essential text for student and researcher alike, advancing our geographical and historical understanding of the making of the world in the twenty-first century."
—Alex Jeffrey, University of Cambridge

"This book is an erudite and broad-ranging exploration of the interplay between logics of the territorial state and globalization in varied forms and contexts. John Agnew convincingly argues that our failure to recognize how 'territorial determinism' and a 'world of flows'" coexist has undermined progress toward understanding and managing global political economy. *Hidden Geopolitics* points toward new realms of interdisciplinary research and should be prerequisite reading for those seeking to lead states, firms, and varied regulatory agencies in the twenty-first century."
—Alexander C. Diener, University of Kansas

"*Hidden Geopolitics* is an intellectual tour de force. Agnew brings a distinguished career of critical thinking about space and power to deciphering how contemporary world politics actually works. What we think of as geopolitics—territorial struggles between Great Powers—obscures the hidden and routine deployments of power over space by a great variety of non-state actors. Geopolitics and globalization are not opposites but entwined co-productions. In case studies of US border politics, Chinese narratives, US federalism, and credit-rating agencies, Agnew exposes the hidden ways in which geopolitics actually works to produce the messy, turbulent, and unjust world of politics we experience every day."
—Gerard Toal, Virginia Tech, Washington, DC

"John Agnew could not have written a more timely and important book. In the midst of a violent invasion of Ukraine by Russia, we need to understand not just the brutal logics of spatial expansionism and the domination of place but also the hidden and messy entanglements of finance, culture, business, energy, and electoral politics."
—Klaus Dodds, Royal Holloway University of London; author of *Border Wars*

Hidden Geopolitics

Governance in a Globalized World

John Agnew
University of California, Los Angeles

ROWMAN & LITTLEFIELD
Lanham • Boulder • New York • London

Executive Acquisitions Editor: Michael Kerns
Assistant Acquisitions Editor: Elizabeth Von Buhr
Senior Marketing Manager: Kim Lyons
Sales and Marketing Inquiries: textbooks@rowman.com

Credits and acknowledgments for material borrowed from other sources, and reproduced with permission, appear on the appropriate pages within the text.

Published by Rowman & Littlefield
An imprint of The Rowman & Littlefield Publishing Group, Inc.
4501 Forbes Boulevard, Suite 200, Lanham, Maryland 20706
www.rowman.com

86-90 Paul Street, London EC2A 4NE

British Library Cataloguing in Publication Information Available

Library of Congress Cataloging-in-Publication Data Available

ISBN 9781538158623 (cloth)
ISBN 9781538158630 (paperback)
ISBN 9781538158647 (epub)

∞™ The paper used in this publication meets the minimum requirements of American National Standard for Information Sciences—Permanence of Paper for Printed Library Materials, ANSI/NISO Z39.48-1992.

Contents

Preface viii

Acknowledgments xiii

Introduction 1

What Is Geopolitics? 3

Hidden Geopolitics Is Not New 7

Globalizing Governance 17

The Logic of the Book 20

Part I: Hidden Geopolitics

1 Geopolitics in a Globalized World 23

Geopolitics versus Globalization 24

Geopolitics of Globalization 27

Geopolitics of Development 31

Geopolitics of Regulation 34

Consequences for Hidden Geopolitics 37

Conclusion 38

2 Beyond Territorial Geopolitics 40

The United States from the Perspective of Land- versus Sea-Powers 41

Hegemony versus Empire 43

Globalization and the Current Global Geopolitical Order 46
US Hegemony and the Roots of Globalization 49
Conclusion 55

3 Making the Strange Familiar 56
Geographical Analogy and Familiarization 58
Why Balkan Analogies? 63
The Two Examples: Macedonian Syndrome and Balkanization 66
Conclusion 69

Part II: Geopolitics of Globalization

4 The Asymmetric Border: The US Place in the World and the Refugee Panic of 2018 72
The US Place in the World and the Asymmetric Border 75
The US Refugee Panic of 2018 80
The US Immigration "Debate" 85
Conclusion 87

5 Putting China in the World 89
"Familiar" Analogies and the Limited Geographic Origins of Thinking about World Politics 92
The Making and the Travels of Dominant Perspectives on World Politics 93
China's Hidden Geopolitics 95
Chinese Narratives on World Politics 96
The Politics of the Narratives about World Politics 100
Conclusion 104

Part III: Geopolitics of Development

6 Territorial Politics after the Financial Crisis 106
The Geography of the 2007–2008 Financial Crisis 108
Spatial Uncertainties of Contemporary Governance 110
World Cities versus State Territories 113
Devolution to Local and Regional Governments 116
Conclusion 119

7 Anti-Federalist Federalism **120**
Dualism versus Polyphony in Federal Governance 124
Donald Trump and National-Populism 127
The Retreat of the Federal Government since the 1980s 131
The Spatial Paradox of Trump's "Populism" and the COVID-19 Pandemic 133
Conclusion 135

Part IV: Geopolitics of Global Regulation

8 Global Regulation **138**
The Rise of Credit-Rating Agencies in Rating Sovereign Debt 140
How Are Ratings Done? 141
Private Authority and State Sovereignty 144
Geopolitical Consequences 145
Conclusion 146

9 Managing the Eurozone Crisis **148**
Popular Accounts of the Eurozone Crisis 149
Analyzing the Eurozone Crisis 152
What Is *Ordnungspolitik*? 157
The Limits of *Ordnungspolitik* in Variegated Capitalism 159
The Territorial Mismatch Thesis and the Eurozone Crisis 162
Conclusion 163

Part V: Hidden No More?

10 Conclusion **165**

References 171
Index 200
About the Author 209

Preface

Ihor Kolomoisky is a massively corrupt Ukrainian oligarch who, by means of US-registered shell companies hiding his identity, has become the largest commercial real estate owner in Cleveland, Ohio. The property was all purchased with money laundered from the bank that the oligarch used to run in Ukraine. But the buildings were purchased as fronts to hide ill-gotten gains and channel other laundered funds elsewhere. The buildings have been left to rot (Michel and Massaro 2021). Unfortunately, there is as yet no global institutional framework for regulating this sort of criminal activity and many states, including the United States, do not seem up to the task of investigating and challenging the massive flows of dubious offshore cash washing into and out of their jurisdictions. The geographic scope of the problem exceeds their individual reach (Dezenski 2021).

The same goes for numerous other contemporary problems from managing global pandemics and the circulation of satellites and debris in outer space; to global supply chains, the registration of most of the world's cargo vessels under flags of convenience that lead to low standards of maintenance and labor regulation; to drug and human trafficking, climate change, and the looting of natural resources (see, e.g., Krishnan 2021; Sun 2021; Hollinger 2021; Acemoglu 2021b; Solingen 2021; Meek 2021; Parkinson and Hinshaw 2021; Peltier 2021; Patrick 2021; Burgis 2015). Even national currencies are under challenge from cryptocurrencies and the decline of cash (Coy 2021). The much-vaunted nation-state, democratic and otherwise, big and small, is increasingly not up to the task of confronting and dealing with problems of planetary range even as many people still totally invest their identities in it (e.g., Gardels 2021).

The current world is filled with stories about flows of capital both licit and illicit that bring both costs and benefits to the places where the capital ends up and those it leaves behind (e.g., Zucman 2015; Obermayer and Obermaier 2016; Spiegelberger 2021; Michel 2021; Collins 2021; Vogl 2022). These are not primarily country-to-country flows but networked ones like those from Kyiv to Cleveland via the offshore tax haven Nicosia (in Cyprus) in the Kolomoisky story. Money makes the world go around, as the cliché would have it. But what it reveals is the extent to which the power bound up with that money—licit more than illicit—also makes for a geopolitics of influence and authority that is largely hidden when we think about the world entirely in terms of states, more particularly the Great Powers, and their relatively open competition over territory and spatial influence. The spatial dynamics of money/power among a myriad of actors rather than the fixity of states and their on-again-off-again banging up against one another in their supposed ineluctable desire for dominance over others of their kind is the present focus of analysis. This book is about taking seriously this "hidden geopolitics." Its progression has happened haphazardly and contingently, so there is no central committee of planners or single force behind the book's narrative. "Covert geopolitics," in that sense, organized by treasonous global cabals capturing "deep states," is conspiratorial nonsense. Nevertheless, there is a historicity and geography to the workings of hidden geopolitics over the past two hundred years or so that the book attempts to trace.

It is not as if the "globalization" that characterizes the contemporary world is a stable enterprise or an end-state that cannot be transcended as it currently operates. Indeed, globalization as the process of increased global economic interdependence has slowed markedly since the 2007–2008 global financial crisis and changes in manufacturing processes (such as the advent of 3D printing and distributed manufacturing) alongside increased questioning of the environmental costs of global supply chains may well produce a reterritorialization of many productive activities, albeit across a mosaic of distinctive localities rather than in terms of national economies per se (e.g., Livesey 2017; Okwudire and Madhyastha 2021). The increased tension between the growing need for global collective action on a wide range of issues (climate change, migration, global supply chains, etc.) and the popular pressures to try and rebuild political communities behind national borders is the "defining challenge" of the day (Pisani-Ferry 2021). But even under this new scenario, thinking about the world entirely in terms of interstate competition between the Great Powers misses much about how the world actually works (James 2021). Blaming foreigners may be a useful political strategy for American, Russian, and Chinese politicians (and other national populists) who cast themselves in a messianic light, but it is problematic when it comes to understanding how the modern world has ever actually worked (e.g., Reich 2021).

Alongside material forces integrating the world across state borders is an increasingly potent planetary consciousness with deep intellectual roots in a number of cultural traditions on the part of significant numbers of people worldwide (e.g., Patomäki 2010). The idea of continental-territorial blocs undermining all of this in a return to the inter-imperial rivalry of the early twentieth century or the Cold War of the later years of that century (e.g., Micklethwait and Wooldridge 2022) misses the fact that across all of these epochs there was still considerable exchange between a host of actors beyond bloc boundaries. The modern world has never been either totally territorialized (as in this vision) or completely networked (as in oversimplified views of globalization) (Agnew 2018).

Recent world history has helped open up the examination of hidden geopolitics. Cataclysmic events like the collapse of the Soviet Union in 1991 and the 2007–2008 global financial crisis provided an opportunity to pose basic questions that usually go unasked during more "normal" times. If in the former case the story was largely one of a failure of the Soviet-style economy to keep pace with the global-capitalist one, in the latter it was put down to savings imbalances between countries or risky financial innovations such as credit-default swaps. Political processes, the legitimation crisis of the state within the Soviet Union in the first case and the US government's obsession with encouraging mass homeownership in the second, are typically introduced as simply functional or instrumental to the economic (the state as the ruling committee of the bourgeoisie, etc.) rather than as a whole series of sites of political contestation. The annunciation of the economic as especially causal has been possible because the social and the political have become defined as somehow "unnatural" or derivative when contrasted to the economic. The end of the Cold War, in particular, could be seen as the closing down of an "unnatural" period in which geopolitics had temporarily trumped economic competition between states and their business interests. Natural order would be restored. Similarly, those perspectives that see an emerging globalization as terminal for any state role also see the eclipse of geopolitics as likewise complete.

It is common, then, to see geopolitics and globalization as opposites with respect to how the world works. Of the six narratives about globalization identified by Roberts and Lamp (2021), for example, only their Global Threats narrative seems even partly attuned to the complexities of a world in which states, businesses, and the planet are locked in a substantial embrace differentially, and not just state-by-state, across the world. The other narratives (the establishment, the left populist, the right populist, the corporate, and the geoeconomic) portray globalization as operating through and across states with varying emphases on how it works but with some winning and others losing as businesses mediate the entire enterprise. They differ mainly in terms of whose "side" they are on in this process: workers in the United

States, peasants in China, businesses, which Great Power, etc. As Roberts and Lamp (2021) argue, a more kaleidoscopic view is necessary to get beyond the world-political-map corset into which the typical narratives are squeezed and yet which somehow is still held mysteriously to portend a less state-centered world. If geopolitics is still associated primarily with geographical determinism (relative location on the earth's surface, sea versus land power, territorial size, etc.) in channeling the universal urge for territorial expansion on the part of all states, globalization is seen as creating an interdependent and increasingly "flat" world in which flows of goods, people, and capital displace the territorialized world of inter-imperial rivalries that characterized the past.

Yet historically such a clear-cut distinction makes little sense. Certainly, the period from 1875 until 1945 can be reasonably characterized as one in which inter-imperial rivalry tended to win out over open trade and so on and the Cold War from 1945 until 1991 involved a major geopolitical fracture between a relatively free-flowing West and a relatively autarkic East. Classical geopolitics—with such ideas as the control over a Eurasian heartland as the key to global command—developed in the first period, in the late 1800s, and represented an effort at justifying imperialism in naturalistic terms of space and race. The threat posed by potent foreigners when they encroached on your crucial space was its leitmotif. But right across the periods in question there were systematic efforts on the part of some governments, particularly in Britain and the United States, and businesses looking to expand beyond home shores, to reduce and remove barriers to trade and investment. These increasingly came to fruition during the Cold War and since the 1990s have expanded to include much of the world. Globalization, then, was *incipient* within the territorialized conflicts of the twentieth century. It was not opposite but in fact a strategic option pursued by some actors within the confines of the geopolitical conflicts that wracked the century. The chessboard approach has been increasingly challenged and supplemented by the networked connections that we associate with globalization (Slaughter 2018). This is the world made by and for hidden geopolitics.

So the presumed superordinate status of the economic to the merely "political" is definitely part of the problem with most understandings of globalization. But the other part has been the definition of geopolitics as restricted solely to interstate competition largely over territory. The dominant image of globalization today relies on seeing something purely economic totally eclipsing the purely geopolitical. The past few years since the financial crisis of 2007–2008 have seen evidence for a renewal of the older style geopolitics of inter-imperial rivalry, for example in the Russian annexation of Crimea and parts of Georgia and saber rattling about and then invasion of Ukraine and in Iranian moves via surrogates and military interventions across the Middle East. Of course, even at the height of globalization, invasions and interventions, such as that of the United States in Afghanistan and Iraq, suggested that military coercion and territorial expansion had not been eliminated from world politics. That these ended badly for the United States is poor consolation. The United States has also used its geopolitical position as a sponsor of globalization for narrower geopolitical ends such as in the use of trade and financial sanctions against its putative "geopolitical" adversaries such as Iran, Russia, China, and North Korea. That territorial expansion and spheres of influence may be increasingly difficult to achieve does not mean that political leaders no longer aspire to try, if only to cover up for domestic problems as much as to acquire resources or display status. Border disputes over policing and demarcation can stir up nationalist mobilization as was obvious in the United States when Trump was president and in Russia as President Putin attempted to use Ukraine as a whipping boy in his rebuilding of a Russian Empire. Perhaps only military failures, such as those of the United States in Afghanistan and Iraq and putatively that of Russia in Ukraine, will seriously undermine pursuing the "right to dominate" (Paris 2020) and the "return of conquest" (Fazal 2022). The self-declared exceptionalism and apparent "messianism" of the United States and Russia (and increasingly China) in relation to the rest of the world is a continuing challenge to true global cooperation (e.g., Agnew 2017a).

This book, then, is about seeing the continuing relevance of the term geopolitics in the sense of interstate competition, particularly that between the so-called Great Powers, but more particularly in extending its usage into the world of globalization. The book is built on a series of studies from the past twelve years or so that together offer a portrait of the world from a geopolitical perspective that goes well beyond the typical usage of that phrase. I label this "hidden geopolitics" simply because it escapes the gaze of those either enamored of the older classical meaning or who do not see anything geopolitical about globalization.

The idea for putting this book together came about as a result of an invitation from Sami Moisio of the University of Helsinki to write a chapter for a book he was editing that challenged the notion that "geoeconomics" was straightforwardly replacing "geopolitics" in the post–Cold War era. A number of others such as Felicity Nussbaum, Heriberto Cairo, Michael Shin, David Kaplan, Scott Stephenson, Anssi Paasi, Patricia Chiantera-Stutte, Matt Zebrowski, Ulrich Oslender, Chengxin Pan, Tom Narins, Steve Rolf, Luca Muscarà, Heather Agnew, and Mat Coleman and many colleagues at UCLA have contributed more than they can know to the work at hand. I absolve them of any responsibility for the final product.

John Agnew
Santa Monica, California

Acknowledgments

I would like to acknowledge the following for permission to reproduce parts of works I have published previously:

Revista Tamaios (Federal University of Rio de Janeiro) for "Geopolitics in an era of globalization," 11, 2 (2015): 4–21, for chapter 1. This is an Open Access journal.

Storia del Pensiero Politico (Il Mulino) for "US hegemony and the limits to territorial geopolitics in the twentieth century," 4, 3 (2015): 407–26, for chapter 2.

Geographical Review (American Geographical Society of New York and Taylor and Francis) for "Making the strange familiar: Geographical analogy in global geopolitics," 99, 3 (2009): 426–43, for chapter 3; "The asymmetric border: The US place in the world and the refugee panic of 2018," 109, 4 (2019): 507–26, for chapter 4; and "Anti-federalist federalism: American 'populism' and the spatial contradictions of US government in the time of COVID-19" (2021), online first, for chapter 7.

"Putting China in the World" (chapter 5) was originally presented as a paper at a Conference on China and International Relations Theory at Deakin University in Melbourne, Australia, on 18 March 2016 organized by Chengxin Pan and Emilian Kovalski.

Spatial Justice and the Irish Crisis (edited by Gerry Kearns, David Meredith, and John Morrissey) for "Territorial politics after the global financial crisis" (Royal Irish Academy, 2014), for chapter 6.

Geopolítica(s) (Complutense University, Madrid) for "'Baja geopolítica': Agencias de calificación crediticia, la privatización de la autoridad y nueva soberanía," 3, 2 (2012): 171–83, for chapter 8; and "La geopolítica de la austeridad europea: 'Ordnungspolitik' y la sombra del modelo económico alemán sobre la crisis de la Eurozona," 6, 2 (2015): 179–200, for chapter 9.

Introduction

We live in a world in which huge companies operate worldwide and generate many of their revenues and have a huge share of their assets beyond the shores of their nominal home countries (AEI 2018). Think of Apple, Google, Facebook, and Tesla, to name just four from the United States, and Nestle, HSBC, Glencore, and Unilever headquartered elsewhere. Yet we confuse the "interests" of those businesses with their home countries as if they were agents of the latter. At the same time, many national governments are in the business of selling citizenship to high earners (Mavelli 2018) and have lost much of their capacity to manage crises like the 2020–2021 global pandemic (Jones and Hameiri 2021a). They are also in competition for investment income and sometimes, as a result, paying for public goods must be sacrificed for lower corporate taxes. Some national governments are obvious fronts for extractive elites looting resources and then investing or spending the proceeds well beyond state borders. To listen to recent geopolitical discourse across the world one would think that none of this counts for much at all. It is all about some sort of anonymous "economics" visited upon us exogenously without any connection to the world of politics and its essential geopolitical roots in a world of competing states that does not admit to the geopolitical potency of actors other than states whatsoever.

Much contemporary political rhetoric concerns oppositions such as that of "nationalism versus globalism," as reflected in the basic campaign slogan of Donald Trump in 2016 of "America First," and claims such as "Taking back control," as in the referendum campaign of the same year in favor of Britain leaving the European Union. They represent *implicit* geopolitical positions about the relative spatial distribution of power and authority, yet are rarely understood in these terms (Abrahamsen et al. 2020). They are more typically seen as simple reflections of a world in which either national sovereignty or its demise will prevail, as if it has always been a question of either/or, one or the other (Agnew 2018). States should be fully autonomous or other states will take over. Understanding the world in its complexity takes a backseat to making sure "your" state remains "secure" or climbs the global hierarchy. At the same time, the fact that globalization, for example, in the sense of a world increasingly integrated by flows of goods, capital, and people, yet by no means that new, is itself the outcome of powerful states and other actors (multinational businesses, banks, and so on) finding significant advantage in a more integrated world is forgotten. Language inherited from previous epochs of inter-imperial competition and the Cold War is recycled to produce satisfyingly familiar scenarios, notwithstanding their irrelevance to the central dilemmas of the time (see chapter 3).

The roots of the recent phase of globalization since the 1970s lie in the profit crisis of many businesses, *not* in inter-state competition, even though it was enabled, among other things, by systematic reductions in import tariffs, the abandonment of a fixed exchange-rate system for floating rates, and the removal of most capital controls on the part of the United States and other governments (see chapter 1). The fact that much of the employment loss in manufacturing industries in the United States is down to the substitution of technology for labor and that much of the increases in income and wealth inequality in the United States are due to dramatic shifts in income tax policy are ignored for an emphasis on "China" (or Mexico or some other foreign country) "stealing" the jobs and leaving behind the working classes of the previously affluent West. Never a word is heard from the state-obsessed about business disinvesting or the policies actively pursued by national governments on its behalf. Thinking about the world solely in terms of states as its singular actors not only misses much about what makes the world go around it is also positively misleading in terms of crafting political responses.

Taken together, however, different spatial fields, such as the national and the global, are not in opposition, based on utterly separate actors and practices, but define overlapping or transversal fields of power in which there is never a strict separation of one scale or level from others, such as the domestic from the international or the subnational from the national (Bigo 2011, 2016). The dialectical geography of global capitalism is not readily reducible to states and their "capitals" (business interests) simply banging up against one another. Think, for example, of how World War II and the Cold War essentially created the basis for a more powerful federal government in the United States as external threats justified increased national-governmental action domestically (Gerstle 2015) or the ways in which US military interventions around the world have returned to the streets of the country in the form of the policing strategies designed for "counterinsurgency" but now directed putatively at US citizens (e.g., Schrader 2019). Meanwhile, the increased competition for mobile capital has put all states, including the United States, and its subnational units, on notice that to attract investment they must adjust their tax and industrial policies or face marginalization (Cerny 2010; Genschel and Seelkopf 2015). The international thus returns back home with a vengeance.

The problem is that the complex transversal geography of power has been neglected because the word that comes first to mind in describing that—geopolitics—has been either excessively restricted in its meaning to the direct effects on politics of the earth's physical geography or lost much meaning at all when used synonymously with words like domination and supremacy on the part of so-called Great Powers. It is also intimately associated with "reason of state" and the "high" politics of strategic foreign policies when much of what moves the world geopolitically is in fact the everyday workings of actors in different places relating across terrestrial space, a sort of "low" but hidden "geopolitics." This book is about recapturing the term in this way and putting it to use as a way of exploring how the geography of power works both globally and nationally to structure and govern the workings of the world's political economy. It is qualified by the word "hidden" in the title to draw attention to the extent to which this usage differs from others and because it often operates silently rather simply publicly or performatively.

Whether hidden geopolitics always works to the betterment of the world as a whole is something else again. That said, we obviously must first understand the way the world actually works if we wish to change it. "Current reality," not some idealized version of the world as it was in the past, should be the guide. Yet it is historical analogies based on a world in structural inertia that tend to be the guide to practice, complete with "predictions" about the future based on the past, rather than a focus on making the future with the materials at hand (Agnew 2019a). This is not to say that competitive Great Power politics somehow counts for nothing or that territorial disputes such as those involving Israel and the Palestinians or China and Taiwan, are passé. Far from it: much of what goes for hidden geopolitics in the workings of globalization and in the expansion of modes of governance beyond states strictly defined is rooted in the actions of powerful states and their governments. At the same time, powerful states continue to view the world in combative "us versus them" terms, even as they perhaps minimize direct military competition as such (e.g., Rid 2019; Leoni 2021). Global complexity, however, is not easily reduced to this alone. That is one of the prime messages of this book.

WHAT IS GEOPOLITICS?

Historically, the word "geopolitics" came to stand for the explicit conduct of foreign policies that are unsentimental, based in the "realities" of the world's physical geography and the singular "interests" of the states into which the world is divided, particularly the militarily most powerful of them, and designed as part of grand strategies that can replace the mere pragmatism and political maneuvering that prevail without geopolitical insight. The word itself was invented in 1899 as part of a normative approach to world politics in which the geo- (facts of relative location to land and sea, etc.) would forever determine the politics. That what mattered had to be disclosed by the divining hand of the geopolitician suggests how much its claims to determinism were duplicitous. Yet, and despite this, the term has long taken on something of a life of its own. Its implicit claim to prescience, using geopolitical claims to predict what will happen, has been one of its main attractions. Beyond this, perhaps the one feature of its definitions that all shared until recently has been a close association with taken-for-granted ideas about the pursuit of domination and supremacy on the part of the so-called Great Powers. This is the so-called modern geopolitical imagination reflecting the worldview of the era of inter-imperial rivalry in the late nineteenth and early twentieth centuries (Agnew 2003). Quite why the term should be required to conform to a meaning it acquired in the period that led up to World War I is never explained except in terms of a conceptual nominalism which insists on giving words essential meanings when such usage is increasingly anachronistic and out of touch with current realities (Agnew 2014). Revealingly, it is not clear, even in the period from 1900–1945 when the term had its greatest efflorescence, that it was much more than a rhetorical reference point to impose sense on Nazi policies in Eastern Europe rather than any sort of accurate guide to how any of the Great Powers actually worked.

Since then, but particularly after being rediscovered by Henry Kissinger and Richard Nixon in the 1970s and 1980s, "geopolitics" has become a term with multiple meanings suggesting heavyweight strategic insight, if usually on behalf of one country or another, or regarded as an atavistic term linking reactionary politics in the past to contemporary right-wing populism. Thus, and in the first respect, Alfred McCoy (2018) says, "Over the past century, countless scholars, columnists, and commentators have employed the term 'geopolitics' (or the study of global control) to lend gravitas to their arguments. Few, though, have grasped the true significance of this elusive concept. However else the term might be used, geopolitics is essentially a methodology for the management (or mismanagement) of empire." This term, he further claims, has been state of the art for empires for time immemorial. In the second respect, geopolitics refers more specifically to the revival of reactionary and aggressive nationalism and the rhetoric of spatial expansion and exclusion that came with it on a par with that of 1920s and 1930s Europe based in part on forgetting where that led. This is the usage intrinsic to Stefano Guzzini's (2012) edited volume on the revival of geopolitical imaginaries in Europe in the aftermath of the Cold War (*The Return of Geopolitics in Europe?*) and in a recent collection of essays under the compelling title *Geopolitical Amnesia* (Tjalve 2020) that tags geopolitics as "reemerging" after being rendered "illegitimate" in "Western political discourse" and "Unlike the paradigm of liberal governance, geopolitics is about the *explicit* parade of power and pride and exclusion: of the deliberate cultivation of nationalist particularism and ethnic exclusion" (Tjalve 2020, 4). It is all about open "antagonism and domination" (Tjalve 2020, 5).

In both respects geopolitics appears as a "scare" term connoting either managing empire without popular consent or the reappearance of a noxious right-wing past that disappeared when a non-geopolitical international balance of power or liberal global order came to reign. The presumption is that geopolitics is lost or disappears unless it is explicitly signaled by invocation of the word itself (as with McCoy and Guzzini) or by signs of the resurrection of what it once represented (as in Tjalve). In my view these are all narrow and ideological uses of the term. They have their uses, for sure. The point is not that they are false but that they are overstated and misleading. In fact, "geopolitics" and "the geopolitical" need not have such connotations at all. Indeed, a substantial literature has developed that insists on using this terminology because global politics is inherently geographical in terms of the constellations of powers distributed across different actors including states and imperial centers but including multinational businesses and regulatory authorities located in different places and acting differentially over terrestrial space. In this neutral usage, phrases such as "imperial geopolitics" and "fascist geopolitics" can be used to flag the more specific usages that currently claim a monopoly but which miss the more pervasive and omnipresent geopolitics *implicit* in all aspects of global politics now and in the past.

Historically, and down to the present day, there has never been anything "natural" about a world divided up into territorial states that are in potential perpetual conflict with one another for additional territory and spheres of influence upon which the claims of "classical geopolitics" rested. This is in fact a world that is provisional and precarious, reliant on presumptions about the permanence of territorialized statehood that miss the extent to which the world has never ever been without a wide range of actors other than states and that many states, if not most, are ineffectual is doing what they claim to do in "protecting" their inhabitants from dangerous adversaries. Many states as we know them are the outcome of secession from others, the product of the accidents of colonialism or settler displacement of existing populations, and the façade for ethnic/tribal/sectarian groups masquerading as something else so they can fly a flag in front of the United Nations Building in New York and field sports teams in international contests. Many of them continue to exist by mobilizing their populations to fear their own imminent collapse. Think of the various fruitless efforts to turn Afghanistan into a "nation-state" without attending to the fact that it has long been a congeries of fiefdoms and a capital city with a self-serving bureaucracy serviced by outsiders (e.g., Tett 2021). Yet there is a distinctive geography to the fragmented territoriality of world politics as it actually exists and the flows through networks (of trade, capital, messages, and people) that bind this world together. This is the world of hidden geopolitics. This focus attends to the messiness of the world rather than to simple nostrums based on its presumed simplicity.

Rather than lost and then resurrected (as in so-called geopolitical amnesia or the return of a land-and-sea geopolitics), therefore, most real-world geopolitics is hidden and taken for granted. The ideas and practices of politics are inherently geopolitical in the sense that geographical assumptions and imaginaries are inevitably at work in animating the everyday statements and acts that ground them (Agnew 2003). This is a geopolitics that is not just about domination by states in relation to one another but also about the workings of power across space in a number of different modalities and with a wide range of actors. It is also about what happens within states with respect to the spatial distribution of the benefits and costs of this or that structuring of power (centralized-decentralized, patronage-ideological, etc.). The understandings referred to earlier see power as invariably centered and geared toward some places and states dominating others or territorially restricting cooperation and popular inclusion. It is not that geopolitical hierarchy based on domination has been eclipsed. Far from it, as we saw with the way in which vaccines were first produced and then deployed during the 2020–2021 pandemic, with poorer countries without much if any access as richer ones monopolized the supply (Tam 2021).

But power is also stretched across mobilizing networks by different actors and involved in the making and organizing of subjects and their consciousness (Allen 2003). There is a geographical materiality to the world that limits and channels these mobilizing networks (Deudney 2000). New technologies of communication and movement can change the networks over time but this is where the relative isolation of some places, the density of infrastructures, and the constraints on flows of physical barriers such as canals, straits, and mountain ranges come into play. The impact on global supply chains by the blockage of the Suez Canal by one large container ship in March 2021 is a good example of this. In a different vein, the "home field advantage" of large US media companies like Google to US government intelligence (Buchanan 2020) can turn to a disadvantage when foreign hackers use the widely diffused surveillance technology in the United States against its private users, as with the ransomware attack on the Colonial Pipeline that delivers gasoline to the eastern part of the United States in April 2021 (e.g., Glenny 2021; McCormick and Murphy 2021). Yet the material constraints in question never operate directly. They take on significance within broader organizational, ideological, and strategic contexts that determine their relative efficacy. Thus conflicts arise over industrial resources such as oil or rare-earth minerals in the context of broader disputes over power and influence rather than in and of themselves (e.g., Stevenson 2021). The world, therefore, is not an even plane in terms of power potential. Yet neither is it simply about the machinations of Great Powers in pursuit of domination or global command on the global "chessboard."

Geopolitics, therefore, as the deployment of power over space, involves authority, seduction, manipulation, and assent as well as domination through coercion. It includes the capacity to build and deploy naval fleets and nuclear weapons but also the authority to impose business and national credit ratings, the organization of global trading and communication networks, the seduction of hearts and minds by advertisers and sales forces, the manipulation of social media to pursue propaganda and sales, the propagation of familiar if misleading historical analogies and logics (including territorialized geopolitical maxims), the evangelizing and organizing of religious doctrines and their organizational forms, and the creativity of agents, including mass publics, in challenging the common sense that they learned in the classroom or on the internet and then sometimes turning this into a basis for political action, however questionable the information this is founded on might be (e.g., Painter 2006; Allen 2020).

Hidden geopolitics, therefore, requires a different conception of power than the typical one in conventional geopolitics and mainstream studies of international relations. This must involve looking at the world from a different perspective. A plausible claim can be made that Machiavelli's and Gramsci's political theories, particularly the former's emphasis on political stagecraft or performance (particularly apparent in his *The Prince*) and the latter's emphasis on *egemonia* (enrollment by consent laced with the fear of shame and guilt), reflecting in part the Italian experience with the quotidian power of the Catholic Church, provide this, whereas elsewhere in post-Reformation Europe Hobbes's view of the state as a military-coercive Leviathan has tended to prevail and led to a different definition of hegemony as simple coercive power rather than the mixture of assent, theatricality, deception, seduction, and coercion that Gramsci had in mind with *egemonia*. It has been argued that Gramsci's perspective is more helpful in understanding the contemporary globalizing world created initially under US auspices than is the completely state-centered Hobbesian one that has always tended to prevail among most students of geopolitics (Agnew 2005).

HIDDEN GEOPOLITICS IS NOT NEW

The famous Enlightenment philosophers Montesquieu and Voltaire saw the ancient Macedonian Emperor Alexander the Great as having created in his day a "great revolution" by having changed the "face of commerce" across the world as then known. Writing in the eighteenth century, they understood "commerce" very widely: it referred not only to economic and intellectual exchange between places but also to the reciprocal relations and exchanges among peoples, states, and sexes. From their perspective, perhaps Alexander's greatest virtue was that even as he conquered he was held to have respected the customs of those he conquered and encouraged commerce rather than fostering the territorial stasis Enlightenment historiography associated with the Persian Empire. Alexander thus provided a model for eighteenth-century European empire-builders to emulate (Briant 2012).

In my view, this "geopolitical-economic" imagination was lost in the late nineteenth century with the rise of naturalized-territorialized understandings of interstate and imperial relations. Dominant powers subordinated other territorial units justified in terms of biological competition conditioned by relative location on the earth's surface. The word "geopolitics" emerged in that context. Since that time the term has had to contend with this original sin. Arguably, however, Montesquieu and Voltaire in their references to Alexander the Great had a somewhat different conception of geopolitics in mind: one in which reciprocity and market-exchange between places as well as the coerced redistribution of resources from colonies to homeland are at work. It is this broader sense of the word that has been revived over the past fifty years in the course of attempts at linking the global political structure of states, empires, and other political authorities to what can be called the "globalization era" (Agnew 2005). This book builds on previous publications (Agnew and Corbridge 1995; Agnew 2005) to provide a timely perspective on current events largely missing from contemporary mainstream debates about the world political economy.

The point here, however, is that even in a time of more territorialized interstate competition, such as the late nineteenth and early twentieth centuries, not all features of global politics and economic governance could be reduced to a struggle for territorial domination. The European territorial obsession, for its part, was based in the importation back home of mapping and partition strategies developed abroad under colonialism where who "owned" what was crucial (Branch 2010). In turn, with the decline of the European colonial empires as a by-product of world wars and nationalist-democratic struggles, "a people could only become sovereign as a state form" (Howland and White 2009, 10) even when "Populations were diverse and often divided, and territories had indistinct borders." Territorial sovereignty is always contingent, not absolute. This is lost on contemporary proponents of sovereigntism, "Taking Back Control," and "America First," who think entirely in terms of the opposition between their states, on the one hand, and the nasty world out there over the horizon, so to speak, on the other (e.g., Agnew 2019b, 2020b). There is nothing transversal about their "reality."

The longstanding contingency of sovereignty, however, has powerful roots in the hierarchical nature of the state system since the nineteenth century. Two aspects of this are worth attention. One is the way in which certain powerful states (and interest groups therein such as businesses) defined international law in terms of legal norms and practices that privileged private property rights worldwide irrespective of nominal jurisdiction where such rights might be located. The conversion of land for useful purpose through labor was the usual justification for imposing defined property rights in colonial territories where they had been collective or absent (Koskenniemi 2017, 362). The domestic territory was just too limited to facilitate the accumulation of resources and capital that colonial expansion could provide. When property disputes arose, they would be settled inevitably at the behest of the more powerful party with the investments and lawyers to enforce their claims. Sovereignty and property have thus always operated together to limit the sovereignty of some and expand it for others (e.g., Fitzmaurice 2014; Ince 2014). Ignoring the pairing of these two concepts/practices has long been a way of maintaining the fiction of equality between states. With the globalization of manufacturing production and financial services, intensifying since the 1970s, if hardly absent before, global centers such as New York and London have become centers for the enforcement of global property rights worldwide (see, e.g., Potts 2020). Corporations, Anglo-American corporate law firms, and trade associations have long exercised powers that are akin to those of states but often even greater in geographical scope and influence (Garrett 2008). Consider the contemporary powers exercised by social media, internet, and logistics companies (Facebook, Google, and Amazon, respectively) that often exceed those of the governments that putatively regulate them. This, of course, is not new. The trend to monopoly is inherent in capitalism unless arrested by antitrust and other governmental actions (Stoller 2019). Some actors are always more sovereign than others. It is just that their identities and origin-locations change over time.

The other root lies in the military-political domination of some states relative to others. This, of course, is what classical geopolitics is all about (plus a directing physical geography). States are neither born equal nor can a dominant position relative to others be equally available to all (Agnew and Corbridge 1995). This is particularly important in relation to domestic sovereignty (efficiently serving public goods to a domestic population equally across its territory), as defined by Krasner (1999), and the capacity to resist external interference (as in so-called Westphalian sovereignty). The long trajectory of invasions and interventions by the so-called Great Powers, from Britain, Germany, and France to the United States, Japan, and Russia, suggests how fictive it is to limit the exercise of sovereign powers to the borders of the colored blocs of space on the world political map. Sovereign powers can be projected over space through alliances and base networks that usually involve the extraterritorial jurisdiction of the distant power trumping the local one. Think of the power exercised by some currencies over the world economy, such as the US$, backed up by the alliances and military infrastructure of the United States worldwide. Such capacity is not easily reversed (e.g., Greene 2022). Sovereignty thereby travels over space for some but not for others (Agnew 2018). Territorial expansion by more militarily powerful states at the expense of others obviously still happens, but it must always be balanced against the much more serious economic-financial and legitimation consequences that claiming "historic" territory, "bringing home co-ethnics," punishing a foe, or controlling strategic resources can involve than was perhaps often once the case with the possibility of sanctions and other restrictions on cross-border financial and resource flows in a world where such flows are more vital than ever (e.g., Lane 2021; Appelbaum 2021; Skidelsky 2021; Graff 2021; Traub 2021; Ignatius 2021; Mulder 2022; *Economist* 2022; Dempsey et al. 2022; Davies 2022). Of course, Great Power elites who perceive their domains as under threat or facing decline could very well ignore such costs in cruelly spiting their enemies, particularly when they are borne by masses of people they literally could not care less about (e.g., Michta 2021 on Russia and China). But decline is not always visible from the inside or when demagogic leaders surround themselves with sycophants (King 2020; Gardels 2020; Blotcky 2021; Edsall 2021b).

Beyond these considerations about persisting interstate rivalries, there are also continuing powerful normative and administrative arguments for locking in some degree of sovereignty into territorial units with which people have familiarity (e.g., Koskenniemi 2011; Rodrik 2013). The recent "backlash against globalization," although it seems in practice to be as much about immigration and the challenge to putative cultural homogeneity that it poses, suggests that there is a substantial basis to what can be called "nation-statehood" (the combination of a social group with a national identity and a state apparatus), where it actually exists (e.g., Streeck 2017). States potentially do things for their populations that are not otherwise provided. In theory they provide security from domestic and foreign threats and dangers. This is often far from being the case. They often visit more violence on their "own" than do foreigners of any stripe. That said, supporting social-democratic efforts at providing decent basic incomes and public services for national populations are as much behind recent questioning of the distribution of the fruits of globalization as the primitive nativism of right-wing populism. Even in the United States, for long the industrialized country with the weakest welfare state, much of the recent political polarization is along social-democratic versus nativist lines (Kuper 2021). Be this as it may, and claims to territorial sovereignty have also frequently been used to frustrate rather than realize anything approaching democracy (Morefield 2005), we are all increasingly aware of emergent threats and challenges from climate change to human rights that cannot simply be addressed *solely* at the scale of the state. Regimes, both democratic and nondemocratic, suffer from difficulties in dealing with such issues because of time horizons involving elections or dynastic succession, questions of responsibility (or not) to mass publics who may be massively ill informed, and the low salience of many so-called global issues in relation to the urgent problems of everyday life (Latour 2016). The COVID-19 pandemic of 2020–2021 revealed these "difficulties" in excruciating detail in relation to travel bans, wearing face masks, organizing lockdowns, and sourcing/organizing vaccinations (Brilliant 2021).

The precise character of statehood and its relative significance in relation to global governance has varied historically according to the nature of the broader cultural-geopolitical order operative at a given time (Sassen 2006). In Agnew and Corbridge (1995), we argued for three epochs of geopolitical order beginning with the Congress of Vienna in 1815 and ending in 1875 (the Concert of Europe–British Geopolitical Order), the Geopolitical Order of Inter-Imperial Rivalry (1875–1945), and the Cold War Geopolitical Order (1945–1990). As of the early 1990s an emergent Global Geopolitical Order was in the offing (Agnew 2003) and for which there is still enormous continuing evidence. But this now seems in some eyes to be under challenge from something that is more akin to the period of Inter-Imperial Rivalry, depending on what happens to relations between the United States, China, Japan, Russia, and the European Union, in particular, in the years to come. Each geopolitical order divided up the world in different ways as the "rules" governing the order were established. Thus in the first order, Britain operated politically to balance power across Europe but its navy and relatively open economy served to both institutionalize colonial rule elsewhere and provide public goods to the world economy such as commodity markets and insurance services. In the second order, territorial geopolitics based on competitive inter-imperial behavior prevailed. In the third one, the United States and the Soviet Union were two imperial states that engaged in ideological and military competition by recruiting client states yet also gave rise to a set of international institutions (particularly on the US side) that by the 1960s were providing the regulatory basis for a more globalized world economy. This only reached its fruition globally after 1990.

Different regimes of trade, investment, diplomacy, and military competition prevailed across the different geopolitical orders. But these were not just the fruit of coercion by singular global hegemons or regional ones. This is often the meaning given to the term "hegemony" (Agnew 2005; Dutkiewicz et al. 2021). Rather, even if countries such as Britain and the United States played outsize roles in different epochs, the different orders resulted from the broad acceptance of common understandings and norms of conduct until these were no longer acceptable to significant constituencies or with the rise of new "powers," such as Germany, Japan, and the United States in the late

1800s, and China and non-state actors today, who try to change the rules to their presumed advantage. "Planning" on the part of the government of a singular hegemonic power was never part of the historical structures that characterized the world during the various geopolitical orders (Woodley 2015).

In the case of what has become the post–Cold War era of globalization, it was the projection of what had been the US historical experience inside the United States (an expanding national market, the reduction of barriers to trade and investment, the creation of a national polity following the New Deal of the 1930s), allied to technological changes such as containerization, satellite-based telecommunications, and new types of ship propulsion, and its appeal beyond US shores, above all in Europe and Japan, allied of course to US political-military power that enabled this projection, that produced the "model" of globalization with US companies leading the charge because of their declining rates of profits in the late 1960s and early 1970s (Agnew 2005; Smil 2010; Stein 2010). What marks off current globalization from the past geopolitical epochs as noted above is twofold: it is based on the rapid diffusion of ideas and information worldwide rather than just trade and it has produced an increased convergence between Europe and the United States, on the one hand, and East Asia, on the other, as the dominant regions in the world economy when they had hitherto had quite different geopolitical roles (Baldwin 2016).

But each geopolitical order has relied on distinctive ways of managing two central processes of the modern capitalist world economy: the dominant scale of capital accumulation and the dominant space of political support and regulation for that accumulation. The former has had two tendencies: the territorial-intensive and the interactive-extensive and the latter has had three tendencies: national-state, imperial-state, and international-state (Agnew and Corbridge 1995, 19–23). Thus, the first geopolitical order (1815–1875) rested on a set of territorial economies and national states in Europe with a growing interactional tendency outside of Europe managed through Britain. In this construction, Britain was the first international state. The second order involved an explosion of inter-imperial rivalries as leading states in Europe plus the United States and Japan competed for dominance over resource- and market-rich territories. As the epoch wore on, the creation of exclusive colonial zones and increasingly protectionist policies at the national level led to the overall primacy of the territorial scale of accumulation in a world of competing imperial states. The third order saw a combination of two imperial states (the US and the Soviet Union) with the United States sponsoring much expanded interactional accumulation as it came to assert its role as an international state, particularly in relation to Western Europe and Japan. Increasingly, the joint impact of extensive accumulation (initially by US-based multinational businesses) and global regulatory institutions gave rise to the globalization of the world economy that emerged into full efflorescence only in the 1990s and early 2000s. In this order many states are internationalized and increasingly intertwined with political regulation that is no longer solely national-territorial but involves supraregional (such as the EU), international (such as the WTO and IMF), and private (such as credit-rating agencies) regulatory bodies. Buried within this order, however, are numerous imperial legacies left over from previous epochs not least such features as the persisting role of London as a global financial center, the Euro-American "export" of the national-state model, and US military bases scattered far and wide (e.g., Halperin and Palan 2015).

The geopolitical order underpinning globalization since the 1980s has been characterized in terms of a mixed model of increased global governance. The conventional schemas used to map global geopolitics during the Cold War era—First, Second, and Third Worlds, East and West, Core and Periphery, North and South—have lost their significance. In their place is an emergent order not based in homogenization, as globalization is sometimes erroneously held to entail, but in relatively novel differentiations. There are three elements to this: increasing US displacement, the rise of other centers of accumulation and regulation, and the jockeying of places hitherto on the margins of the global system to find their way into it.

For one thing, the US core at the heart of the processes of globalization begun during the Cold War has hollowed out on a number of fronts, even if, for example, its overall numerical military predominance still prevails (Agnew 2005). The use of that power in recent conflicts suggests that it is not what it has often been alleged to be in terms of efficacy or performance (Ullman 2018; Lamb 2021; Coll and Entous 2021). Indeed, the entire rhetoric of US global dominance is now utterly delusional (Wertheim 2021). The US role in the world economy as represented by trade and investment flows is much reduced over forty years ago and not simply in the face of the rise of China but more generally (e.g., Posen 2021). The mismanaged 2020–2021 pandemic and the growth of right-wing extremist organizations encouraged by a sitting US president to the extent that they attacked the US Capitol in Washington DC on 6 January 2021 in support of his challenge to the legitimacy of the 2020 presidential election suggests that problems at home will finally take precedence over interventions abroad (Glasser 2021; Baccini and Weymouth 2021). The threat of reactionary politics overtaking the country and undermining its history of innovation and productivity for the sake of white-nationalist nostalgia has not gone away with Trump's 2021 ejection from the US presidency (e.g., Ganesh 2021b).

At the same time, US monetary centrality has become increasingly tenuous beginning with the abrogation of the Bretton Woods currency system in the 1970s down to the financial crisis of 2007–2008. Even if the US$ is still the main currency in many global transactions and in foreign-exchange reserves worldwide, its use is increasingly challenged by other national currencies and the onset of cyber-currencies such as Bitcoin (Foroohar 2021; *Economist* 2021b). The 2007–2008 financial crisis called into question what had become "common sense" about the US emphasis on investment in financial products rather than in the real economy of production and services (e.g., Kirshner 2014). The contemporary US global tax system encourages the proliferation of offshore tax havens as US-based companies shift their profits offshore, and this then encourages foreign investment in place of domestic and a decline in revenues for governments at all levels, as well as money laundering by business tycoons and their political stooges/protectors in the United States and elsewhere (e.g., Sharman 2012; Burgis 2015; Zucman 2015; Sandbu 2019; Obermayer and Obermaier 2016; Sharman 2017; *Economist* 2021d).

The country also suffers from serious institutional dysfunction as witnessed by the difficulty of achieving much of any policy consensus across a bitter national partisan-political divide and the breakdown of the eighteenth-century federalism at the heart of the regime as the states and national governments head in mutually exclusive directions on multiple issues (Agnew 1999; Agnew 2005; Brigety 2021). The catastrophic response of the Trump administration to the pandemic in 2020 was more about the continuing breakdown of US federalism than just about Trump's narcissistic personality and managerial incompetence (see chapter 7). The national infrastructure of roads, bridges, railroads, airports, electricity grid, education, and healthcare has suffered from massive deferred maintenance and underinvestment since the 1980s (e.g., Waldmeir 2021; Witte et al. 2021). Many of its largest businesses (Amazon, Facebook, Microsoft, Tesla, and so on) make as much or more of their profits abroad as at home and to a considerable extent are not in any meaningful sense "American" at all. This is not to say that the United States as a force in world politics is in some sort of terminal decline or that China is the single beneficiary of the shifting dynamics of the world economy (Winecoff 2020; Hass 2021) but that thinking solely in terms of fixed territorial entities with self-evident labels is no longer, if it ever was, adequate to the task of understanding how power works geographically.

All this has led, in turn, to the rising importance of global and supranational organizations in which many other actors, both state-based, public, and private, hold sway, even though this is by no means all totally new (e.g., Cammack 2003; Büthe and Mattli 2011; Auld 2014; Yates and Murphy 2019; Tan 2021). This has been so even as the US government under Trump turned its back on the wider world. This trend also creates opportunities for smaller and hitherto more marginalized states and other actors to assert their roles in accumulation and regulation both separately and collectively. The rise of China should be seen in this context as challenging—because of the highly state-regulated character of its capitalism—the prevailing orthodoxy about the entirely "private" character of global capitalism (Carney 2018). It also calls into question the presumed invariably "autonomous" character of much European and American business when it too has often depended heavily on home-governmental favoritism. Consider the huge subsidies that firms like Boeing and Airbus receive from, respectively, the US government and the European Union. Yet the focus on capital accumulation remains central. But as China's initiatives such as the transport infrastructure One-Belt-One-Road show, this cannot be realized just within national borders, irrespective of public/private ownership or the existence of effective local regulation. As long as capital is accumulated, the search for the highest rates of return and routes out of domestic debt crises leads to ever-expanding frontiers. Many states are now so internationalized that turning them into old-style territorial states will be more than a little difficult. Since 2012, however, China's government seems to want to keep absolute command over its domestic territory at the same time that it profits as much as possible from external ties (see chapter 5). Unless this tension is resolved, the possibility of its completely replacing the United States at the center of world politics seems unlikely (Christensen 2021a; Jentleson 2021; Rachman 2021b). Unless it can persuade the world that its ways are more attractive than current ones and they can be packaged in terms of some sort of "rules-based" language (however hypocritical), debt-based financing of infrastructure projects will not be enough (on what is needed, see, respectively, *Economist* 2021f; Beinart 2021). As of 2021 China's military capacity and strategic alliances are hardly of a scope to challenge existing arrangements without it first becoming a more attractive pole to others (Gilli and Gilli 2019; Goldstein 2020).

In this context, much contemporary national-populism in Europe and the United States, rather than challenging the overall contours of globalization as such, should be seen as based in nostalgia on the part of different constituencies (in northern Italy or the US Midwest, for example) for their having been "knocked" down from previous heights of favor and influence (Agnew and Shin 2019). It reflects anxiety about declining status globally and in relation to other groups such as racial minorities or immigrants who look different from them (e.g., Smith and King 2021). Indeed, it is the net failure of conventional political parties and national governments to practically address the combined sense of decline and nostalgia that encourages supporting the national-populist cause notwithstanding its essentially oppositional rather than practical or policy-based character (Trubowitz and Burgoon 2022). Elsewhere, poorer states and businesses with local rather than multinational or global economic bases face the challenge of organizing to resist and accommodate decisions emanating from more powerful sites. Much of the time, they end up supporting the broader system through their presence in the system rather than doing much to undermine it. It may well be that it is in the places where globalization operates in the most obviously predatory fashion and with the most questionable local outcomes that the possibilities for challenging it are greatest. But in a world where separate national development is something of a mirage, except for countries large enough and/or well organized enough to manage a renaissance through working up the global "food chain," joining a globalizing world economy turns into a fateful embrace. The alternative then is to try and reform it rather than working against it by, for example, challenging the prevailing order within international organizations like the WTO (e.g., Hopewell 2016).

Much recent talk about the "crisis" of globalization rests on the notion that—with the fading of its American sponsor, the rise of China's state capitalism, and the efflorescence of national populism in the face of malign foreign influences, immigration waves, and pandemics—the world will retreat into territorial and regionalized enclaves (e.g., King 2017; O'Sullivan 2019; Cooban 2022). A recapitulation of the epoch of Inter-Imperial Rivalry could be in the offing. The Russian invasion of Ukraine in 2022 suggested as much. Yet it also showed how vulnerable a presumed relatively autarkic imperial-territorial country could still be to its own military incompetence, organized resistance from its supposedly weaker opponent, and external economic pressures (e.g., Jones, S. et al. 2022; Watling 2022; Mittal 2022; Osipovich 2022). Russia's reliance on oil and gas exports turned out to provide less leverage over the world at large than many believed it would be in limiting an external response (Johnson and Ustenko 2022; Wintour 2022). If the expansion of NATO had given some basis to its government's paranoia about being surrounded by adversaries (Agnew 2009), the fact that so many of the putatively Russian soldiers who were killed in the early phases of the invasion were from non-Russian minorities and Russian President Putin was avowedly messianic in declaring Ukraine an integral part of Russia, rather than the independent state the world of states had recognized, suggests how much the war itself was about defending/expanding a multinational empire rather than entirely a defensive maneuver against foreign aggression by means of invading a neighboring country, as its apologists inside and outside of Russia tended to claim (e.g., Zafesova 2022; Zakaria 2022; Wood 2022). Whether "Russia" simply reduces to the murderous whims of one man, Vladimir Putin, is also open to question (e.g., Frye 2021). Time will tell, of course, how this all works out.

Yet a global infrastructure of production chains, financial flows, global nongovernmental organizations, regulatory organizations, and interconnected communication networks will not easily be disentangled and replaced (e.g., Sandbu 2021; Khanna and Srinivasan 2021). If anything, the 2020–2021 pandemic points toward the increased importance of global cooperation and regulation in the face of emerging threats that will be global-planetary (from pandemics to climate change to migration flows) and not best managed on a piecemeal national or local basis (e.g., Monti 2021 on pandemic management). The so-called vaccine nationalism of 2021 in relation to the COVID-19 pandemic will probably have less influence than meets the eye. Hoarding vaccines when foreigners could still reinfect you with adaptive variants makes no sense. The need to attend to distant events explains, for example, the increased worldwide diffusion of law governing such matters as transnational crime and human trafficking (e.g., Simmons et al. 2018). The genie of global interdependence will not be easily returned to the bottle. "Most people's lives today dangle on ten thousand different global strings" (Keane 2003, xii).

GLOBALIZING GOVERNANCE

It is helpful to list some of the features of the contemporary governance of the Global Geopolitical Order. Some of these, of course, are inherited from previous epochs. These features will crop up repeatedly across the body of the book.

The first of these is the need to resist seeing governance entirely in terms of idealized states. Governance is more than just administration by a centralized state bureaucracy but usually involves less-intensive regulation than a term such as governmentality usually suggests, which covers the granular regulation of personal conduct through management of populations rather than solely by means of disciplinary measures and sovereign power (Foucault 2010). Governance can thus be engaged by a range of actors operating across networks and territories to encode and enforce rules, norms, and actions that meet with the active acquiescence of those organizations and entities that come within the scope of the actors in question (e.g., on the internet, O'Hara and Hall 2018; and on the global oil market, Goldthau and Hughes 2021). Particularly as issue agendas extend to define "global publics," concerned with pollution, public health, underdevelopment, human rights, and climate change, to name a few, politics is not readily contained within tight territorial parameters (e.g., Keane 2003). It need not include coercive power but relies mainly on participation and assent. Enforcement, therefore, rarely if ever involves much more than the imminent threat of expulsion from the "club" or refusal to admit to membership without at least some acceptance of the major rules at issue. Examples beyond states and international organizations (like the WTO and IMF) include such institutions as non-majoritarian regulators (NMRs) of markets enforcing competition and antitrust rules at national and international levels (Coen and Thatcher 2005); global corporations managing complex networks of affiliates and subsidiaries (Garrett 2008; May 2015); multinational businesses engaging with and lobbying international organizations like the WTO and ILO (Louis 2018); churches and religious organizations, particularly worldwide ones like the Catholic Church and organized Islam (e.g., Agnew 2010); and transnational nongovernmental organizations enforcing international law (Eilstrup-Sangiovanni and Sharman 2021).

The second feature is that governance is largely "mixed" rather best thought of in terms of the simple opposition between states and markets that has prevailed in much thinking about geopolitical order (Acemoglu and Robinson 2019). China is much more "capitalist" than many Americans think (its economic growth is down more to private enterprises than the state-owned sector and it is a relatively open economy except for retaining controls on outbound capital) and the United States is much more "socialist" in some respects (say, in terms of taxing capital gains and providing social security in old age) than is China (Ignatius, A. 2021). States themselves have always had important differences in the depth and scope of their bureaucratic apparatuses relative to private-public bargains, patronage links, and the molding of society to facilitate capitalist enterprise (e.g., Sayer 1992). Today much reference to "neoliberalism," for example, tends to suggest that market transactions happen without any institutional mediation and regulation. This is anything but the case (Slobodian 2018). It is in fact more the type and degree of mediation that is at issue rather than its presence or absence (e.g., Offner 2019). Different "varieties" of capitalism and global value chains thus entail different sets of regulatory practices. But none exists without them (Morgan and Whitley 2012). Notwithstanding ideological positions about the "magic" of the marketplace, there is no such thing as a market for a good or commodity completely without political voice and regulation (e.g., Smith and Burrows 2021). Public programs and administration can also be privatized and yet be subject to regulation (Verkuil 2007). Of course, much of this is not new. A good argument can be made that the modern world economy was partly made in the eighteenth and nineteenth centuries by the activities of state-licensed companies such as the British East India Company that mixed together all manner of accumulative and regulatory actions in the regions in which they operated, including military ones in this case (Stern 2011; Dalrymple 2019; Phillips and Sharman 2020). Much of what goes for technological innovation is likewise the fruit of government initiatives and spending followed by private exploitation. Think of the Apple iPhone (Mazzucato 2013).

A third feature is the difficulty of reinstating borders and rigid state-mandated governance in the face of the increased hollowing out of territories by communication and business networks emanating from beyond national shores. Corporate elites are increasingly transnational in outlook and interests even if still tied into home-country lobbying (Murray 2017; Robinson 2018). If contemporary China, Russia, and Turkey represent the best examples of efforts at reinstating borders and taking advantage of the relative openness of the rest of the world to pursue foreign-policy objectives, much of the rest of the world finds itself on the crux of a dilemma between maintaining their openness to investment, trade, and communication but protecting their territories from foreign interventions oriented to inciting public opinion to affect elections, penetrating corporate and government communication networks, and otherwise undermining governmental authority (e.g., Buchanan 2020; Perlroth 2021). During the Trump administration the United States acquired a national government intent on withdrawing from international organizations, active engagement with established allies, and commitment to relatively open borders.

Yet at the end of the day, the US model of engagement with the world, particularly the role of US business and finance globally, militates against this sort of withdrawal without enormous costs (James 2021a). Examples of this would include the utter failure of Trump's tariff policy on Chinese products (many made for US-based business) and the diminished reputation of the United States as an honest broker worldwide because of the incoherence and incivility of Trump's approach to governance (Irwin 2020; Gramm and Toomey 2021; Chazen Institute 2019; Kirshner 2021; Steil and Della Rocca 2021). The soaring US trade deficit under Trump is exhibit A for the difficulties facing efforts at reinstating a territorial-mercantilist economy (Palmer 2021). The fact that US-China investment flows flourished even as the US government was openly hostile to China's role in the world economy speaks to the continuing allure of a relatively open world economy (Kynge 2021). The United States is also still heavily involved, as are many other states, in contractual agreements with one another over supraregional agreements (such as in the reformed NAFTA and the European Union) as well as bilateral agreements over military bases and resource sharing (Cooley and Spruyt 2009).

At the same time, the 2007–2008 financial crisis and the pandemic of 2020–2021 suggest how many individual states have lost much of their material ability and significant reputational credibility in responding to crises. At least one current of what goes for contemporary populism is directed at drawing attention to state failure in governance, of which some is down to overreliance on private actors and the weakness of current national regulation (Agnew and Shin 2019). This is often expressed more vehemently in some regions and localities than others (such as the US Midwest) because of increased unemployment and job insecurity as a result of shifts toward more automation in manufacturing and the failure of new inward investment to compensate for other job losses due to foreign competition. Sometimes it is actually foreign firms that provide something of a substitute by way of branch plants (Knox et al. 2015). The state versus globalization narrative, then, is not a one-way street. Foreign influence is not always as malignant as populists allege.

Finally, a fourth feature of global governance is the production of an increasingly globalized space for regulation, assertion of expert knowledge, and legal practice (Hoffmann 2021; Innerarity 2016). There is an entire "background" world of lawyers, physicians, engineers, managers, and assorted technocrats devoted to specific projects that extend into spaces well beyond those of the average state or supranational organization (such as the EU). Rather than a "jungle out there," it is a heavily regulated world based on negotiated arrangements that require expertise to manage its plurality and dispersion. As lawyer David Kennedy (2008, 848) puts it by example: "every crate travels with a packet of rights and privileges, every transfer depends on a network of institutions and rules." This works within countries, particularly ones with federal and decentralized tiers of government, as much as across them.

By and large, this is an unruly and ongoing process rather than the result of some static constitutional compact made at a conference in Geneva or wherever. Powers change, as do their authors, as influence shifts among actors. This is what seems to be happening, for example, within the WTO, but extends also into the realm of the governance of transactions and standards governing products. None of this is to suggest that this system is just to all of the parties involved in it. It is very much the outcome of who has the powers within the various regulatory arenas. Increasingly, for example, and with the active withdrawal of US governments from multilateral and global spaces, the European Union has picked up the slack. Anu Bradford (2020) speaks of what she calls "The Brussels effect" with respect to the imposition of rules on, for example, data protection, 5G technology for telecommunications, and taxing social media companies that then become global standards because firms wish to retain access to the EU space.

In a real sense such processes are not so much regulating a given space as producing new ones (Liste 2016). This usually does not give rise to a level but more to an uneven surface as local/regional biases in knowledge and interpretation lead to "regime collisions" over specific areas of law (human rights versus environmental law and so on) and geographical differences in how the different spheres of regulation are practiced. But this real world of potentially global but differentiated and fragmented spaces is very different from that of the world political map with exclusively territorial states banging up against one another (Bagaran et al. 2016).

THE LOGIC OF THE BOOK

The book consists of five parts, the fifth of which is a conclusion. Part I is devoted to developing the dimensions of hidden geopolitics. The first chapter lays out the argument for the overall framework of the book of geopolitics in a globalized world. Starting with a discussion of how geopolitics and globalization have been mutually entailed down the years, the chapter then develops the threefold focus of the volume as a whole on the geopolitics of globalization, the geopolitics of development, and the geopolitics of global regulation mentioned previously. The other two chapters in this section concern the ways in which hidden geopolitics has been obscured by the continuing obsession with a territorialized geopolitics even as it has retreated and with using historical analogies, often very misleading ones, to invariably argue for the continuities rather than the changes in the workings of geopolitical order.

Having cleared the field, so to speak, subsequent sections provide case studies oriented to the three main themes highlighted in the first chapter. If that chapter makes a case for how much contemporary globalization was the outcome, contested and episodic as it may have been, of initiatives coming from within the United States, the continuing reverberations of US government and business involvements beyond its borders and the specificities of China's rise within the current global geopolitical order deserve close attention. So the two chapters in part II address, respectively, the 2018 US-Mexico border crisis as representative of the former and the question of what China brings to the global order that is different from what came before as key to identifying its overall future contours.

Part III has two chapters concerned with various aspects of how states adjust, compete, and manage their domestic territories in the face of the global geopolitical order. The first chapter examines how different levels of government responded to the 2007–2008 financial crisis. The second chapter in part III addresses the relative dysfunction of the US federal government during the 2020–2021 pandemic to raise questions about the difficulties of national-populism in the face of a large population suspicious of the federal government and, even if anti-globalist, hostile to the idea of the sort of governance that could do much about that or the pandemic.

Part IV includes two chapters that offer case studies of the global regulation around which much of the current global geopolitical order has come to rely. The first one explores the role of credit-rating agencies in relation to the selling of sovereign bonds by central banks across the world but places them in the context of the broader topic of globalized regulation and the forms that this takes. The second one considers the aftermath of the 2007–2008 financial crisis in terms of the so-called Eurozone crisis and what this revealed about the workings of the European Union as a major example of the institutional mediation making the current geopolitical order so distinctive from previous ones. Part V offers a brief concluding chapter that attempts to sum up the pros and cons of thinking about current world politics in terms of the motif of hidden geopolitics.

I

HIDDEN GEOPOLITICS

1

Geopolitics in a Globalized World

It is common to see geopolitics and globalization as opposites with respect to how the world works. If geopolitics is associated primarily with geographical determinism in channeling the universal "urge" for territorial expansion on the part of all states, globalization is seen as creating an interdependent and "flat" world in which flows of goods, people, and capital displace the territorialized world of inter-imperial rivalries that characterized the past (e.g., Friedman 2005). This distinction makes little sense.

In this chapter I discuss four aspects of the connection between geopolitics construed in its broadest meaning and the globalization that the world economy has experienced over the past fifty years. The first is to challenge the idea that geopolitics is "opposed" to globalization. This contention reflects adherence to the territorial "necessity" of state expansion characteristic of the classical nineteenth century understanding of geopolitics. I then turn to what I see are the three dimensions of geopolitics in an era of globalization: the geopolitics of globalization, the geopolitics of development, and the geopolitics of global regulation. These, respectively, involve discussing the historic role of the United States in enabling and stimulating much of what goes for economic globalization (increased trade and investment around the world and so on), identifying the capacities of different states in light of different colonial histories and histories of statehood to engage in successful strategies of economic growth and thus capture the presumed benefits of globalization, and showing the new agencies of global regulation, both public and private, that are addressing and enabling current patterns of globalization, often independently of any single state or grouping of states.

GEOPOLITICS VERSUS GLOBALIZATION

Brian Blouet (2001) devoted an entire book to justifying this opposition. He writes:

> Geopolitical policies seek to establish national or imperial control over space and the resources, routeways, industrial capacity and population the territory contains, whereas globalization is the opening of national space to the free flow of goods, capital, and ideas. Globalization removes obstructions to movement and creates conditions in which international trade in goods and services can expand. (Blouet 2001, 1)

Capital has somehow completely replaced any sort of political enterprise, state-based or more extensive, in driving world politics.

Yet historically such a clear-cut distinction between geopolitics and globalization is problematic. Certainly, the period from 1875 until 1945 can be reasonably characterized as one in which inter-imperial rivalry tended to win out over open trade and so on and the Cold War from 1945 until 1991 involved a major geopolitical fracture between a relatively free-flowing West and a relatively autarkic East. Classic geopolitics developed in the first period and represented an effort at justifying imperialism in naturalistic terms of space and race (Ashworth 2013). But right across the periods in question there were systematic efforts on the part of some governments, particularly in Britain and the United States, and businesses looking to expand beyond home shores, to reduce and remove barriers to trade and investment. These increasingly came to fruition during the Cold War and since the 1990s have expanded to include much of the world. Globalization, then, was incipient within the territorialized conflicts of the twentieth century. It was not opposite but in fact a strategic option pursued by some actors within the confines of the geopolitical conflicts that wracked the century.

The opposition relies on posing two spatial ontologies as necessarily antithetical: a world of territorial and self-aggrandizing states and a world of networked flows of capital, goods, and people independent of states. These are seen as competing paradigms of modernity. In this construction, territorialization is opposed to open circulation. In fact, they have always coexisted with one another, if historically either one or the other has had periods of relative ascendancy. More specifically, the territorial state has had a historical geography to its formation and diffusion that suggests anything other than a straightforward historic victory of territorial containment over open circulation (e.g., Vergerio 2021). Global and territorial spaces have long coexisted (Agnew 2016). The modern state system did not appear overnight and fully formed as a result of the settlement of the European religious wars enshrined in the Treaty of Westphalia in 1648 and globalization did not spring up instantaneously and spontaneously in the 1970s or 1980s. If globalization discourse tends to suffer from hyperbole: "portraying the transformation from the modern Westphalian to the globalized postmodern world system in terms of a caesural rupture of extremely short duration" (Larkins 2010, 199), geopolitics is seen as anachronistic because of its association with early twentieth-century imperial rivalries. This logic continues in the distinction often made recently between a geopolitics that prevailed historically before the onset of a geoeconomics in which states now weaponize trade and investment for strategic purposes (e.g., Blackwill and Harris 2016). But trade sanctions and exchange-rate manipulation are hardly as novel as this perspective contends. The "geopolitics" in question remains as totally state-centric even without the previous emphasis on military force (Agnew 2020a).

The purpose of this chapter is to show what each of them—geopolitics and globalization—actually owes to the other. There is a passing affinity between this approach and that of Carl Schmitt's writing on *The Nomos of the Earth* (2003 [1950]). It is worth mentioning here to distance the approach from what might seem to be an apparent alternative. In *The Nomos*, Schmitt, a German conservative legal scholar and erstwhile supporter of the Nazi regime, conceived of geopolitics in terms of competing spheres of influence in which a regional hegemon would dominate within a given area beyond its own territorial borders (Elden 2011). Modeled on the way the US Monroe Doctrine had evolved to limit interventions in the Western hemisphere to the United States, Schmitt attempted an integration of the geopolitical and the economic by positing that dominant powers should not seek to annex territory but to integrate surrounding areas within their *spatiale Bereich* or spatial sphere of influence.

Arguably, this is more or less what happened to large parts of the world during the Cold War. The emergence of the European Union as a supraregional authority has reinforced the attractiveness of the logic. This gives Schmitt's work an apparently prophetic quality. Yet there are three major problems with this approach beyond the problematic reputation of its author. One is that it is resolutely ignorant of the role of actors in world politics other than states in general and the presumably dominant regional powers (such as the United States, Russia, or Germany) in particular. A second is that the proposed *Grossräumen* or regional spheres identified as such may exist but the role of singular dominating powers is far from obvious in most possible ones and geopolitical considerations may not always be more important than economic or cultural ones (as in South Asia or the Middle East, for example).

Finally, globalization as a set of processes potentially operating worldwide through technological changes in communications and transportation technologies and stimulated by government policies encouraging trade and investment across state borders nowhere figures in Schmitt's theoretical calculus. Even while eschewing annexation as the motivation for *Raumhoheit* or spatial supremacy, Schmitt cannot escape from the territorialized logic of economic autarky that he inherited from his longstanding commitment to the political theology of the *Volk* or people (German or otherwise). His anti-liberalism trumps his ability to think of a world in which a state-centered geopolitics not only coexists with but guides planetary political-economic order. It is the sense of a fading or lost world that informs the overall perspective of Schmitt and other apostles of absolute territorial sovereignty on the part of dominant powers: "Territorial sovereignty was transformed into an empty space for socioeconomic processes. The external territorial form with its linear boundaries was [legally] guaranteed, but not its substance, i.e. not the social and economic content of territorial integrity" (Schmitt 2003 [1950], 252 quoted in Coleman 2011, 137).

It is useful perhaps to make the case for the geopolitics *of* globalization in empirical terms. Using different terminology, a range of features of contemporary world politics can be ascribed to geopolitics. These include the incidence of interstate conflicts, the occurrence of civil wars, and the unevenness of economic development around the world. These always have putative geopolitical as well as economic causes. In other words, acts of governments and other public and private authorities have profound effects on both country-by-country and local differences in conflict potential and economic development. Globalization is also thus far from being a spontaneous, purely economic process. It is also the progeny of geopolitical action.

The three ways in which geopolitics actually underpins globalization can be identified as constituting geopolitics in the contemporary era of globalization. The first, at the global level, is the geopolitics of globalization or the way in which the world's most powerful state for the past seventy years, the United States, has facilitated the opening up of the world economy (see chapters 2 and 4). This has obviously not been without resistance as can be seen, for example, in the Arab World, with efforts by militant Islamist groups to turn away from any paradigm of modernity as irredeemably tainted by its foreign and/or Western origins and in Russian government efforts to reestablish Russia as a regional hegemon even if this imposes massive costs on its own territorial economy. The contemporary world is not one without contradictions. The second, at the national and subnational levels, is the geopolitics of development with reference to the differences between states and localities with respect to their mobilization of populations to pursue economic development and the investment in public goods and infrastructures to enable this pursuit (chapters 6 and 7). In the face of globalization, some countries, China and South Korea would be examples, have managed to reorganize their economies to benefit from the changes (see chapter 5). Other governments have been much less able and willing to do so. The final is the increasingly complex system under globalization of what can be called "low geopolitics" or the economic-regulatory activities carried out by relatively independent private and public agencies and the emergence of intermediary jurisdictions, particularly tax havens and global financial centers in world cities through which the invoices of world trade and investment increasingly circulate (chapters 8 and 9). In total, this is geopolitics without the drama of military strategies involving carrier task forces and so on but with real impacts on everyday lives around the world.

GEOPOLITICS OF GLOBALIZATION

Globalization as we understand it today began in the nineteenth century, even if it had earlier roots in European colonial expansion (Wallerstein et al. 2013). The growth of world trade as a share of global GDP is one indicator of this long-term trend (see figure 1.1). The technological and managerial changes following the industrial revolution led to massive increases in demand for resources, outlets for markets, and returns on investments, all facilitated by foreign expansion. If in Europe a balance-of-power regime encouraged inter-state competition outside of the region, the arrival of new state actors such as Germany, Italy, Japan, and the United States onto the global scene disrupted the British-dominated globalization of trade and finance worldwide. British governments provided the international legal and financial rules including the monetary gold standard that greased the wheels of nineteenth-century global commerce. This ended badly when up-and-coming powers such as Germany with more territorialized conceptions of political-economic organization and feeling closed out of existing imperial arrangements challenged the political-military status quo. Much of the twentieth century was spent fighting and

Figure 1.1. Value of Exports as a Share of Global GDP, 1827–2014 (Fouquin and Hugot, 2016)

recovering from the wars that this geopolitical system of inter-imperial rivalry entailed (Agnew and Corbridge 1995).

In the aftermath of World War II, the United States took on the global role of sponsoring a return to the sort of open world economy relinquished by a now-declining Britain. The impetus to this came both from the desire of US industry to benefit from worldwide expansion and the perceived threat to this from the Soviet Union and its autarkic model of economic development. The roots of contemporary globalization can be said to lie, at least in part, in the containment of the Soviet Union: the putative strategy at the center of US Cold War policy. The internal decay of the Soviet model meant that by the 1980s, the United States had become the world's most important country economically and militarily. Its military capacity, at least if measured by share of national economy devoted to military spending, is without peer: equal to the next twelve largest spenders put together. Whether this always guarantees equivalent success in specific conflicts, from the Vietnam War to recent fiascos such as the 2003 invasion and occupation of Iraq and the inability to coerce Russia in Ukraine in 2014, is open to much doubt. Nevertheless, US economic and cultural influence around the world has generally proved very successful, even though openly challenged during the Cold War until 1991 by the competing political-economic model of the Soviet Union based on central government economic planning as opposed to the private ownership of land and industry championed by the United States.

US governments were compelled by their ideological struggle with the Soviet Union to favor lifting restrictions on trade and commerce, though historically protectionist of their own domestic market. The United States replaced Britain in using its financial and military power, both acquired as outcomes of World War II, when the other world powers were very largely exhausted, to support the development of the global legal and financial norms necessary for the overall expansion of commerce. Pushing for this were American businesses that saw opportunities for both investment and consumer markets around the world. Four examples of institutional/technological changes serve to show how much the organizational and technological infrastructure of post-1970s globalization has relied on US geopolitical status and capacity (Eckes and Zeiler 2003).

First of all, removing barriers to trade such as tariffs and quotas became an important goal of US foreign policy in the 1950s and 1960s. US governments sponsored all of the major rounds of the General Agreement on Tariffs and Trade (GATT) to open up world trade in manufactured goods. On agriculture and services, the strategy remained much more circumspect, showing how much it was US industrial corporations and banks that favored an opening of the world economy more than other business interests. Table 1.1 shows the net reduction in GATT member average tariffs between 1947 and 1991 that paralleled the course of overall trade and economic growth (figure 1.1). Trade amounted for an increasing share of overall global economic growth over this period. Thus was laid the groundwork for the explosion of world trade, the expansion of manufacturing supply-chains for parts and components across international borders, and the dramatic opening up of previously closed economies such as that of China.

Table 1.1. Tariff Reductions during the GATT Rounds, 1947–1994

	% Cut in All Tariffs	*Average Tariff Level as % of 1931 Level*
Negotiations between 1934 and 1947: over 1931 level		66.8%
1st Round (Geneva, 1947)	21.1%	52.7%
2nd Round (Annecy, 1949)	1.9%	51.7%
3rd Round (Torquay, 1950–1951)	3.0%	50.1%
4th Round (Geneva, 1955–1956)	3.5%	48.9%
Dillon Round (Geneva, 1961–1962)	2.4%	47.7%
Kennedy Round (Geneva, 1964–1967)	36.0%	30.5%
Tokyo Round (Geneva, 1974–1979)	29.6%	21.2%
Uruguay Round (Geneva, 1987–1994)	38.0%	13.1%

Source: Real Phillipe Lavergne (1983), *The Political Economy of US Tariffs: An Empirical Analysis*, Ottawa: North-South Institute, 32–33. Updated for the Uruguay Round.

Second, as the world's largest economy in 1945 and thereafter, the United States also came to provide the world's main currency for world trade. This made the US central bank, the Federal Reserve, the world's most important monetary institution. The value of other currencies in world commerce was fixed to the value of the US dollar with central banks managing the process of rate setting within narrow bands of fluctuation. The decision by the US government in 1971 to shift from the governmentally managed monetary system established in 1944 by the United States and other countries (as a result of the Bretton Woods Agreement) to a free-floating exchange rate in which the value of the US dollar would fluctuate relative to other currencies as a result of competitive bidding in open markets was crucial in creating the global financial system we have today. It was not a deliberate decision to change the global monetary system so much as a tactical maneuver by the administration of President Nixon to reduce the US balance-of-payments deficit and encourage US exports by devaluing the currency (Perlstein 2008, 601–3; Gowa 1983). Nixon's decision to unilaterally abrogate the Bretton Woods Agreement of 1944 for fixing exchange rates was arguably one of the most important geopolitical decisions of the late twentieth century, whatever Nixon himself intended, but has rarely been seen in this light (Blackwill and Harris 2016, 168–69). Since then the world monetary system has been based increasingly around floating exchange rates as the relative values of more and more currencies are set in foreign-exchange markets rather than by governments or national central banks. This set the scene not only for a globalized financial system (when floating exchange rates were joined by removals of controls on capital movements) but also for the global transmission of financial risks as with the 2008 global financial crisis brought on by worldwide bank purchases of US subprime mortgage securities. With the rise of other economies under globalization, such as China, Brazil, and so on, the question arises of how long the US dollar can continue to dominate as the medium of world trade (Eichengreen 2011).

Third, large US-based and other multinational businesses and banks were important sponsors and beneficiaries of this opening up of the world economy under US government auspices that has in turn enabled the global supply chains and massive changes in global patterns of economic development since the 1970s. But the actual technologies used in this process, labeled generally by the term "logistics," such as the use of shipping containers and the organization of supply chains bringing together components from multiple sites for assembly and sale elsewhere, have relied on models drawn very much from the US military and its preparations for projecting and managing forces on many fronts at once. Indeed, the nuts and bolts of globalization as a means of organizing the production and circulation of goods, capital, and people rely fundamentally on logistics. By way of example, containerization was first used on a large scale by the US military. Only later did its radical reduction in time taken to load and unload ships lead to its widespread civilian adoption. Containerization is an absolute prerequisite for the just-in-time (JIT) system at providing components through the global supply chains that now connect computer manufacturing across the United States, Japan, Taiwan, and China. Thus, as Deborah Cowen (2014, 41) argues:

> For JIT to become a globalized system, inputs and commodities had to be coordinated and transported quickly across space. U.S. military procurement laid many of the infrastructural foundations for this work during the Korean War. With the military's use of containers to manage massive supply chains during the Vietnam War, container shipping became firmly entrenched.

Japanese companies were arguably the first private enterprises to seriously adopt global supply chains allied to JIT management. The opening of Japanese-owned car assembly plants in the United States in the 1980s, following the imposition of US quotas on vehicle imports, was arguably the beginning of the whole transition to the massive flow of parts and final goods across the world as they combined Japanese and US suppliers together for their assembly plants (e.g., Jozuka 2019; Maswood 2021).

Fourth, and finally, the very possibilities of cross-border corporate and financial ties have been realized because of the spread of legal norms and procedures that are managed by global law firms, based primarily in New York and London, that mediate in stock offerings, inter-firm disputes, and mergers and acquisitions activities (Sokol 2007). One reason London has retained its central role in the world economy is the inertia associated with its development of a court system and legal norms governing corporate law that date back to the nineteenth century. But New York is increasingly important as the source of the law that is central to globalization. US legal norms and practices now dominate globally in relation to many transnational transactions (e.g., Trubek et al. 1994; Buxbaum 2006). US procedural practices such as class action and pretrial discovery have spread worldwide. This is not so much by the explicit adoption by states of such procedures but more in terms of the private practice of law involving primarily non-state actors. The geopolitical status of the United States obviously informs this diffusion process. Legal systems have always been syncretic or absorptive of foreign practices to one degree or another even when primarily, for example, civil (statutory) or common (judges make law) law traditions. What is novel is the extent to which today the wheels of globalization are oiled by the transnational movement of US legal practices (Brake and Katzenstein 2013). Such as it is, this transfer of US practice into transnational law fosters rather than limits corporate power (Barkan 2013).

These trends all suggest, however, that once under way and with sufficient support worldwide, globalization does not necessarily need continuing "geopolitical support" from a single state sponsor. The frequently voiced view in the United States is different. As Thomas Friedman (2000, 467–68) puts it "the globalization system cannot hold together without an activist and generous American foreign policy." Yet it is undoubtedly the case that globalization requires underlying institutional direction and practical support. Whether international institutions and regulatory agencies can do this remains moot. If US and other governments turn away from globalization, as some including the US government under Trump seemed to be doing, the lesson from the early twentieth century suggests that globalization itself could falter.

GEOPOLITICS OF DEVELOPMENT

Globalization works through as well as around state-governmental institutions. It is a myth that globalization leads to the "end" of the state (Mann 1997). This is a frequent corollary to popular conceptions of globalization: states and all other forms of governance decline in power as markets come to rule everywhere unimpeded (Van Creveld 1999). In fact, much of the impetus behind globalization lies in taking advantage of differences in factor endowments and fiscal and monetary policies within and across different countries. In this context, some governments (national and subnational) have been more adept than others at exploiting the opportunities provided by a more open world economy. The map of the most globalized countries, according to one set of empirical indicators, reveals that the world is far from "flat" or uniform in terms of active involvement in the world economy. Small European economies tend to be the most open followed by other European countries, the United States and Canada, New Zealand, Singapore, Hong Kong, and Malaysia. In terms of trade, holdings of foreign assets (particularly US Treasury bonds) and "weight" within the world economy, South Korea, Japan, and China are also very important.

Given its rapid rise from negligible significance as a player in the world economy before 1987 to its growth as the world's second largest economy by 2012, China's story is particularly interesting as an example of the geopolitics of development. China's great success in improving its level of economic development and reducing its number of poor people is not simply just a question of exploiting its vast pool of relatively cheap labor. Mobilizing populations and organizing insertion into global markets have been particularly important. The first, dependent in part on a degree of cultural homogeneity and acceptance of government popular legitimacy, makes it possible for foreign and domestic investors to expect maximum political stability and minimal workplace disruptions. The second requires a clear sense that some economic activities, banking, for example, need considerable government regulation, even as the country is opened up globally to exploit its comparative advantages in land, labor, or capital. Perhaps even more crucial is investment in infrastructures such as ports, railways, and highways and public goods such as general education and healthcare to produce propitious settings for profitable private investment. There is a clear connection between successful efforts at popular mobilization and infrastructure investment, on the one hand, and dramatic improvements in economic development, on the other. Proposals to shrink the "administrative state" popular in conservative circles in the United States rely on the notion that the public goods and infrastructures in question are not needed to produce competitive advantage or they will arise spontaneously by private action when there is no historical evidence that either of these is true.

Somewhat ironically, therefore, the charge made by many sovereigntists that globalization rides roughshod over states, as in Brexit and America First sound bites, precisely misses the point that dealing effectively with globalization requires more rather than less government. Of course, the more culturally defensive versions of sovereigntism see anything foreign as dangerously alien and the more politically and economically oriented versions see globalization overwhelmingly in terms of either democratic deficits or setting rigid limits on governmental macroeconomic policies, respectively (Agnew 2020b). But the possibility of being alone in the world quickly encounters the reality that it cannot but be on terms necessarily shared with others absent either autarky within a large territory (as in the former Soviet Union) or sealing off from the world at large (as in North Korea) (Agnew 2019b). When different regions or subnational units have radically different experiences and expectations about being in the world and the policies needed to pursue their goals (as between

Scotland and England, Catalonia and Castile, or the southern US states and much of the rest of the country) the possibilities of a one-size-fits-all national mobilization are increasingly limited (see chapters 6 and 7). In the United States, for example, the national capacity to pursue a common policy toward globalization is crippled by the dysfunction of its contemporary federalism and the geographical polarization of its national politics (e.g., Kreitner 2020; this book chapter 7).

But a number of different development strategies can make sense depending on size of economy (population, infrastructure demands, etc.), resource base, governmental structure, and governmental efficacy. Large home economies allow for both economies of scale in production/consumption and import substitution. Historically, Brazil, India, and Mexico followed this approach. Russia, after having flirted with the world economy after the collapse of the Soviet Union, may be heading back in this direction. Regional supranational authorities such as the European Union and NAFTA can provide such benefits while also maintaining state-level autonomy of various sorts (see chapter 9). Countries with large resource bases, particularly ones with relatively inelastic demand but subject to depletion (such as oil), can bank on using sovereign-wealth funds to invest in assets both nationally and globally (Xu and Bahgat 2011). Many of the world's major oil-producing countries, from Kuwait and Venezuela to Norway, have such funds. But countries such as Singapore, Malaysia, China, and South Korea have also followed this strategy to a degree. Smaller states can turn themselves into tax havens. Some US states (such as Delaware and Wyoming), Caribbean island neocolonies (such as the Cayman Islands), Luxembourg, Switzerland, Ireland, the Netherlands, and Britain (since the 1980s) have taken on at least some of the attributes of tax havens: allowing foreign companies and wealthy persons the advantages of domiciliary status to lower or eliminate income taxes, facilitating tax inversions (after mergers or acquisitions moving to the lowest tax jurisdiction available), and through transfer-price invoicing lowering taxes by means of booking revenues to the lowest tax jurisdiction in which a corporate subsidiary is located (frequently solely for this purpose) (Shaxson 2011). Obviously, these development strategies tend to be at the expense of other jurisdictions. But the lobbying power of the businesses and individuals that benefit from them is such in those other jurisdictions that little or nothing can be done to eliminate the tax avoidance strategies upon which they are based without government-to-government cooperation to limit tax competition (e.g., Hakelberg and Rixen 2021).

At the other end of the continuum of development are many quasi- or even "failed" states that are unable to manage the possibilities on offer from globalization (Acemoglu and Robinson 2012; Jackson, R. H. 1993). Some of this incapacity can be put down to the colonial histories of many states, particularly the lack of mapping between nation on the one hand and state on the other. While corruption is hardly a monopoly of such regimes, it is endemic in many postcolonial states, at least in part because of seeing government office almost entirely as a source of patronage. Colonies that later became independent states were often carved out by colonial powers (such as Britain, France, Spain, and so on) with little or no attention to their ethnic or national homogeneity. This makes establishing political legitimacy for national institutions especially difficult. At the same time, political institutions imposed from the outside rather than developed indigenously do not always travel well, so to speak. This is particularly the case when the economic recipes imposed by outside lending agencies discourage public investment and impose austerity budgets. In the aftermath of the Cold War, the ending of those pressures from the United States and the Soviet Union that kept certain states together through massive infusions of aid as a result of complementary competition have opened states up to a "hollowing out" as different sects, tribes, clans, and regional groups vie to establish their own political dominance or secession. This latter trend, of course, is not restricted to weak states but also afflicts such long-established strong states as Britain and Spain where the European Union provides a broad overarching governance framework within which quite small states can flourish.

Whatever the precise strategy of development chosen, it is clear that economic growth in the era of globalization depends crucially on the capacity to find a niche within the wider global economy. While this is particularly true for smaller states, larger ones can also benefit enormously from collective mobilization on behalf of clear goals. Regions and localities within countries likewise have different economic potentials and political capacities for development depending on the nature of the political regime (centralized versus federal, etc.) and the exploitation of agglomeration economies (returns to specialization) across economic sectors. Think of the extent to which British governments have crafted national economic policies since the 1980s favorable to London and its economy but damaging overall to rest of the country (Ingham 1984; Agnew 2013; Agnew and Mantegna 2018). The structural impediments imposed by global geopolitical realities, however, make some options more available than others across the world. For a large subset of the world's states, particularly those with the most negative and long-lasting colonial experiences, largely located in Africa and the Middle East, the fruits of globalization, if they are such, remain a distant goal (Robinson 2018).

GEOPOLITICS OF REGULATION

With the onset of globalization since the 1970s, world economic development is increasingly regulated not just by governments within countries but also by increasingly influential private, quasi-public, and international organizations (e.g., Cammack 2003; Bartley 2018). Arguably the growth in private and quasi-public agencies is the product of the erosion of the public-private divide with the revolving door in personnel between government and private business, popular and business hostility (particularly in the United States) to government regulation (at least before the financial collapse of 2008), the absence of much intergovernmental regulation, and the explosion of transnational transactions to which established states are ill-equipped to respond (Cooley and Spruyt 2009). As Janine Wedel (2004, 217) describes this trend: "Spurred by two decades of deregulation, public-private partnerships and a worldwide movement toward privatization, non-state actors now fulfill functions once reserved for government. Moreover, the inclination to blur the 'state' and 'private' spheres now enjoys global acceptance. An international vernacular of 'privatization,' 'civil society,' 'non-governmental organizations' and other catch terms de-emphasizing the state is parroted from Washington to Warsaw to Wellington." The decisions of the myriad of new transnational organizations can have major effects on the course of globalization. They constitute the actors in what can be called "low geopolitics" to distinguish it from the "high geopolitics" of interstate hierarchy and inter-imperial rivalries. Even though this trend has powerful sponsors in the United States, the European Union, and among the businesses that lobby in the traditional corridors of geopolitical power, it gives rise to actors who are only accountable indirectly to any recognizably public political masters.

In the first case are international standard-setting and regulatory agencies. These are arrayed across two dimensions: whether they are essentially private or public (in terms of responsibility) and whether they are market or nonmarket driven (in terms of decision mechanisms) (Büthe and Mattli 2011) (table 1.2). International financial and development organizations such as, respectively, the International Monetary Fund and the World Bank are the best known of these. They are intergovernmental organizations but follow their own agendas set by their professional staffs with votes weighted toward their major funders, in particular the United States. They support governments in difficult economic circumstances in return for those governments following policy prescriptions designed by those organizations. An important example of the private/market organizations would be the major credit-rating agencies, which rate the riskiness of bonds issued by businesses and governments (see chapter 8). Their decisions are based on the claim that they have specialist knowledge and "independence" not available to governmental organizations. When governments try to raise revenues by selling bonds, therefore, they are subject to the authority exercised by private credit-rating agencies such as Moody's, Standard and Poor's, and Fitch when doing so. The recent Eurozone crisis showed their importance relative to that of public agencies such as the IMF and the European Central Bank whose decisions reflected anxieties over decisions by the credit-rating agencies. In the public/market category are

Table 1.2. Categories and Examples of Global Standard Setting and Regulatory Agencies

Public/Nonmarket	*Private/Market*
International Labour Organization (ILO) International Monetary Fund (IMF) World Bank Kyoto Protocol	Credit Rating Agencies (CRAs) Microsoft (Windows) Forest Stewardship Council (FSC) Corporate Social Responsibility (CSR Setters)
Public/Market	*Private/Nonmarket*
EU Competition vs. Federal Trade Commission (US FTC) US Securities and Exchange Commission (SEC)	International Accounting Standards Board (IASB) International Electrotechnical Commission (IEC) International Organization for Standardization (ISO) International Swaps and Derivatives Association (ISDA)

Source: Büthe and Mattli (2011).

organizations that regulate mergers and acquisitions and the monopoly pricing and insider trading practices of giant businesses often well beyond home shores such as the US Federal Trade Commission and the Securities and Exchange Commission. Finally, there is a host of standard-setting organizations that fit into the private/nonmarket category. These are the organizations that have come into their own in recent years as filling regulatory roles simply not addressed by public bodies of any stripe. They set accounting rules, product safety specifications, rules about derivatives and other financial products, and so on. They may seem mundane in terms of what they do. But they are exactly the agencies that Büthe and Mattli (2011) dub the "new global rulers."

In the second case, most national central banks today have a high degree of political independence from their governments. For example, the Bank of England, long subject to close supervision by the British Treasury, has been independent of such influence since 1997. The European Central Bank, invented in 1999 to govern the new euro currency, likewise exercises a power separate from that of the member states in the Eurozone (the 19 members of the European Union that since 1999 have come to share the same currency). This means that they make decisions about how much currency to issue, interest rates, and exchange-rate supports with an eye on global markets rather than just their own governments (see chapter 9). At the same time, much of the world's private financial economy is increasingly moving "offshore" to avoid as much national and global regulation as possible. To take advantage of low or nonexistent corporate and personal income taxes, many transnational businesses now incorporate in tax havens such as the Cayman Islands. Major global financial institutions in New York and London provide the nerve centers for this cross-jurisdictional circulation of corporate profits. Central banks increasingly try to coordinate their activities to manage these offshore flows. In the Bank for International Settlements they even have their own joint bank to coordinate their efforts at regulating global finance (Lebor 2013). The contradiction between the desire of large countries with dependent populations and development plans to retain tax revenues and the increasing desire and opportunity of wealthy individuals and businesses to avoid or evade taxes plagues the contemporary system of international financial regulation. A major crisis is brewing in that the massive avoidance of taxes not only creates opportunities for "money laundering" of illegal activities, it also reduces the revenues that governments need in providing the public infrastructure investments necessary for successful economic development.

CONSEQUENCES FOR HIDDEN GEOPOLITICS

What does this all mean for hidden geopolitics? For one thing, it leads to seeing the contemporary world as *not one of states as single unified actors*. While that image was always problematic for most states it is now utterly misleading, even for the most powerful ones. Increasingly, in the same epoch in which the big three credit-rating agencies, for example, have come to exercise such authority as they do, central banks, for example, have become more independent of their respective governments. Regulation of money and finance has become increasingly driven by private and quasi-private actors rather than by states per se. Governance has been reconstructed to meet the needs of increasingly globalized private actors such as banks and industrial corporations rather than the needs of the territorialized populations of states (Pistor 2019). State bonds underwrite this system and socialize risk onto domestic populations in return for back stopping the speculative activities of private banks, hedge funds, and other investors. "Technocrat-guardians," as Roberts (2010) terms them, in the central banks and credit-rating agencies, shielded from democratic influences thereby guard the marketplace and defend its stakeholders from fiscal and monetary policies of a socially redistributive or nationally oriented quality. Governance as the exercise of technocratic control has in fact become the modus operandi not just globally but at all spatial levels including the national, the regional, and the municipal (Marazzi 2011, 121). Beyond all of them loom the differentials of bond revenues determined in the international financial markets and evaluated by the credit-rating agencies.

Second, *the meanings of such key terms in political and geopolitical discourse as private versus public and markets versus states have undergone revision*. No longer can the political be seen as uniquely deriving from states or from societies defined in national-state forms. Rather, the spatial boundaries governing states themselves are no longer the national ones. They are profoundly the boundaries defined by the investment and regulatory activities of private/public businesses, pension funds, banks, international law firms, and standard-setting and credit-rating agencies. Even as the economic crisis of 2007–2008 could be seen as calling the roles of all of these into question, they have, if anything, emerged from the crisis more strongly entrenched than they entered it (e.g., Mirowski 2013; Zacarés 2021). Too much money was spent bailing out those "too big to fail" for the influence of the giant banks and industrial corporations that are the prime movers behind this heavily financialized system to suddenly dissipate (Crouch 2011). Indeed, their interests are increasingly the ones at stake as governments compete with one another to acquire their largesse. The inability to demarcate where the public ends and the private begins is exactly what produces the inability to address how to move beyond the Scylla of undemocratic transnational regulation and the Charybdis of increasingly globalized investment and monetary flows and their legal empowerment.

Third, and finally, in this context *the expropriation of land that has lain at the heart of conventional geopolitical thought is thrown into doubt as a transcendental signifier*. If classically, sovereignty was intimately associated first with the body of the monarch and then with a people occupying a territory, the Manichean them-versus-us logic which this entails no longer makes sense when the very basis to sovereign decision lies in the interstices between states in the capacities and identities of non-state actors rather than in states banging up against one another. This suggests, inter alia, that we have little to learn from excavating theorists such as Schmitt and Mackinder whose logic relies precisely on the expropriation of land/territory (e.g. Legg 2011; Kearns 2009). In a world in which authority is increasingly outsourced by states and in which states "instrumentalize" sovereignty to serve given ends but increasingly thus come under the dominion of transnational actors whose goals thus become theirs, sovereignty has not ended but has been transformed into a new "game" quite different from those old-fashioned geopolitical thought insists on constantly reproducing as somehow "essential" to understanding how the world works (Adler-Nissen and Gammeltoft-Hansen 2008).

CONCLUSION

Geopolitics and globalization have always gone together rather than been antithetical. The claim that they have been opposites over the course of the past century or so does not bear close examination. In this chapter I have tried to show how they have been mutually entailed by focusing on three moments of geopolitics' relationship with globalization: with respect to the origins of contemporary globalization in the policies pursued by successive US governments after 1945; the close connection between geopolitical history and status and the capacity to exploit the possibilities of globalization; and the emergence of new regulatory and standard-setting agencies under the sponsorship of major geopolitical powers but growing in authority in recognition of dominant states' limited ability to manage the explosion of transnational transactions on their own. Whether this virtual circle of geopolitics and globalization will continue into the future or in precisely the form it has taken so far is in the lap of the gods. What seems clear is that thinking of geopolitics in the limited territorialized-competitive terms characteristic of its early twentieth-century iteration offers little or no grasp of what has happened since. It is time to move on from the narrow inter-imperial cast of geopolitics and the foolish policy advice it often leads its proponents to proffer. At the same time we should avoid seeing contemporary globalization as somehow without geopolitical underpinnings along the lines of much writing in economic geography and economic sociology.

Yet it is hard to escape the confines of traditional thinking. The next two chapters in this first section provide evidence for the two most powerful ways by which thinking about the world remains trapped: the exclusively territorialized conception of space that informs most if not all understandings of "geopolitics" and the familiar terminology and historical-geographical analogies that this then draws on to characterize the world at large. We have been there before and foreigners are always to blame.

2

Beyond Territorial Geopolitics

The United States is a peculiar Great Power, and this had profound effects on twentieth- and early twenty-first century world politics. That is the basic premise of this chapter. The United States brought into existence the first fully "marketplace society" in history. This is a territorial society in which politics and society operate largely in terms of exchange- rather than use-value. A distinction first made by Adam Smith but developed in various ways by later thinkers such as Karl Marx and Karl Polanyi, it revolves around the idea that social and political relationships can be based predominantly on either their instrumental value (i.e., as if a price could be put on them) or their intrinsic value (i.e., as if they had unique qualities). Previous societies had elements of both, but with the rise of capitalism value-in-exchange increasingly eclipsed value-in-use. Only in the United States, however, were there so few barriers to the spread of exchange value into all areas of life and so many new incentives for acceptance of the market norms that accompanied this. In particular, the nascent country had none of the feudal-monarchical remnants that were important to modern state formation in Europe. The contradictory quality of the United States as being both just another state and one whose national government became an agent of a globalized marketplace society is one noted in accounts of how much the possibility of a world outside the bounds of the international state system inevitably encounters the difficulties of ever getting there (e.g., Walker 2010).

This is not to say that there are not profound social divisions within the United States that reproduce almost caste-like differences in access to public goods and private opportunities and thus violate the code of a pure marketplace society. But they are overwhelmingly justified in terms of merit, work ethic, or familial attributes. Rather than the openly class-based character of

European politics, at least down until recently, in the United States everyone is at least potentially "middle class." As a consequence, popular ideology tends to obscure the deep-seated inequalities based on race, ethnicity, and class. Thus, and in relation to the 2020–2021 COVID-19 pandemic, two approaches to the management of the pandemic were apparent with origins in historic divisions within US society over appropriate policy responses by federal and state governments:

> For middle class white people and elites, public health policy typically reflected liberal sanitationist values [focused on voluntary efforts at overcoming disease] . . . At the nation's borders, however, and for the disadvantaged and for most people of color, the United States has been more often authoritarian and quarantinist [exerting forceful control over bodies and lives]. (Witt 2020, 9)

So there is no need to romanticize the real operational limits of the effects of exchange-value on undermining status hierarchies of one sort or another. After all, African American slaves had by definition always had prices on their heads. The United States has had a long history of making things into property that should not be property without acknowledging that fact yet still valuing some people more than others.

In the United States, "the state" was designed by its founders in the late eighteenth century to be the servant of society, in particular its property owners and entrepreneurs, not the instrument for perpetuating aristocratic rule in an increasingly capitalist world economy. The size of the country and the increasing ethnic diversity of its population combined with the peculiarity of its form of statehood, federalist and with divided central institutions, to create material and ideological conditions propitious to exchange value as the basis for all social and political *not just economic* relationships. So, even as the United States expanded territorially into North America and through trade and investment into the rest of the world, its process of exercising power has been through bringing places to market, both materially and ideologically, rather than simply through coercive control over territory. That has been supplementary if episodically highly significant.

THE UNITED STATES FROM THE PERSPECTIVE OF LAND- VERSUS SEA-POWERS

Yet much scholarly and popular discussion of the US role in the world insists on seeing the United States as either simply just "another state" (albeit a bigger, more powerful one) or as an empire, by stretching the manifestly territorial meaning of that term to include non-territorial influence and control. Neither approach is satisfactory. Recently, classical geopolitical arguments have undergone somewhat of a revival in response to the impasse between rival liberal and realist theories of international politics (e.g., Clover 1999; Kaplan 2010). What seems most attractive in these accounts is one or more of the following: the so-called return of the global geopolitics of resources with the economic rise of China, the pedagogical simplicity of global mapping of seemingly total "opposite" types of political regime, and the appeal to the materiality and spatiality of the earth as a whole implied by the elemental antagonism of land and sea.

In classical geopolitical thought from the early twentieth century, the United States is typically classified as a quintessential sea power because of its offshore location relative to Eurasia (the geographical centerpiece of all classical geopolitical thought) and thus a potential base for a maritime empire drawing in scattered territories worldwide along the lines of the European seaborne empires such as those of Portugal and Britain. Yet this belies the fact that the simple opposition of sea- and land-powers does not match the case of the United States as a Great Power in any meaningful way. For one thing, given the traditional emphasis of the land-sea opposition on coercive or military power, the military capacity of the United States since its rise to global prominence has always involved the organizational ability to project land forces using sea- and air-power rather than a singular dependence on naval power or "gunboat diplomacy." Moreover, the United States was not born as a "sea-faring nation," which is the basic trope behind representing Britain as the quintessential sea-power. In fact, the United States was born as a territorial enterprise involving coast-to-coast settlement of European and African immigrants within a continental framework. Finally, the land-sea opposition, if with obvious origins in ancient Greek struggles between supposedly sea-powered Athens and land-powered Sparta, became popular as a simplification of emerging global struggles for primacy in the context of the period from 1875 to 1945 of intense inter-imperial rivalry between established and rising Great Powers. This was before the rise of air-power and the advent of nuclear weapons. More specifically, the present-day world is significantly different, above all in its geography of power, from previous epochs. Often labeled as the era of "globalization," this label signals the rise of actors (multinational firms, global NGOs, international institutions, etc.) and processes of development (globalized financial markets, global commodity chains, etc.) that cannot be linked to a single territorial address (Fettweis 2003).

This is a world that the United States has by design and through unintended consequences helped to bring about. If this is an "empire," then it is the only decentered one in history, which I would think makes it something else. For another thing, this world has not been brought about predominantly through direct coercion or by territorial rule but through socioeconomic incorporation into practices and routines derivative of or compatible with those first developed in the United States. The best word to describe these processes is "hegemony." Drawing from my previous book (Agnew 2005), this chapter tries to make the case for this by pointing to the ways in which the United States developed an interactional/non-territorial approach to capitalist development rather than the ways in which empires relied on direct territorial control. In turn, this laid the groundwork for the shift away from the territorial geopolitics that is the stock-in-trade of conventional geopolitics.

HEGEMONY VERSUS EMPIRE

There has recently been much debate over which of two words—hegemony or empire—best describes the relationship between the United States (more specifically, the US governmental apparatus) and the rest of the world today. Much academic debate is about words and it often seems scholastic and of little practical concern. In this case that is anything but true. The two words offer profoundly different understandings of American power and its contemporary manifestations, not least in terms of how such power can be challenged. Interestingly, in much usage the two terms are not readily distinguished from one another; either way an Almighty America is seen as recasting the world in its image. From this viewpoint, hegemony is simply the relatively unconstrained coercive power exercised by a hegemon or seat of empire. I want to suggest that this usage is both problematic historically and unhelpful analytically. More specifically, the terms have distinctive etymologies and contemporary meanings in English and other languages that when used analytically can help to give precision to what has happened to US relations with the world at large, for example as a consequence of the 2003–2007 war on and occupation of Iraq. Taken together, they also provide a take-off point for the historical relationship between US hegemony and globalization considered subsequently.

By way of example concerning the two words, it is possible to have empire without hegemony. Good cases in point: Spain and Portugal after the sixteenth century. Neither country had much if any control over world politics after 1600 but did have territorial "possessions" left over from their early roles in European world conquest. It is also possible to have hegemony without empire, as with the United States after World War II, when US governments exerted tremendous influence over world politics but with little or no contemporaneous territorial extension. US governments, in line with their own republican and anti-colonial origins as well as a new material interest in free trade, identified themselves largely with anti-colonial movements around the world. The distinction between hegemony and empire can help today in addressing whether or not securing US hegemony after the end of the Cold War will require increased reliance on seeking empire. In other words, will continued US hegemony depend upon creating an empire somewhat like that ruled by Britain at the end of the nineteenth century as opposed to continuing to work multilaterally through international institutions and alliances, particularly when US economic troubles raise the possibility of a globalized world order in which the United States is no longer paramount? The hegemony/empire distinction also enables us to see two distinctive impulses within US geopolitics that have historically characterized American national self-images and their projection outward: what can be called domestic "republic" and foreign "empire." On the one hand, the popular idea that the United States represents a new type of polity and, on the other, that its security as such depends on interventions and influence worldwide including, but not being restricted to, territorial occupation and control.

The US influence has been particularly widespread and potent compared to previous epochs that might be identified with the "hegemony" of other states. Some commentators claim that Britain was more committed to hegemony than the United States has been and that the United States has increasingly and successfully substituted coercion for hegemony since the 1970s (Silver and Arrighi 2003), and others that both have been empires for which the word "hegemony" is simply a euphemism (Ferguson 2003). Needless to say, this chapter argues otherwise.

In the first place, US hegemony has been based on a rejection of territorial limits to its influence, as would necessarily come with empire. In this sense it has been a more ambitious non-territorial enterprise, notwithstanding periods when territorial strategies have been pursued, such as during the Spanish-American War. The United States is not just the latest in a long list of hegemons achieving global "power" and then all behaving the same way. In previous epochs, such as that of British hegemony in the nineteenth century, the influence exerted was much more geographically circumscribed. Indeed, Britain had little or no hegemony in Europe. Outside of Europe, its empire was central to its enterprise, although there was considerable investment in and trade with the United States, Latin America, and elsewhere as well. The whole world has become America's oyster, so to speak, such that, at least until recently, it has brought even its erstwhile challengers such as Russia and China within its cultural-economic orbit.

Second, American hegemony has been a potent brew of cultural and political-economic doctrines and rules of conduct enforced up to a point but usually the outcome of assent and cooperation more than direct coercion. Except within their empire, think of cricket and tea, and among certain groups of "anglophiles," the British never had anything like the same influence around the world. More importantly, to see the resulting globalization as simply based on coercion is profoundly mistaken. It is the result of the self-mobilization of people around the world into practices, routines, and outlooks which they not only accept but think of as their own. This has been the "genius" of US hegemony: to enroll others in its exercise. But this brew did not simply appear out of thin air once the United States came to use its power resources to make itself a global superpower. It was already brewing domestically in a cultural-political-economic context that has had any number of important historic similarities to the larger world: a history of serious and persistent social and geographical conflicts, a system of government founded on the institutional division of power, an industrial-capitalist system that evolved without much central direction or negative regulation, a population of multiethnic origins, weak political parties and organized labor, and from the 1890s onward the first political economy devoted to turning production and consumption into a virtuous circle (under the rubric of Fordism).

The term hegemony understood in this manner figures prominently in some accounts of modern geopolitics proposed previously (Agnew and Corbridge 1995; Agnew 2005). These accounts see the modern world as experiencing a succession of hegemonies associated with different dominant states but with recent American hegemony slowly giving way since the end of the Cold War to a hegemony without a hegemon; hegemony exercised increasingly through global markets and international institutions by a growing transnational class of business people, lawyers, and bureaucrats. In this construction, hegemony is absolutely *not* equivalent to simple domination (territorial or otherwise) but refers to widespread assent to principles of conduct that are the "common sense" of world politics and that emanate from distinctive cultural-economic sites with potentially global reach.

The transformation of US hegemony into something outside its hands can be seen as predating the end of the Cold War but intensifying thereafter. Increased US unilateralism since 1970, beginning with abrogation of the Bretton Woods Agreement governing fixed currency exchange rates in 1971, is viewed as evidence for a crisis of rather than a strengthening in *American* hegemony. Unwittingly, however, this and other unilateral acts by US governments have all had the net effect of spreading and deepening the impact of globalization. For example, US recognition of Communist China in 1972 has had the long-term effect of bringing China into the world economy as a major producer and consumer, the support for Islamic fundamentalists in Afghanistan during the period of Soviet occupation helped to create the global terrorism that relies on the technologies of globalization but is ideologically at odds with the marketplace society that the world was told by President George W. Bush to be "for or against," the imposition of import controls on Japanese cars in the 1980s brought Japanese car companies to produce in the United States. In this construction, hegemony is extremely reliant on soft power, the active assent to and agreement with international standards of conduct governing economic and political transactions, largely the rules of marketplace society, even as US governments rail against the very institutions and rules (such as the UN, for example) they first sponsored. Osama bin Laden and Al-Qaeda knew this very well.

GLOBALIZATION AND THE CURRENT GLOBAL GEOPOLITICAL ORDER

The post–Cold War geopolitical order, however, is still organized geographically. No longer is the geographical structure that of US and Soviet blocs and a Third World in which the two central powers competed. Rather, it is that of a profoundly uneven or fragmented global economy with a patchwork or mosaic of local and regional areas connected together through or marginal to the control centers based in the world's major cities and governmental centers. But states are, if anything, even more important to this economic hegemony without centralized political control, to paraphrase Ellen Wood (2003), than they were to the Cold War geopolitical order. From this perspective, recent US-government actions post–11 September 2001 can be seen as an attempt to reestablish the United States as central to contemporary hegemony by using the one resource, military power, in which the United States is still supreme. Though the attacks of 11 September can be construed as directed as much at the values and practices of the world economy in general as at the United States per se, the George W. Bush administration chose to see them in a nationalist light. To a significant degree this response is related to the fact that the Bush government was dominated by people with business and political ties to US defense industries as well as to the militarist attitudes of the American South. Unfortunately, it is not clear that the United States can economically afford to prosecute a war without end on terrorism or its perceived cultural and political opponents without the active cooperation of its previous allies and without sacrificing the very values and interests that its war is supposedly all about. Empires always seem to end up undermining exactly what it was they were initially supposed to sustain. From this perspective, empire is both unsustainable and counterproductive as a strategy for resecuring US hegemony.

States and other actors in world politics are increasingly part of global arrangements that point beyond both US hegemony and US empire. The world economy today is truly global to a degree never seen before in its geographical scope, the pace of transactions between widely scattered places within it, and its hollowing out of simple territorial forms of political authority across a wide range of issue domains (economic, social, and political). And it has become so in the way it has, subsequent chapters will argue, because of the nature of US hegemony. That hegemony, however, has made itself increasingly redundant. The influence of capital is now mediated through global financial markets, the flow of trade within multinational firms, and the limited capacities of global regulatory institutions. Its benefits and costs now fall on all parts of the world. The corporate form created and nurtured in the United States has become the global model abetted by the abandonment of governmental responsibility for limiting corporate power through antitrust and other means (Winkler 2018). If the benefits and costs still fall unevenly, the unevenness is no longer on a country-by-country or bloc-by-bloc basis. Geographical variation in economic growth is increasingly local and regional within countries. But it is not the global that is "new" in globalization so much as there is a changing geographical logic to the world economy. In other words, it is not its "globality" that is new but its combination of global networks and localized territorial fragmentation. Under the "previous" global, the world economy was structured largely (but never entirely) around territorial entities such as states, colonial empires, and geopolitical spheres of influence. The main novelty today is the increasing role in economic prosperity and underdevelopment of *cross-border flows* in relation to national states and to networks linking cities with one another and their hinterlands and the *increased differentiation* between localities and regions as a result of the spatial biases built into flow-networks.

Rather than the "end" of geography, therefore, globalization entails its reformulation away from an economic mapping of the world in terms of state territories toward a more complex mosaic of states, regions, global city-regions, and localities differentially integrated into the global economy. There is geopolitics to contemporary globalization, therefore, both with respect to its origins and with respect to its continuing operation. Culturally, the world is also increasingly "creolized" rather than simply Americanized (Pells 1997). This is not surprising given the increasing cultural heterogeneity of the United States itself and the need for businesses, be they American, European, or whatever, to adapt their products to different markets at home and abroad. Crucially, for the first time since the eighteenth century the "cradle of capitalism"—Western Europe and the United States—"has as much to fear from the rapidity of change as does the periphery" (Desai 2002, 305). More specifically, the most important political change is the dramatic decline in the autonomy of even the most powerful states in the face of the globalization of production, trade, technology, and communication.

State power always has had two aspects to it: despotic power and infrastructural power (Mann 1984). If the former refers to the power exerted by socioeconomic elites that occupy political office, the latter refers to the power that accrues to the state as such from its delivery of infrastructural or public goods to populations. Historically, the rise in relative importance of infrastructural power, as elites have been forced through political struggles to become more responsive to their populations, led to a territorialization of political authority. Until recently, the technologies for providing public goods have had built-in territorial bias, not least relating to the capture of positive externalities. Increasingly, however, infrastructural power can be deployed across networks that, though sited in discrete locations, are not necessarily areal or territorial in the externality fields that they produce. Thus, currencies, systems of measure, trading networks, educational provision, and welfare services need not be associated with exclusive membership in a conventional nation-state. New deployments of infrastructural power both deterritorialize existing states and reterritorialize membership around cities and hinterlands, regions, and continental-level political entities such as the European Union (Scott 1998). There is a simultaneous scaling-up and scaling-down of the relevant geographical fields of infrastructural power depending on the political economies of scale of different regulatory, productive, and redistributive public goods. Consequently,

> the more economies of scale of dominant goods and assets diverge from the structural scale of the national state—and the more those divergences feed back into each other in complex ways—then the more the authority, legitimacy, policy-making capacity, and policy-implementing effectiveness of the state will be eroded and undermined both within and without. (Cerny 1995, 621)

In the US case, this is exacerbated by the difficulties of coordination of purpose and direction within the country's governmental system.

Using the example of currencies, the United States has encouraged the use of the US$ in world trade and finance since the collapse of the Bretton Woods system in the early 1970s. Initially designed by the Nixon administration to make US exports more competitive and to staunch the US balance-of-payments deficit, the floating of the US$ against other currencies has been a major if unintended stimulus to globalization, both in facilitating trade and in encouraging the explosion of global finance. Although the US government, insofar as it can influence the Federal Reserve (the US central bank), can still use its $ to manipulate the world economy to the benefit of its producers and consumers, there are real limits to this when the United States depends on massive inflows of foreign-originated investment, when such a large proportion of the US$ in circulation is outside the territorial boundaries of the United States, and when other governments (such as China) peg their currencies closely to the dollar and build up large reserves that they can use to maintain the peg and thus keep the prices of their exports competitive in the US domestic market. As a result, the US$ and other currencies of wider circulation (such as the euro and the Japanese yen) have slowly eroded the independent monetary infrastructural power of both the states in which their currencies circulate and themselves, to the extent that they, and not just the bearers of less-potent currencies, are now on the receiving end of currency shocks from "outside." Global markets increasingly determine the relative values of what are still nominally national-state currencies. Indeed, the "inside" and the "outside" of the state are increasingly in question as to their material significance. Thus, in a major area in which the United States has previously exercised economic hegemony, there are increasing signs of hegemony—that of global currency markets—without a singular state hegemon that can *effectively* intercede in them.

US HEGEMONY AND THE ROOTS OF GLOBALIZATION

The story of American hegemony, therefore, is not that of the simple rise of yet another hegemonic state in succession to previous ones but rather the creation of a global economy under American auspices, reflecting the content of a hegemony arising from the development of the United States, and the feedback of this system on the behavior of US governments. In this section I endeavor to show why the later hegemonic strategies of US governments in world politics favoring the "soft" power of assent, cooperation, co-optation, and consensus, even if invariably self-interested and backed up by coercion, grew out of the particularities of American historical experience, especially the divided political institutions and marketplace society that made it distinctive from other states. This does not involve endorsing the exceptionalist claim that the United States is not simply different from but *better* than other places. Rather it is to replace the narrative of hegemony as essentially one Great Power indistinguishable from others substituting for another now in decline, a mechanical model of hegemonic succession, with a narrative that gives hegemony distinctive content depending on which state or society exercises it. Globalization is the outcome of the geographical projection of American marketplace society allied to technical advances in communication and transportation.

It is in the domestic history of the United States, therefore, that the roots of the US hegemony exercised later around the world can be found. To reiterate, this is not an argument for the superiority of the United States, as those who confuse arguments about the specificity of the American experience with American "exceptionalism" tend to claim. It is, rather, that world history has its roots in specific places, not everywhere at once or in behavioral imperatives that emanate from some global totality such as "capitalism" or "land- versus sea-power." This is not, therefore, an argument for either an overarching *telos* (such as physical geography, capital accumulation, technological change, or liberalism) or a single cause that lies "behind" everything else. I emphasize, rather, the sedimented experiences of the American population, particularly in relation to critical junctures, such as the late nineteenth century, and the cumulative effect of these on popular practices and attitudes.

In this connection, it is a commonplace now to see the genius of the American Constitution of 1787, as expressed most eloquently and persuasively in the writings of James Madison, as tying freedom to "empire." Madison maintained that in place of the British colonial system the best solution for the American rebels would be the creation of a powerful central government that would provide the locus of security for the survival of republican government. The central government would oversee geographical expansion into the continent and this would guarantee an outlet for a growing population that would otherwise invade the rights and property of other citizens. In this way, republican government was tied to an ever-expanding system. Madison had brilliantly reversed the traditional thinking about the relationship between size and freedom. Small was no longer beautiful. Of course, Thomas Jefferson and others less tied to the fortunes of land acquisition and growing markets initially opposed the logic of expansionism. But eventually they too came around. Indeed, when he became president, Jefferson justified the acquisition of Louisiana and the prospective addition of Canada and Cuba by claiming the extension of "empire for liberty."

Although couched in the language of political rights and citizenship, the association of freedom with geographical expansion reflected two important economic principles. The first was that expansion of the marketplace is necessary for political and social well-being. The second was that economic liberty is by definition the foundation for freedom per se. So the totally new political system after independence was designed to combine these two principles: the central government guaranteeing the capacity for expansion into the continental interior and into foreign markets and lower-tier government (the states) and the division of powers between the branches of central government restricting the power of government to regulate and limit economic liberty.

Each of the political-economic principles can be seen as emerging from stories about American "national character" and the model of citizenship offered by the vision of American exceptionalism. Although Americans celebrate some historic occasions, such as Independence Day (the 4th of July), and founding documents, such as the Declaration of Independence and the Constitution, they have not had much history to define themselves by. America has been defined not so much by a common history, as most imagined communities of nationhood seem to have (Anderson, B. 1983). Rather, Americans have defined themselves through a shared geography expressed in the future-facing expansion of the frontier by individual pioneers. The Founding Father, Thomas Jefferson, said he liked "the dreams of the future better than the history of the past."

The founders of the United States could find ready justification for their institutional creation in the timely publication of Adam Smith's *An Inquiry into the Nature and Causes of the Wealth of Nations* in 1776. Smith stood in relation to the founding as Keynes was to do to the political economy of the New Deal in the 1930s: a systematizer of an emerging "common sense" for the times. The Constitution is open to contrary interpretations on the relative powers of both federal branches and tiers of government (Lynch, J. M. 1999). Following the Civil War and particularly from the 1930s until the 1980s, the federal level expanded its powers much more than any of the Founders, including its greatest advocate, Alexander Hamilton, could have foreseen. At the federal level, and reflecting the essential ambiguity of the Constitution, the Supreme Court has also come to exert great power through its capacity for interpreting the meaning of the founding document.

The "culture of the market" directly challenged and quickly overwhelmed that of "the land" in the early United States and opened up localities to long-distance movement. The market revolution of the early nineteenth century, however, had older roots (Sellers 1991). The commercial outlook of many US farmers had its origins in the spatial division of labor organized under British mercantilism, in which they came to serve distant markets rather than engage in subsistence agriculture. Much of the basis for American independence lay in the struggle to expand the boundaries for individual economic liberty within a system that was more oriented to a sense of an organic whole: the British Empire. American "marketplace society," therefore, was not a pure intellectual production or entirely postindependence in genesis but arose out of an evolving material context in which it served the emerging identity and interests of a dominant social group of capitalist farmers (Agnew 1987). As the industrial bourgeoisie rose to prominence in the nineteenth century, they inherited the hegemony of marketplace society already in place but expanded it both geographically, into every nook and cranny of the expanding country, and functionally, into every part of everyday life.

The common sense of American society, therefore, is a profoundly marketized one. Everything and everyone has their price. But this does not mean that there has ever been total agreement about how far to push this or whether government is solely its instrument or can be its restrainer. Certainly, the excesses of the marketplace have never been without resistance or challenge from the Age of Jackson in the late 1820s and early 1830s to the present. Indeed, within the broad parameters of marketplace society, American politics has always oscillated between attempts at policing and disciplining the marketplace in the interests of this or that group through the use of governmental power and letting market forces loose from tighter institutional moorings (Earle, C. 2003). Generally, it has been during times of economic distress or in response to perceived political threats (internal, as with the Civil War, or external, as with the world wars) that the balance has shifted toward restraint. The two ramshackle political parties that since the Civil War have tied American society to its political institutions, however, both accept the marketplace model but have had shifting attitudes toward managing it. With the exception of the Democratic Party during the 1930s, however, which profoundly increased the federal role in the US economy and society, both parties have tended to shy away from interfering much with the political dominance of private economic interests.

Certainly, by the 1890s the United States had, in the eyes of influential commentators and political leaders from all over the country, fulfilled its "continental destiny." The time was propitious, they believed, to launch the United States as a truly world power. One source of this tendency was a concern for internal social order. Not only did the late nineteenth century witness the growth of domestic labor and socialist movements that challenged the preeminence of business within American society, it also saw a major period of depression and stagnation, the so-called Long Depression from the 1870s to 1896, in which profit rates declined and unemployment increased. This combination was seen as a volatile cocktail, ready to explode at any moment. Commercial expansion abroad was viewed as a way of both building markets and resolving the profits squeeze. Unemployment would decline, popular consumption would increase, and the appeal of subversive politics would decrease. Another source was more immediately ideological. US history had been one of expansion: why should the continent set limits to the "march of freedom"? To Frederick Jackson Turner (1996, 289), the historian who had claimed the internal "frontier" as the source of America's difference with other societies, the United States could only be "itself" (for which one reserved the term "America," even though it applied to the entire continent, not just the part occupied by the United States) if it continued to expand. An invigorated American foreign policy and investment beyond continental shores were the necessary corollaries.

The outburst of European colonialism in the late nineteenth century was also of importance in stimulating American designs for expansion beyond continental limits. Home markets were no longer enough for large segments of the American manufacturing industry, particularly the emerging monopolies such as, for example, Standard Oil and the Singer Sewing Machine Co. Without following the Europeans the fear was that American firms would be cut out of overseas markets that exercised an increasing spell over the American national imagination, such as China and SE Asia. The difference between the Americans and most of the Europeans, however, was that for the Americans, business expansion did not necessarily entail territorial expansion. Guaranteed access was what they craved. Indeed, colonialism in the European tradition was generally seen as neither necessary nor desirable. Not only was it expensive for governments, in many cases it also involved making cultural compromises and deferring to local despots of one sort or another; costs many Americans were not anxious to bear. There was also the difficulty of squaring empire with a national identity that had long had a considerable anti-imperial component (Heiss 2002).

It took some time for the United States to react to the outburst of European imperialism beginning in the 1870s. Indeed, not until the 1890s did the United States embark on an explicit imperialist project, as the post–Civil War integration of the US economy concluded and the industrial and agricultural sectors entered recession. Undoubtedly for a time, and as a result of both economic imperatives and the desire to avoid lagging behind the Europeans (and Japanese) in "imperial prestige," US governments did pursue territorial possessions. From around 1910 until the 1940s, however, a reaction against this set in (at least as far as territories outside Latin America are concerned!) with a return to suspicion of territorial expansion. After the Second World

War, considerations of security and stability in the Cold War with the Soviet Union tended to trump anti-imperialism but now in the context not so much of pursuing American territorial empire as in restricting the development of regimes seen as sympathetic to the Soviet Union: from Iran and Guatemala in the 1950s to Cuba, Chile, Nicaragua, Angola, South Vietnam, and a myriad of other countries later on.

From the 1890s, the American approach to economic expansion tended to favor direct investment rather than portfolio investment and conventional trade. Advantages hitherto specific to the United States in terms of economic concentration and mass markets—the cost-effectiveness of large plants, economies of process, product and market integration—were exportable by large firms as they invested in overseas subsidiaries. For much of the nineteenth century, capital exports and trade were what drove the world economy. By 1910, however, a largely new type of expatriate investment was increasingly dominant: the setting up of foreign branches in other industrial countries by firms operating from a home base. US firms were overwhelmingly the most important agents of this new trend. They were laying the groundwork for the globalization of production that has slowly emerged, with the 1930s and 1940s as the unique period of retraction, since then. It is the globalization of production through direct investment and strategic alliances and an allied loosening of financial markets from national-state control that constitute the truly most-significant driving forces behind contemporary globalization. The globalization of production has its roots in the American experience of foreign direct investment from the 1890s onward.

But American expansionism after 1896 was never simply economic. As with hegemony at home, it was also always political and cultural. There was a "mission" to spread American values and the American ethos as well as to rescue American business from its economic impasse. These were invariably related to one another as parts of a virtuous circle. Spreading American "values" led to the consumption of American products, American mass culture broke down barriers of class and ethnicity, and undermining these barriers encouraged the further consumption of products made by American businesses. American foreign policy largely followed this course thereafter, with different emphases reflecting the balance of power between different domestic interests and general global conditions: making the world safe for expanding markets and growing investment beyond the borders of the United States. America itself was sold as an idea (Rosenberg 1983, 37).

The movement from a territorialized marketplace society to globalization was based on the prior existence of the "open borders" that characterized the American experiment. Notwithstanding the periodic political pressures to close the national territory to foreign products, people, and capital that emerged into prominence during times of declining firm profitability, rising unemployment, and social upheaval, the general trajectory of American politics from 1890 onward was toward opening up the national economy in relation to the rest of the world.

This reflected the origins of the United States as a set of settler colonies in which space was open to expansion rather than enclosed in defense of outsiders. Spatial orientations are of particular importance to understanding America, therefore, whether this is with respect to foreign policy or to national identity. It could be argued that a geographical imagination is central to all national political cultures. Imagining a coherent territorial entity containing a group of people with a common attachment to that territory has been crucial in the making of all national states. However, if all nations are imagined communities, then America is the imagined community par excellence (Campbell 1992). The space of "America" was already created in the imaginations of the first European settlers en route to the "New World" as a space of openness and possibility (Dolan 1994). It was not constructed and corrupted by centuries of history and power struggles as was Europe. Even now, America is a country that is easily seen as both "nowhere" and "pastless," constructed as totally modern and democratic against a European (or some other) "Other" mired in a despotic history and stratified by the tyranny of aristocracy. The ideology of the American Dream, an ideology which stresses that anyone can be successful in acquiring capital and goods given hard work, luck, and unobtrusive government, marks out the American historical experience as unique or exceptional. The dominance of this liberal ideology has meant that America has never had either the revolutionary or reactionary traditions so prevalent in modern Europe. In narrowing the political field, the American liberal tradition protects the goals of the individual against the state and social collectivities (Hartz 1955). Narratives of the history of America as a country of migrants successfully seeking a better way of life provide practical evidence for this imagination. The enslaved Africans and conquered "Indians" who made constructing the New World possible are not surprisingly largely absent from this vision except as incidental characters or as barriers to be overcome.

The mindset of limitless possibility was reinforced by the myth of the frontier experience of individual social mobility, of the energy of a youthful country in contrast to the social stagnation and economic inequality of "old" Europe. Americans were free to set themselves up in the vast expanse of "empty" land available on the frontier, discounting the presence of natives whose self-evident technological and religious "backwardness" justified the expropriation of their land. All settlers were equal on the frontier, so the myth goes, and those who were successful succeeded due to their own hard work, not through any advantage of birth. Clearly there are historiographic problems with this national myth, not least the violent erasure of other people and their pasts that occurred as part of this geographical movement (Shapiro 1997). However, the myth has long remained as a powerful aspect of American culture. The initial presumption was that as long as the frontier continued to expand, America would flourish.

This mindset remained influential beyond the physical expansion of the United States across the continent as "the frontier" was reconfigured around the necessity to expand the "American way" and "American good" beyond American shores, especially in the years following the end of the Second World War when another power (the Soviet Union) offered a competing utopian rendering of political economy. Importantly, the frontier story is not simply an elite construction told to the population at large but one retold and recycled through a variety of cultural forms: most obviously through mass education, but more importantly through the media and in popular culture.

The "frontier" character of the American economy—expanding markets for goods and opportunities for individuals beyond previous limits—figures strongly in the American stimulus to contemporary economic globalization. As I have argued, this is itself tied to a particular cultural image: the ethos of the consumer-citizen. The American position in the Cold War of defending and promulgating this model ran up against the competing Soviet model of the worker-state. The resultant geopolitical order was thus intimately bound up with the expression of American identity. This was spread through ideas of "development," drawing clearly on American experiences, first in such acts as the Marshall Plan to aid the reconstruction of Europe immediately after World War II, and then in the modernization of the "Third World" following the elements of a model of American society pushed most strongly during the short presidency of John Kennedy (1961–1962). The Age of High Mass Consumption that President Kennedy (and Johnson) advisor Walt Rostow proclaimed as the end of history, and as such the goal of worldwide US development efforts, was a reflection in the mirror that America held up to the world (Rostow 1960).

CONCLUSION

This selective historical narrative points to how the foundations for globalization and the new geography of power associated with it were laid down initially in the United States in the late nineteenth century. This came to fruition with the rise to Great Power status of the United States after World War II and the capacity of the United States to project its political economy into the rest of the world. Thus contemporary globalization undoubtedly does have a geopolitical basis to its origins, albeit no longer predictably congruent in the benefits it delivers to its place of origin. From this viewpoint, the contemporary global geopolitical order is not best thought of in terms of classical geopolitical motifs such as land- versus sea-powers but must attend to the ways in which hegemony interpellates with empire and how global hegemony develops from prototypes reflecting the institutions and values of dominant Great Powers. Timeless geopolitical metaphors offer little purchase on understanding this spatially complex process.

3

Making the Strange Familiar

Historical-geographical analogy has been crucial to perpetuating the image of geopolitics inherited from the era of inter-imperial rivalry and imposing it on current reality. We are all familiar with the invocation of the Munich syndrome for the dangers of appeasing radical adversaries referring back to British prime minister Neville Chamberlain's taking Hitler's promises at face value in the buildup to World War II. In 2003, for example, it was freely invoked to justify the US invasion and occupation of Iraq. In the United States in 2021 it became widely acceptable to speak of "containing" China and in 2022 of doing the same to Russia. Of course, this is an effort at going back to the "good old days" of the Cold War with the former Soviet Union, even if current circumstances—China is deeply involved in the world economy and Russia's "business model" is one of oligarchs looting domestic raw materials and investing the proceeds abroad; the Soviet Union was profoundly isolated; and the internal political cohesion of the United States to face off against an implacable enemy—are nothing like in the 1950s. This is not just a poor historical trope but also a misleading and dangerous analogy that risks self-fulfilling conflicts (Ganesh 2021a; Kopper and Peragovics 2019). It can also suggest that China and Russia are not so much agents of their own destiny as pursuing courses of action that are entirely down to the mistakes and culpability of the United States (and "the West" in general) who have hitherto "run" the world for time immemorial (Ganesh 2021c). Old appeasement analogies are then trotted out as if their relevance were self-evident. Irrespective of immediate geographical circumstances or historical change, the analogy serves to give support to the claim of perpetual territorial animosity rooted in the "timeless desire" of Great Powers to control global space.

Given the relatively important roles of the European countries and the United States in recent world politics, it is no coincidence that many of the most popular geopolitical analogies in current circulation are drawn from the edges of Europe. This is the near abroad where much of the foreign policy of the Great Powers was focused during much of the twentieth century. As a result, terms such as "Finlandization" (neutralization in the face of a hostile and more powerful neighboring state; it made a spectacular comeback as a proposed solution to the 2022 Russian invasion of Ukraine (e.g., Spiegel 2022)), "beyond the Pale" (referring initially to the area inhabited by the native Irish beyond a fenced district conquered by the English around Dublin and later to the area most Jews were confined to within the Russian Empire), "Dutch disease" (referring to the macroeconomic consequences of a sudden resource bonanza), "the Switzerland of [this or that world region]" (meaning a country whose once severe internal ethnic conflicts have been resolved institutionally), "Macedonian syndrome" (the prospect of irredentism and subsequent unstable borders leading to intractable ethnic conflict), and "balkanization" (the fission of multiethnic empires into successor national states) have come into a certain linguistic currency among politicians and scholars alike to refer to and putatively explain situations well beyond the original context of use but carry with them loaded meanings that expose the specificity of their origins as political terms based on geopolitical stereotypes. To complicate matters, some of these, beyond the pale, for example, are also used more abstractly or as turns of phrase to refer to mental states, modes of thought, or intellectual divisions of one sort or another.

In this chapter I focus on the latter two—Macedonian syndrome and balkanization—as not only drawing from the same well of analogies but as also profoundly illustrative of the process of geographical naming and political blaming. This is how the territorialized version of geopolitics is reproduced notwithstanding all of its deficiencies in relation to historical as well as current reality. When they "travel" or are applied around the world, the turns of phrase conjure up a particular vision of conflict as akin to that associated with the region from which they are taken: atavistic and presumably intractable ethnic-national conflict. The term "ethnic" conflict is itself often vague yet all-inclusive in covering everything from religious and linguistic to nationalist-based conflicts but equally often without reference to external sponsors and interventions whose roles are thus completely obscured by the analogies and research/policies that emanate from them (e.g., Wimmer et al. 2004).

As we shall see, if the first analogy about the Macedonian syndrome has a largely academic application, the second, balkanization, has been applied more broadly and by a wider range of commentators and actors in Europe and North America. This critical analysis of geographical naming reflects a recent trend toward understanding global geopolitics as an active process of naming, blaming, and acting on the basis of geographical labels and the meanings they encode (e.g., Ó Tuathail and Agnew 1992; Ó Tuathail 1996; Agnew 2003; Bialasiewicz and Minca 2005).

GEOGRAPHICAL ANALOGY AND FAMILIARIZATION

In his book laying out a geopolitical strategy for a post–G. W. Bush US foreign policy, Zbigniew Brzezinski (2006) made extensive use of the idea of what he calls a "Global Balkans" stretching from Turkey to the farthest reaches of Central Asia and down into South and SE Asia. In this construction, a zone of political instability yet of economic importance, not least because of its large deposits of fossil fuels, will be at the center of world politics for years to come. Previously, Brzezinski (1997) had made reference to a "Eurasian Balkans" that had a similar role but which excluded South and SE Asia. What Brzezinski leaves unsaid is *why* he uses the term "Balkans" to describe the regions he defines as he does. Brzezinski's own eminence within US foreign-policy circles and the success of his books suggest, however, that there is something self-evident to some audiences about invoking the word Balkans at some considerable distance from its home location. Long associated in Western Europe with irrational ethnic hatreds among intermixed ethnic groups, the Balkans as a geographical analogy works to make a stranger world somehow more familiar and consequently both more understandable and manageable because it conjures up the image of a place with a "known" past of internecine conflict and historical trauma that can be projected elsewhere. Needless to say, this vision of a world lends itself neatly to a geopolitics in which the United States and other Great Powers are largely benign, exogenous actors rather than active agents of conflict in the regions in question. The naming involved thus gives rise to both a model of the process that produces conflict, akin to the ethnic enmities of the Balkans, and those who are to blame, the locals, and not the distant and apparently disinterested and blameless outsiders.

Seemingly unbeknownst to him, Brzezinski's works appeared at a time of spreading interest in metaphor and analogy among students of world politics (see, e.g., Chilton and Lakoff 1995; Beer and Hariman 1996; Beer and de Landstheer 2004). Some of this is motivated by the so-called literary turn in the social sciences which has drawn attention to how all thinking and practice is mediated by language (and reasoning with language) and by the need, felt equally by theorists, teachers, and politicians, to turn the unfamiliar into the seemingly familiar (e.g., Lakoff and Johnson 1980; Der Derian and Shapiro 1989; Drulák 2006). From this viewpoint, metaphor and, more particularly, analogy are not simply stylistic conventions or rhetorical devices. They are fundamental to all thought, communication, and, because much political action is collective and thus reliant on communication, to mobilization and behavior. Representation is not the dead letter that it is often portrayed to be by exponents of geopolitical and/or economic determinism. Because metaphor is fundamental to all thought, pretending that one can transcend it is dangerously misleading. From one viewpoint, indeed, metaphor is *the* crucial human talent. Yet, in awe of metaphor's power to frame thought, some other thinkers have come to believe that metaphors are all-powerful (e.g., Lakoff and Johnson 1980). But, as Pinker (2007) argues, this is going too far. Metaphors are implicit generalizations whose implications can always be tested against both natural and social reality. Consequently, some metaphors can be judged as more fruitful and helpful than others. Thus, for example, much of the recent explosion of writing about the United States as "empire" is based on the explicit invocation of historical analogy to this or that prior empire without much—if any—attention to minimalist criteria for what makes an empire, the changed circumstances of the day, and whether other terms or concepts might not better capture the realities of the moment. A story of historic continuity or repetition through the use of a specific historical-geographical analogy thus trumps one of change or adaptation in the nature of political forms (Agnew 2005, chapter 2; Kennedy, D. 2007). So, in much of contemporary international politics and in analysis of it, a seemingly dead metaphorical geography trumps a living history.

Some of the recent interest in analogy is inspired not so much just by the terms used in explicit theorizing (such as this or that state as an "empire" or interstate relations as "anarchic") as more specifically by the practical reason of politicians and intellectuals of statecraft, as the presumed experience of some times and places is projected onto the world in order to facilitate communication with or performance directed at target audiences (e.g., Shapiro 1989; Khong 1992). In this way a set of often "doubtful particularisms" are turned into universal truths to justify this or that action without much immediate connection to the time and place to which the particular metaphor or analogy is now being applied. Analogies are metaphors that involve comparison with a supposedly exemplary, similar, or congruent situation elsewhere and/or at another time.

If metaphors are indirect descriptions, then, analogies are indirect arguments. The precise nature of the comparison implied by an analogy is usually left obscure because to make it more specific would be to betray its inevitable ambiguity in relation to the case at hand. Increased specificity about its appropriateness would point up its limitations. Some historical analogies from recent world politics are undoubtedly familiar: for example, that to the US Bush administration in 2003 Saddam Hussein was a reincarnation on the Euphrates of Hitler and those who might question precipitate military action in relation to Iraq were equivalent to Neville Chamberlain and the appeasers of Hitler in the 1930s. Yet implicit in the analogy is the problematic notion that Iraq somehow enjoyed a similar role in world politics and a capacity to change its course as did prewar Germany. Of course, opponents of the Iraq War were similarly caught up in analogies to the Vietnam War and other "quagmires" of different vintage and location (Korea, Central America, Philippines) whatever the significant differences with these other cases. Much of the political disputation in the United States and Europe about the Iraq War was a verbal war between historical analogies. When Russian president Vladimir Putin referred to the government of Ukraine as "Nazis" in the build-up to Russia's invasion of that country in 2022, he was using the powerful memory of the Soviet Union's World War II struggle with Germany and putative Ukrainian collaborators to deny Ukraine its status as a sovereign state (e.g., Pomerantsev 2022). To Putin this analogy is no mere rhetoric (Krastev 2022). It had become commonplace among his apologists long before the invasion (e.g., Dobrokhotov 2021). The myth of the Great Patriotic War was thus used to justify disciplining the wayward Ukrainians and point the way back to past imperial grandeur (Guénard 2022; Sorokin 2014). Amazingly, that the president of Ukraine was Jewish with ancestors who had been murdered in the Nazi Holocaust seemingly reinforced rather than contradicted the claim that Ukraine was a province in revolt against Holy Mother Russia. It is exactly the geopolitical and intellectual uses of such historical and, more specifically, geographical analogies, not unmasking the disciplinary metaphors (anarchy, containers, empire, etc.) that guide thinking about world politics tout court, that concern me here; although they obviously matter too.

Indeed, one type of analogy that has received much less attention than the use of historical analogies is the recycling of geographical terms or names in order to familiarize unfamiliar situations in terms drawn from some salient and presumably familiar prior geopolitical experience or situation. This could be called domesticating the exotic. Numerous such analogies have come into common linguistic currency to refer to and putatively explain situations well beyond the original context of use but carry with them loaded meanings that expose the specificity of their origins as political terms based on geopolitical stereotypes. What is most important about them is that they carry conceptions of the nature of a given place projected onto new ones and thus implicitly identify parties from the original place as analogous to ones in the place of application. In this way, accounts of "what happened" in one place are projected as putative explanations onto another place. We thus come to "understand" one place in terms of a familiar (but not necessarily empirically accurate or even plausible) account of another. In this chapter I wish to focus on two geographical analogies that seem to have spread widely among pundits and scholars alike in the United States and elsewhere since the 1990s—Macedonian syndrome and balkanization—as illustrative of the process of geographical naming and political blaming.

There is a mock-geographical quality to the geopolitical reasoning that involves recycling geographical names in new contexts. One feature of so-called critical geopolitics is about drawing attention to how world politics is "spatialized" or rendered geographically meaningful by political leaders and through media representations but, in so doing, often devalues particular places and the people who inhabit them, so much the better to commodify them economically or pacify them politically and militarily (Ó Tuathail and Agnew 1992). The use of geographical names from one place exported as a geopolitical analogy elsewhere is obviously only one aspect of this process. But it is a largely unexplored one. Here I wish to emphasize the important role of "familiarization" in the application of geographical names in new contexts. By this I mean to stress the communicative more than the constitutive function of analogy. Various factors may well be "driving" a particular policy or action but they must be readily related to some *prior meaningful collective group experience elsewhere* that is memorable, commonplace, and seemingly familiar so as to better explain or justify them. What is most attractive from this viewpoint, then, is not some new poetic metaphor or novel analogy indicative of the newness of a situation but precisely the opposite. In this construction, it is, rather, "dead" or familiar metaphors that have been repeated endlessly over time and that have acquired a taken-for-granted status as home truths that are preferable. Finlandization (for enforced neutrality) and balkanization (for endemic primordial hatreds), for example, are both of this ilk. From this perspective, drawing attention to the geopolitical analogy in question involves a defamiliarization of commonsense understanding, designed to interrogate the origins and appropriateness of a specific geopolitical analogy and its applications. Defamiliarization is the act of reassessing our perceptions of analogies, stock phrases, and clichés that have become mundane and taken-for-granted as self-evident. The word defamiliarization seems to originate with the Russian critic Shklovsky who argued in 1916 that a key purpose of art and literature was "making strange" what was familiar so as to call into question the perception of everyday things and life that had become routinized (Hawkes 1977, 173–4). But Karl Marx, among others, would have readily understood the point in question. Unfortunately, much of western social science has long had something of a deaf ear to such concerns.

The two geographical analogies I have selected for illustrative purposes are the Macedonian syndrome and balkanization, both of which refer to Europe's southeastern geographical margins. As has become well known over the past twenty years, in general usage the two terms have come to refer, in the case of Macedonian syndrome, to "confused, mixed or impure" (in Italian and French, for example, mixed fruit or vegetable salad is invariably "Macedonian") and, in the case of balkanization, the "spatial segmentation or partition along violent lines based on primordial hatreds." Both terms are applied, usually pejoratively even as they appear as analytic, across a range of geographic scales usually to signal immanent threat or warning of danger from ethnic or national "separatism" and division. Fear of contagion from ethnic atavism far away may seem far-fetched, but everywhere in the world long histories of abuse of racial and ethnic categories for material and symbolic advantage raise the specter of an ethnic revanchism that is anything but simply far away. To choose just two random examples, recall the tortured history of race relations in the United States and the ethnic cleansing of the Scottish Highlands in the eighteenth century. But it is the usage at the level of world politics that is my concern here, not so much such applications as the "balkanization" of the internet or the "balkanization" of America resulting from immigration by Spanish- and other non-English-speakers.

In a fascinating survey of the balkanization analogy as used in relation to US immigration, Mark Ellis and Richard Wright (1998), do, however, note two features of its use that are fundamental to its wider geopolitical popularity. One is the *concreteness* that is conveyed by its "spatiality." Even though the application is often a geographical and cultural "stretch" from the original context, the abstraction involved is hidden by the apparent concreteness of the cross-reference to a real place. Another is the way in which it captures in a geographic name a process that, it is claimed, has long-standing roots of a primordial cast. A sense of *dreadful fate* is implied because the Balkans, the region from which the term derives, is said, problematically I hasten to add, to be one of ancient and implacable hatreds. The past then becomes a sure guide to the present and future even when that past is of somewhere thousands of miles away. Consequently, once under way, as the geographical fate of the Balkans itself is held to testify, balkanization is not readily reversed. There is also, therefore, an air of *futility* implied by the term. It says: "these people" are just like that and nothing much can be done to reverse their vendettas and blood lusts. As Albert Hirschman (1991, 43) shows, this is an important strategy in the "rhetoric of reaction" by which the very possibility of *really* changing the world is put off limits: "any alleged change is, was, or will be largely surface, façade, cosmetic, hence illusory, as the 'deep' structures of society remain wholly untouched. I shall call it the futility thesis."

In the global context, balkanization and similar analogies also have several other political and communicative advantages. One, as noted previously, is that they privilege *adjacency* in the genesis of conflict because Balkan conflicts presumably involve locals sparring with and then killing one another without much if any initial direct involvement by distant outsiders. Such analogies lead away from placing conflicts or wars within a wider geographical frame of reference, particularly that of global political hierarchy (Slater 1999). As well as reducing geopolitical complexity to local animosities, however, they also *depoliticize* conflicts. Use of the term "balkanization" substitutes a psychocultural account of conflict for a political one. Implicit in it, as we shall see presently, is the idea of the Balkans as a region grappling with the cultural disruptions introduced into local "traditional" society by modernity (tribe versus state, patronage versus transparency, etc.) rather than with the global realities of geographically defined economic, political, and social disadvantage and exploitation which stimulate local political engagement (Robin 2004, 151). The net effect is that "blame" is localized. In this way, the analogies contribute what can be called a "rhetoric of evasion" (Welch 2003).

Such analogies also tap into the tendency, particularly marked in US politics but not absent elsewhere, to "dumb down" geopolitical complexity into *easily communicated sound bites*. Good examples of this in recent years are such phrases as "war on terror," "axis of evil," "clash of civilizations," and "end of history." During the Cold War such vague ideas as "containment" and "domino effect" performed similar purposes (Ó Tuathail and Agnew 1992). Such slogans reflect the need to explain and justify foreign policies to largely unsophisticated and often ignorant populations in simpleminded terms. More specifically, the round-the-clock news cycle of mass media catering to ephemeral and uninformed consumers lends itself to compression of complex issues into simple analogies. But they also indicate the increasing importance of slogans in all aspects of life, reflecting the widespread penetration of advertising and marketing practices. As a result, superficial ideas are rewarded and specialist analysis based on real local knowledge placed in a wider frame of reference is penalized (Halper and Clarke 2007).

Finally, the "strangely familiar" character of the analogies is crucial to their success. They involve a particular constellation of power, knowledge, and spatiality based not on outright opposition between Them (over there) and Us (over here) as alleged in so much contemporary geographical philosophy as leading to the geographical imagination of western imperialism and colonialism (Gregory 1994, 165–205). In a globalized territorializing of Hegel's master-slave dialectic, so much of this writing leaps too quickly from Britain to India or from France to the Middle East. Rather, it is the very *liminality* of the Balkans, Ireland, Finland, etc. on which the analogies draw, as being places *between* the dominant states where the analogies originate, on the one hand, and the subordinated regions of the world, on the other, that gives the analogies their power when applied to the latter. At one and the same time, the familiar places are ones that are different if seemingly known yet also redolent of faraway places yet unknown but made familiar when assimilated to the different but known. It is the half-barbarian and half-civilized nearby that brings the distant into focus, not a simple "othering" through total opposition of a distant Them with nearby Us (Dainotto 2000, 2007).

WHY BALKAN ANALOGIES?

There is a "Balkan discourse" about the words and names used to describe the region and its constituent places and people in SE Europe (e.g., Garde 2004). Part of this is about how the region became associated with a certain kind of political pathology in the early years of the twentieth century in the minds of Western European politicians and intellectuals and how this underwent a revival, particularly among American and European pundits and politicians in the 1990s (see, e.g., Todorova 1997). The breakup of the Ottoman Empire during the nineteenth and early twentieth centuries had not been seen as the splitting up of "natural states" into "unnatural" statelets even as it was dubbed as "balkanization." Anything but: it was widely viewed as marking the beginning of the end for the Muslim Turks as overlords of a significant portion of Europe and the emergence of SE Europe into the modernity of nation-states. From the beginnings of Greek independence in the 1820s down until the 1890s, Macedonia was in play as the border-zone between the competing nationalisms of Greece, Bulgaria, and Serbia (Agnew 2007b). Mixed ethnically between Slav, Albanian, Vlach, Romani, and Greek groups with a lack of clear criteria for distinguishing one from the others, Macedonia was a paradigm for the larger region. With the first Balkan War of 1912, the Ottoman Empire was almost entirely removed from the map of Europe. But when the second Balkan War of 1913 pitted the Greeks, Bulgarians, and Serbs in a conflict among themselves and the process of political dismemberment was extended to the Austrian and Russian Empires after World War I, the term took on a new negative connotation that it has never subsequently lost (Todorova 1997, 32).

The precise boundaries of the Balkans, however, are not always clearly defined. Thus, if for some an Ottoman past is a necessary requirement of "Balkanism," for others any political connection with that past, even if only because of membership in the former Yugoslavia as for Croatia and Slovenia, extends potential membership. If many Slovenes and Austrians, for example, have tended to the former, seeing Slovenia as central European rather than Balkan, most Italian commentators have tended somewhat more to the latter viewpoint (Patterson 2003). In both cases, of course, Balkan still serves as a negative standard about what one either is or is not. More importantly, in the present context it is precisely the labile character of the boundaries of the region that helps to make the Balkans such a fruitful source of geopolitical analogies. The Balkans always threatens to escape neat containment in southeastern Europe.

The Ottoman and Austrian empires that long ruled in southeastern Europe never insisted on cultural and linguistic unification. Their rule also varied in its directness and effectiveness from place to place (Jesné 2004). If in Western Europe the quintessential states such as France and England preexisted their respective nations, in southeastern Europe "the idea of the national sovereign state was imported from the west by the growing middle classes born in the empires or on their periphery" (Jesné 2004, 166). The coming of the modern territorial state in this region (as in most of the world beyond Western Europe), therefore, has always involved drawing borders across complex ethnic settlement patterns and sometimes using anachronistic arguments about the present-day national affiliations of long-gone polities (such as the ancient Macedonian Empire, an ancient Hindustan, or the ancient Israelites) to justify who should control a given territory and the naming rights to it. But a philosophical geography already posited such regions as lacking in the attributes needed for self-confident, locally generated statehood. These had little if anything to do with economic development per se but reflected the taint of despotism, imported from the Ottoman and Russian empires, and, in the case of southern Europe, the need for a renewed *reconquista* for an idealized "Europe" of places that were clearly identified as the seats of that very European civilization (particularly Greece and Macedonia). In other words, in the "mind of the Enlightenment," to use Wolff's (1994) apt turn of phrase, and as expressed by such intellectual luminaries as Montesquieu and Hegel, "The South is what Europe, simply, *was*" (Dainotto 2000, 383). If in one interpretation, in particular that of Montesquieu, a fallen South stood in need of rescue by a progressive North, in another, for example that of Rousseau, the South represented an "older" Europe that had to be reincorporated to fulfill a European identity grounded in "multiplicity" (Dainotto 2000, 385–7). In both cases, in order to complete Europe as a region defined as a multiplicity of states and as a balance of power, these southern places were to be the showcase in which the initial spread of the European model of statehood would take place. With the end of the Cold War and the breakup of Yugoslavia, the Balkans has again been rediscovered as a missing part of the European "body politic"—only this time, it seems that the "malignant nationalism" of the region is seen as a barrier to integration into the contemporary project of European unification (Luoma-Aho 2002). The Balkans can never win.

The irony in all this, therefore, is that Macedonia and balkanization are both associated with a region in Europe which has long been in the process of being "completed" rather than being a region which was ever truly completely alien or foreign. Nevertheless, the negative connotations seem to follow from the way in which this completion of the nation-state model has always apparently been achieved through local internecine violence and ethnic cleansing. Of course, this requires simultaneously forgetting about all of the vicious ethnic cleansing and forced population removal that has also gone on elsewhere in Europe and in North America. The revival of such processes in the 1990s as the former Yugoslavia split apart, however, only seemed to confirm the atavistic basis to Balkan politics. "Balkan" and derivative words, then, have become shorthand in Western Europe and North America for ethnic violence, religious intolerance, and fixation on historical trauma notwithstanding the nonethnic, contemporary, and external sources of much of the political violence. Crucially, external actors and the wider geopolitical situation are necessarily exempted from much if any role in the region's political problems by this association of the Balkans with recurrent haunting from a primordial and fanatical set of ethnic identifications.

In a recent essay, Slovene Marxist philosopher Žižek (2005, 116) makes clear that in fact many of the elements of the Balkan drama were introduced to the region from the West through the imitation of statehood mandated against the occupation of the region by the Turks. He notes, inter alia, in alluding to the former Ottoman masters in much of the Balkans, "Let us not forget that the two great ethnic crimes imputed to the Turks in the 20th century—the Armenian genocide and the persecution of the Kurds—were not committed by traditionalist Muslim political forces, but by the military modernizers who sought to cut Turkey loose from its old-world ballast and turn it into a European nation-state." The Balkans is thus blamed for what outsiders had long desired for the region. Although it may be going too far to suggest, following Žižek (2005, 116) once more, himself citing another Slovene philosopher, Mladen Dolar, and his reading of Freud's references to the region: "that the European unconscious is structured like the Balkans, is thus literally true: in the guise of the Otherness of 'Balkan,' Europe takes cognizance of the 'stranger in itself,' of its own repressed." Undoubtedly, however, irrespective of the value of a Freudian interpretation, Western Europeans' (and Americans') *apparent* familiarity with the Balkans and what they have taken as its main characteristic, primordial ethnic conflict, has bred a fateful contempt.

THE TWO EXAMPLES: MACEDONIAN SYNDROME AND BALKANIZATION

I choose two examples from an array of possible ones to show how, by means of geographical analogy, the presumed characteristics of one place come to inform geopolitical understanding of other ones. The term "Macedonian syndrome" is a specific locution of relatively recent vintage with an initial theoretical purpose behind it. The sentiment and understanding it conveys about an ethnically mixed-up/confused place has much older usage going back at least to the Balkan Wars just before World War I. The locution itself was first coined by Myron Weiner in 1971 in an article that has since become widely cited both with respect to Macedonia and its neighboring countries and also to places in all directions and at all distances from its original site of application. But Weiner intended that this be so. His entire purpose was to develop a theoretical model based on Macedonian experience that could be applied to what he called "the newly independent states of Asia and Africa" (Weiner, M. 1971, p. 665). Weiner was not a Macedonian or Balkan specialist but a student of India. He chose Macedonia, first and foremost, because it and its neighbors were the European countries most like the "new states" of Asia and Africa (former colonies, economically backward, etc.) Most importantly, he drew attention to the mélange or *macedoine* aspect of religious and linguistic groups resident in the country. Though disavowing that he was engaged in drawing analogies—that would immediately call his "model" into question as to its presumed universality; he preferred to say he was building a "descriptive model"—Weiner was indeed using the Macedonian case as he saw it to describe a syndrome of characteristics, particularly the irredentist nature of local political disputes with ethnic groups distributed *across* existing state borders, to suggest the future course of conflict elsewhere around the world. Parenthetically, as is well known, the role of irredentism has in fact been relatively unimportant in many interstate conflicts and civil wars (Holsti 1991; Lake and O'Mahony 2006). Yet the "model" has recently picked up many new citations (164 total as of 04/2021 since 2000, with only 195 overall since 1971) after a long latent period, suggesting that the analogy to Macedonia still has considerable geopolitical mileage notwithstanding its central focus on an issue of limited importance beyond Macedonia except, perhaps, in Kashmir.

On Google, for example (04/12/2021), there are 153 hits for "Macedonian syndrome," of which all but a few are geopolitical in nature; and in Google Scholar there are 195 hits, all of which are geopolitical. Although some of the latter are studies of the Balkans that use Weiner's model (such as Larrabee 1990–1991), most are applications of the analogy to such disparate locations as the Baltic states, Afghanistan, Iraq, SE Asia, Kashmir, and India, as well as worldwide. In every one of the "applications" that I examined, the Macedonian syndrome provided the template for assessing local conditions, notwithstanding Weiner's (1971, 683) own caveat about how "a given effect can have many causes." Most of the articles and presentations covered in this sampling date from the 1990s through 2018, indicating that, more than fading away because of doubts about the efficacy of how well the syndrome might travel or the limits of any geopolitical analogy across time as well as space, there has been a recent revival of such thinking (see, e.g., in the flagship journal of US sociology, Wimmer and Min 2006—an article which is explicitly based around the logic of the "Macedonian syndrome" applied to wars around the world over a 175-year period, but which is missing any analysis of state hierarchy or imperialism as causes of wars and denies any historical pattern to ethnic conflict that may be connected to worldwide trends such as globalization, even though elsewhere Wimmer (2004, 2) claims a clear "rise and fall" of ethnic conflicts across the years 1945–2002). The analogy has been revived, therefore, even as the empirical "reality" it purports to explain strongly suggests, at best, both its historicity and its increased redundancy.

"Balkanization" is both a more venerable and a more diffuse term in use since the 1920s and with reference to a much wider range of phenomena (e.g., Earle, E. M. 1926). With 1,010,000 hits on Google, only about one-third of which qualify as geopolitical, and 24,300 hits on Google Scholar, where about 25 percent qualify, this term is less singularly geopolitical than is

Macedonian syndrome. What is clear, however, is that the geopolitical usage has increased dramatically over the past forty years with most applications to the United States since the late 1990s but with many other places (in order, after Iraq and the US, SE Europe, Africa, Indonesia, and Iran) not that far behind. A speech President Clinton made on 24 March 1999 as NATO pilots began the bombing of Serbia over the Serbian treatment of Kosovo's Albanians used some well-known tropes of Balkan representation, such as "a fault line" between civilizations and "small countries" wedged between larger ones without actually invoking "balkanization" itself. But the thought was there. More explicit usage is now fairly common.

The first geopolitical usage beyond Balkan shores I have found is in an article in the *Economist* in 1960 (216) warning that "African leaders . . . owe it to themselves . . . to grasp what there is in the majority report for them before they opt for balkanization" and in an essay by political geographer Charles Fisher in 1962 in which SE Asia is described as the "Balkans of the Orient." Since that time, particularly since the breakup of the Soviet Union and Yugoslavia in the early 1990s and in the face of the US debacle in Iraq, the geopolitical usage has exploded. The arc of usage on Google suggests that conservative US bloggers and politicians have been particularly drawn to the analogy. For example, such US conservative and nationalist websites as Enter Stage Right, NoWorldSystem, and American Free Press were frequent users between 2005 and 2012. From 2000 to 2009 much of the application was to the United States and Iraq. But scholars also make considerable use of the term, with *Politics Professor*, for example, defining balkanization as a "theory of the fragmentation of states" and others trying to make use of the analogy in an analytic way (e.g., Roshwald 2007).

Some of this usage of "balkanization" probably reflects widespread speculative debate about globalization and its relationship to renewed instability of international political borders in the late twentieth century (see, e.g., Kahler and Walter 2006). In one account, widely diffused among geographers, Fredric Jameson (1991, 50–54), for example, has seen political fragmentation and nationalism as an emerging if baleful alternative to a globalizing "late capitalism." He associates such postmodern capitalism with both a loss of centralized control and the emergence of a sense of a perpetual present in which space replaces time. In this account, then, the recycling of geographical analogies like balkanization, if not of directly historical ones like appeasement, could make sense, because of the spatial element in the comparison. In the intellectual world of a clean break between modern and postmodern capitalism, only spatial analogies should have continuing currency. Temporality has ended. Others, however, see evidence of increasing political fragmentation not only as a direct result of a *centralizing* globalization more than an alternative to it but also as necessarily involving a fateful recycling of stories about the past (and stereotypes of other places associated with that past) analogously into the present (Agnew 2005). In this construction, geographical analogies are not simply spatial ones; as well as a spatial reference they also have all sorts of historical memories and stereotypes embedded in them. It is but a small step to render stories about the explosion of ethnic enmities under postmodernity or the increased fungibility of borders with globalization, if ultimately mischievously and misleadingly, in the more colorful terms of balkanization or other analogies involving geographical naming and political blaming. Familiarizing of the unfamiliar thus becomes ever more insistent in a world of seemingly escalating geopolitical instability.

The following are some typical web-based stories from 2006–2007: comparing the prospects for a unified Iraq with the Balkans, raising the alarm among non-Iranians to the threat to Iranian territorial unity from US-sponsored balkanization, and warning of the dangers to this or that African country (the DRC, the Sudan, Somalia, etc.) from foreign-sponsored balkanization. The term travels far and wide but seems to be particularly prevalent wherever "events" seems to be especially unstable and prone to resist outside control. Usage relative to the United States is often also not without geopolitical relevance. Thus immigration, particularly from Latin America, and affirmative action programs to promote different racial and ethnic groups are seen as not just as socially problematic but also as potentially territorially divisive within the United States, which will then have knock-on effects on the global standing of the United States. President G. W. Bush made the point in his own inimitable manner when he referred to "however they delineate, quotas vulcanize society." I think he meant to say balkanize or perhaps "volcanize" (in relation to volcanoes). He must have misheard the pronunciation from whoever briefed him, hearing a "v" when a "b" was in fact spoken. Obviously, his use is not one of those on Google. I didn't look up "vulcanize."

CONCLUSION

"Macedonian syndrome" and "balkanization" have become popular geopolitical terms to signify, respectively, mixed/impure and marginal/fragmented/chaotic, often in far distant contexts from the original places to which they refer but reflecting a specific understanding of distinctiveness from a European/American standard. The terms represent particular readings of the original places of reference without which they could not "travel" elsewhere. These typically involve emphasizing the local sources of conflict—typically ancient hatreds—to the occlusion of the larger geopolitical field of imperialism and diffusion of political models of nation-statehood that the Balkans can also be taken to represent (Agnew 2007b). Such language, therefore, is not simply an innocent writing strategy substituting directly empirical with more evocative terminology. The Macedonian syndrome and balkanization analogies implicitly carry with them models of the Balkans that are then imposed elsewhere. Crucially, in a geopolitical context this means identifying *local* actors as those entirely responsible for whatever conflict the actual usage is connected to. Ironically, Great Power geopolitics has long been oriented to seeing both interstate conflict as the singular center of world politics and the locals as invariably pawns in the larger game. The repetitive invocation of the familiar analogies, therefore, reveals how hollow such claims frequently are. As they become second nature, however, they become self-fulfilling propaganda rather than meaningful metaphors for understanding complex situations (e.g., Chait 2022).

The Balkans, of course, is the long-suffering source of the analogies in question in this extended example. To the Balkans, then, we should return in questioning their efficacy. In a joke going the rounds in the Serbian capital Belgrade around the time President Clinton made his speech on Kosovo in March 1999, the Serbs were held to complain that they were under bombardment from a country that had no history, to which the US President was said to have replied: "Soon, you'll have no geography." There's more truth to that joke than to either of the analogies (balkanization and the Macedonian syndrome) that helped to produce the geopolitical setting for the joke in the first place.

II

GEOPOLITICS OF GLOBALIZATION

4

The Asymmetric Border

The US Place in the World and the Refugee Panic of 2018

The summer and fall of 2018 brought to light a distinct change in US government immigration practices at its southern border with Mexico. In October 2018 a five-year-old girl sitting alone was asked to sign a plea deal in a Texas courtroom to bar her from seeking asylum in the United States (Stillman 2018). Earlier in the year, thousands of other children were held in private facilities separate from parents and family members arrested with them until they could have hearings that would lead to rapid deportation. Initially the US government denied that they had a family separation and detention policy (Herrera 2018). The US Department of Homeland Security when pressured publicly to end this practice as a result of news reports could not find some of the children they had detained and many more of the parents had been summarily deported before any possibility of reunification with their offspring. In October 2018 the US administration again raised the possibility of separation, detention, and deportation as alternatives to releasing asylum seekers prior to legal proceedings as was long the official policy if not the actual practice (Miroff et al. 2018).

Yet this was only an escalation of what has long been symptomatic of US controls along its southern border: the lack of capacity to distinguish and then manage different categories of potential entrants into the land territory of the United States or to integrate the "border question" into the broader question of US immigration policy. Well-sourced accounts suggest that in response to the panic, border-control agents were often intercepting possible refugees before they reached ports-of-entry to prevent them from presenting themselves as potential asylees in the United States (Lind 2018). By November 2018 the Trump administration was looking to the Mexican government to intercept potential refugees in complete disregard of legal commitments to provide hearings to those seeking refuge from potentially deadly circumstances back home. This disregard for established law and norms governing refugees is increasingly shared across the world irrespective of the formal obligations of the governments in question (Fisher and Taub 2018).

A more muted version of the 2018 crisis erupted in early 2021 as migrants and refugees trapped in Mexico as a result of Trump administration policy and new ones heading north from Central America and elsewhere as a result of lives disrupted by disastrous hurricanes and drug trafficking anticipated a more humanitarian response from the new Biden presidency in the United States (Narea 2021; Tharoor 2021; Kerwin 2021). Yet again there was much confusion in the US media and among US politicians about the dimensions of the crisis, including the extent to which this was a problem about unaccompanied children when most of the interceptions of illegal border crossings were of young Mexican men and refugees from Haiti and elsewhere and not Central American children and families (Miroff and Sacchetti 2021; Montes and Caldwell 2021).

The categories of immigrant (all those who move from one country to another typically assumed to be for mainly economic reasons), refugee (those who move because of wars and fear of persecution), asylee (those in the US illegally or arriving at ports of entry who wish to apply for asylum), and asylum seeker (those who claim to be refugees but whose legal right has not been established and who applied for asylum outside the US) have become increasingly confused. Even though these are not always neat categories in practice, they are in law. For example, in theory, immigrants can return home without fear of imprisonment or death; even though they are returning perhaps to relative poverty, they will not face immediate violence or imprisonment. Some of the confusion about categories is not simply the result of ignorance. For example, it is not always clear when apprehended at the border whether people are simply undocumented immigrants or potential asylees. But political and media discourses have also contributed by deliberately using the existing reality of undocumented immigrants in the country to treat asylees and refugees as indistinguishable from the former because they are using a sort of legerdemain to gain entry to the country. At the same time, even as the total numbers of people overall seeking entrance along this border have declined, there has been a rising level of panic in the United States over immigration in general and the position of refugees/asylees in particular as potential terrorist and criminal threats, notwithstanding massive empirical evidence from official sources in the United States that neither is true (e.g., Lusk et al. 2012; Warren 2021).

More importantly, immigrants in general (including refugees and so on) are increasingly seen as a source of demographic and cultural change in the United States that challenges the historic status hierarchy between people of European heritage on the one side and those originating in other parts of the world on the other. Though such concerns have long characterized US immigration practices going back to the exclusion of people of Chinese heritage in the late nineteenth century, rarely has partisan politics in the United States been so singularly focused on the demographic-political implications of immigration across its southern border. Simultaneously, immigrants are also seen as simply showing up uninvited and without good reason to look to the United States for their salvation, as if its relative adjacency and the political and military actions of US governments around the world and of other US-based actors like agribusinesses and banks play absolutely no role in the pressures that produce streams of immigrants and refugees heading to the US-Mexico border. Many Americans seem either oblivious to or simply disingenuous about the consequences of the "catastrophic decisions" made by their governments that now show up on their doorsteps (Todorov 2010, 188).

The blurring in recent US political discourse of refugees, illegal immigrants, terrorists, and people of Muslim heritage, as if these notions were not readily distinguishable and the United States were just an innocent bystander in a world over which it exercised little or no influence, represents the latest iteration in a long-standing popular refusal to acknowledge the asymmetric quality of the US border: that the US has a very long geopolitical reach beyond it but does not recognize that what comes to pass in human terms as people wash up at that border has anything at all to do with that reach (Nevins 2001). This is not a defense of one national territory from incursions from others, as it is usually framed, but the outcome of an essentially lopsided extraterritoriality in which the United States exercises power well beyond its borders but refuses to see that this then creates conditions in which affected populations have little alternative to escape those conditions other than trying to cross the US border (Restrepo 2021). Even much of the writing about justice for refugees tends to regard all states as interchangeable, one with the other, as if all were both potential sources and destinations (e.g., Gibney 2015). Yet we know that this is not the case. Refugee flows are clearly asymmetric with causes that are not entirely local but also geopolitical and spatial connections that follow from this. In other words, the sovereignty exercised by the United States is not simply territorial but also extends well beyond US shores by means of control and regulation of major global financial and monetary processes as well as through the ability and practice of military and political intervention in other "less sovereign" territories (Agnew 2018). This is by now a familiar and frequently told story but it is not one that is typically related to the asymmetric quality of the US southern border in relation to the question of immigration. The United States and Mexico, not to mention the United States and the states of Central America, are not equal border "partners."

This chapter has three related parts. The first part provides an effort to explain why US governments and substantial segments of the population have conceptions of space that encourage a dual vision of US history that at one and the same time has a conception of a compact national territory as wrested by a governing group of settlers from an unwilling continent and a conception of geopolitical space that projects the defense of that space into the rest of the world based in an expansive mission to make the world over in America's image. This dualism raises questions about to whom the rights enshrined in the US Constitution really apply and whether the population of the territorial United States bears any responsibility for acts beyond its borders carried out by its government (and allies) and American businesses in its name. The second section describes the refugee panic of 2018 involving policies of separating children from parents and incarcerating them as reflections of the failure to recognize the dualist vision and its consequences described previously. But its timing also represents the use in US domestic politics of fears about the changing ethnic composition of the US population more than an actual uptick in the numbers of refugees/asylees (or all so-called illegal immigrants, for that matter) attempting to cross the US southern border. The third part therefore relates the conundrum of the 2018 refugees/asylees, overwhelmingly from Central America, to the contemporary way in which all immigration is discussed in the United States and the rise since the election of Donald Trump to the US presidency in 2016 of a white populism in the United States that sees refugees as a threat to the political-cultural dominance of the white settler groups that hitherto also saw the United States as a project that potentially knows no boundaries. The border fixation of 2018 perhaps heralds the immanent collapse of the unconscious pretense that a territorialized society exercising global geopolitical scope produces no consequences "back home."

THE US PLACE IN THE WORLD AND THE ASYMMETRIC BORDER

The historical geopolitics of the United States should not be understood as just that of the rise of yet another hegemonic power at the expense of previous ones (see chapter 2). This is frequently as it is viewed in various theoretical frameworks focusing on each period with which a dominant superpower can be associated (Spain, the Netherlands, Britain, and the US) as essentially equivalent in character. From my viewpoint, the territorial United States has provided a prototype for a universal project that would know no earthly boundaries yet would be grounded in the relative global isolation of North America (Agnew 2005; Bâli and Rana 2018). As a settler-colony society, it developed as an indigenous marketplace-society in which American freedom was tied to ever-expanding market enterprise. No political borders really set limits to this. As a result, many Americans have seen the United States in a mystical light as an "exceptional" country founded in universal principles that they could then impose on others. A major question today is whether the population can put this behind them for a collective vision that is both more pragmatic and less messianic (Cooley and Nexon 2020; Manson 2021).

From the birth of the United States as a political-economic project (argued in more detail in chapter 2), two principles underpinned the association of freedom with geographical expansion. First of all, the conception of statehood that evolved in the United States was not one of limits or borders but of an ever-expanding zone or frontier in its quintessential American sense. This differed significantly from contemporary European understanding of a frontier as just another word for boundary. This principle reflected the settler-colonial origins of the country. Geographical expansion initially into the continental interior and later beyond would release the economic and political tensions that might otherwise undermine the social status quo upon which US independence was based with power in the hands of propertied and financial interests. The second principle was that economic freedom more than political citizenship was the root of freedom tout court. As this has been put previously: "From the start . . . the United States was a profoundly economistic society, reflecting the values and interests of the merchants, bankers, and plantation owners who were the architects of its political institutions" (Agnew 2005, 74). The freedom to own property without political mediation or government mandate, and potentially worldwide, was the leitmotif of a frontier-oriented society.

Until the 1890s its "continental destiny" occupied most energy—not least because of internal differences over the role of slavery in the agrarian economy of the southern states and the expansion of infrastructure, such as canals and railroads—to bring this vast land area to market. Both material interests, such as profit decline and stagnation, and ideological sources relating to the "closing" of the continental frontier, in the influential writings of Frederick Jackson Turner, for example, openly raised the question of why North America should set limits to "the march of freedom." Earlier signs such as the Monroe Doctrine and the Mexican-American War were now to be fulfilled in full-blooded efforts at expanding commercially and, if necessary, militarily beyond continental shores. The Spanish-American War and subsequent military interventions in Mexico and Central America are examples of this impulse.

The First World War was crucial in beginning the transition of the United States to superpower status albeit with major limitations when the United States failed to join its own invention, the League of Nations, in the aftermath of the war. Of course, US global expansionism came to fruition only after the Second World War when the United States became the center of one of the world's two most important spheres of geopolitical influence. The long-term shift from a territorialized marketplace society to globalization was based in the prior experience of "open borders" that were central to the American experiment.

> The space of "America" was already created in the imaginations of the first European settlers en route to the "New World" as a space of openness and possibility. It was not constructed and corrupted by centuries of history and power

> struggles, as was Europe. . . . The enslaved Africans and conquered Indians who made constructing the New World possible are largely absent from this vision, except as incidental characters or as barriers to be overcome. (Agnew 2005, 90)

At the same time, of course, by dint of its massive resource base and exploding industrial capacity, the United States was also moving from a peripheral toward a central position within the world economy and global geopolitics. The main difference between the United States and other settler-colonial societies, such as Australia and Canada, lies in this geopolitical fact, even though they share other features relating to myths about the heroic character of founding groups and difficulties in imagining or, until recently, even acknowledging that their territories were in fact long occupied by other peoples as such rather than just as bit-part actors in morality tales about brave settlers overcoming the odds. Many years were to pass to produce a match between the potential and actual US geopolitical roles at a world scale. But what it did produce was an increasingly contradictory relationship between, on the one hand, a territorialized image of the United States and an expansive world-changing image of the country abroad, on the other. The domestic space, if you will, needed defending militarily and through the expansion of American mores abroad, and as a servant of US business interests, yet the political status of the United States was still apparently that of "just another" country with a government like others, a seat at the United Nations, and a flag and anthem among others. Since the end of the Cold War and the perpetual geopolitical "emergency" that this signified for many Americans and along with the fact that the globalization initially sponsored by US governments and US-based businesses has increasingly had deleterious effects on some places and social groups inside the United States, the "open borders" motif of US history has come under increasing cross-pressure. As a result,

> [T] he United States has an increasingly ambivalent position within its own hegemony. . . . The US commitment to external expansion to manage conflicts at home and serve the commercial ethos of dominant social groups has come back to haunt its creators. The United States now appears as an "ordinary" country subject to external pressures more than simply the source of pressure on others. (Agnew 2005, 223–4)

The historical relationship between the United States and Latin America represents perhaps the most pertinent example of the inside/outside tension that has lain at the heart of the US geopolitical imagination since the founding of the United States. The emergence of the idea of the linear international border as signifying a simple switch from one territorial sovereignty to another, arguably a central feature of international law only since 1900 or so, should not obscure the degree to which some borders such as that between the United States and Mexico are more important than others such as those between the countries of Central America (Foucher 2007; Agnew 2018; Goettlich 2018). Woodrow Wilson's imagined world of independent territorial nation-states based on national self-determination has never been effectively realized. Some remain more sovereign than others. It is not just a question of differential priority to policing of borders but of the relative powers and potential for projecting those powers geographically of the governments behind the borders in question (e.g., Adamson and Tsourapas 2019).

Three empirical cases illustrate this conundrum in relation to the US-Mexico border. The first has been the long-term tendency of US governments to intervene across the hemisphere to arrest or direct political change deemed unfavorable to the United States as a whole or to specific US business interests. Central America has been a specific focus of these efforts on and off for many years. The litany of such interventions is so long that I could not possibly list all of them in the pages available to me here. Suffice it to mention the 1980s US interventions against insurgencies in El Salvador and Nicaragua (Garcia 2006). More recently, the United States has supported governments in Honduras and Guatemala for geopolitical reasons, even when those governments have been displacing and killing indigenous people and rural populations that stand in the way of the expansion of agribusiness and other firms often with important American connections (Frank 2018; Kline et al. 2018). These dramatic impacts have created rounds of refugees seeking shelter outside the countries in question and sowed the seeds of local crime when some refugees have returned home and extended their gang networks locally even if their headquarters remain in the United States. Their activities have further encouraged other rounds of refugees as parents try to rescue their children from gang recruitment efforts and the violence intrinsically related to gang activities.

The second has been the so-called "War on Drugs" in which US government agencies (particularly the DEA or Drug Enforcement Administration) have extended their energies directly into Mexico, Central America, and Colombia to potentially limit the supply of narcotic drugs, particularly cocaine and marijuana, into the United States. Since 2006 these efforts have overwhelmingly focused on the southern border rather than in the Caribbean and more generally as was the case hitherto. The overall failure of this effort from its beginnings in the early 1970s should not lead to neglect of the dire effects such intervention has had in militarizing and otherwise disrupting traditional communities across the entire region, particularly in recent years, in southern Mexico and Central America. The 2018 arrest in Miami of the brother of Honduras's president for drug trafficking points to the extent to which American "allies" in the region are a source of the very instability that produces refugees on the run from the narco-gangs that terrorize their neighborhoods and try to recruit their children (Ernst and Malkin 2018; Whelan 2018). The president himself has been named as profiting personally from narcotics trafficking (Anderson, J. L. 2021). In late March 2022 the Honduras Supreme Court ruled that the now ex-president should be extradited to New York to face drug-trafficking charges (Perez 2022). The methods developed in policing the drug war have in turn come back to the United States in the militarized models of policing and attitudes of the police (often veterans of US military interventions abroad) back home (Schrader 2019).

The third example is the export of guns from the United States to Mexico. Mexico has some of the strictest laws governing gun ownership in the world. How is it then that Mexico has one of the world's highest rates of gun-related fatalities? On average about 253,000 guns are smuggled into Mexico from the United States every year. Most of these are seemingly purchased legally in the United States. Mexico's recent homicide rate, fueled mainly by conflicts between and within drug-trafficking gangs (moving their product northward to US consumers), at 25 deaths per 100,000 people compares to 5 per 100,000 in the United States and 60 per 100,000 in El Salvador (among the world's highest) (Linthicum 2018). US gun culture still apparently knows no boundaries even as other features of US expansionism are called into question at home (Blitzer 2018a; Krauze 2021). The US southward reach beyond its borders remains enormous. The asymmetric border between the United States and Mexico is such that the government of Mexico or Mexican society has tremendously less capacity to influence what goes on across it than does the power from the north. It is this asymmetry that makes it more than just any old border.

The United States is a signatory to the Universal Declaration of Human Rights of 1951 in which seeking asylum is defined as one such right. Under the 1967 Protocol Relating to the Status of Refugees, the United States is prohibited from returning refugees to persecution and the US 1980 Refugee Act set up a formal process for applying for asylum (Gorman 2017). In 1996 the United States brought into effect the Illegal Immigration Reform and Immigrant Responsibility Act (IIRIRA) that created a number of new barriers to asylum. Previously, the US authorities rarely detained anyone for any length of time in violation of immigration laws. The shift began following the Mariel Boatlift from Cuba and the migration of Haitians in the 1980s. The fact that some of the Cubans were released convicts tainted the entire cohort (Minian 2018). The presumption of the 1996 legislation was that established asylum procedures had provided an incentive for the burgeoning cross-border undocumented immigration at that time from Mexico to the United States.

Be that as it may, the Act introduced a number of barriers such as "expedited removal" if applicants have not passed through screening at an official port-of-entry prior to application, "mandatory detention" of certain asylum seekers depending on their demographic status and country of origin, and filing deadlines if genuine refugees have not filed a formal application for asylum within one year of gaining refugee status upon arrival in the United

States. These all violate the spirit and letter of the treaties on refugees to which the United States is party, particularly returning many of those claiming refugee status to dangerous situations and detaining others, including children separated at arrival from their parents, in harsh conditions and with lack of access to immigration lawyers and courts (Acer and Byrne 2017). In this frame of reference, the responsibility in the border-crossing equation lies largely if not entirely with the putative refugees and not with the US government as a party to what may have turned the people into refugees in the first place (Drake and Gibson 2017; Higgins 2021). This raises the question of the culpability of the United States, both its government and population, in ways comparable to those of European countries with former empires, as to the relative priority to be given in asylum proceedings to so-called postcolonial migrants whose direction of movement as refugees retraces that of the spatial reach of the former empires (e.g., see Amighetti and Nuti 2016).

THE US REFUGEE PANIC OF 2018

In the 1990s through the early 2000s, millions of undocumented Mexican citizens crossed the US border. In 2000 the US Border Patrol apprehended 1.6 million Mexicans trying to cross. Few if any declared themselves as refugees seeking asylum in the United States. Over the next fifteen years, the numbers at the border slowly plummeted. By 2017 the number apprehended was 127,000 Mexicans for the year, with 176,000 coming from other countries, overwhelmingly those of Central America. So the overall rate of attempted crossing is much lower and by and large other nationalities have replaced potential Mexican immigrants. 2017 had the lowest rate of apprehensions at the southern border since 1972 (McGinty 2018a). It is unclear how many undocumented immigrants succeed in gaining entry to the United States either across the border or, more frequently, by overstaying visas after arriving legally through airports or other ports of entry. Drawing on a number of sources, the *Wall Street Journal* (Tam and Caldwell 2018) estimates that illegal border entries from Mexico into the United States dropped 90 percent between 2000 and 2016 (figure 4.1). As of 2014 the US Department of Homeland Security estimated there were 12.1 million undocumented immigrants living in the United States of whom 6.6 million were from Mexico. Of course, nearly 45 million US residents are foreign-born, so three-quarters of US immigrants are in the country fully documented. Far more immigrants all told now arrive from Asia than from Latin America but this is also not well known. A majority of Americans when polled (55 percent) say that most immigrants are in the country illegally, opening up a significant slice of the population to political misinformation about the whole topic (Bump 2018).

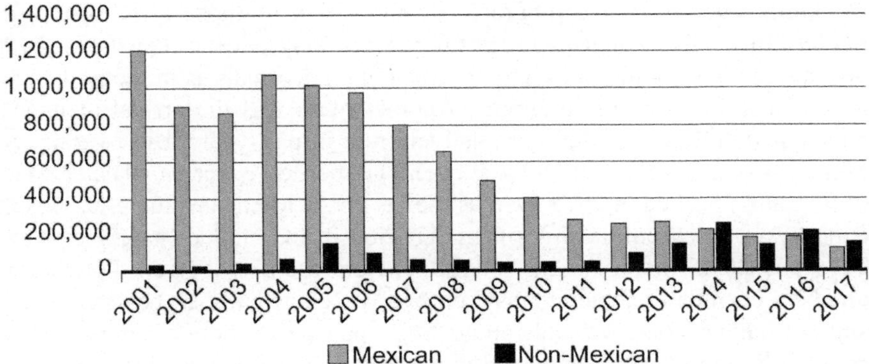

Figure 4.1. Apprehensions at the US-Mexico Border, 2001–2017, Mexicans and Others (US Customs and Border Protection, 2017 Border Security Report, Washington, DC: US Government)

Beyond the dramatic decline in numbers apprehended before 2017 suggesting, given the increase in border policing, that this did not mask some hidden surge in border crossing, and the decline in numbers from Mexico, the most important change is that most of those coming from Central America were both better educated and more affluent than previous Mexican border crossers and many arrived wishing to enter as refugees rather than as economic immigrants per se (Alden 2017). Many more of those recently crossing the border at official ports-of-entry and elsewhere were now potential asylees. The weekly numbers, however, were in the thousands rather than the tens of thousands of undocumented immigrants tout court in the 1990s and early 2000s. The overall numbers were still small compared to the number of apprehended border crossers ten or twenty years ago. In 2019–2020 the numbers increased dramatically back to those experienced in the early 2000s, reflecting the buildup at the US-Mexico border over the previous two years and the arrival of new groups, particularly Haitians (Chishti and Meissner 2021; Bolter 2021; Gramlich and Scheller 2021). In 2017–2018, the increase in asylees at the border paralleled the increase in the numbers of Central Americans applying as refugees for affirmative status as asylum-seekers while still at home between 2013 and 2016. In fiscal year 2017 there were 99,035 asylum requests compared to 13,880 in 2012. Of these, 24,337 asked for asylum at a port of entry, the rest after being apprehended. Fully 62,609 of the total were from Central America. Hondurans and Salvadorans in particular report that it is increased crime and violence in their homelands more than the prospects of a "better life" that motivate their attempts at reaching the United States. This gives a basis to the "credible fear" standard that underlies the international law of asylum. Indeed, US statistics report that most applicants reach this standard. The system then bogs down because it takes so long after this decision to actually reach affirmative adjudication on the asylum requests

(McGinty 2018b). The demographic composition of those arriving at the border reflects the changed nature of border crossing. Most of the 2017–2018 arrivals came as family units and not as single individuals as in the past with predominantly economic migrants. Another trend was the arrival of unaccompanied children, something relatively rare in past years. But overall arrivals of Central Americans at the southern US border (covering all categories of migrants) peaked in 2014 even as they eclipsed Mexicans numerically so, contrary to much politicizing of immigration in the United States between 2016 and 2018, there was no "invasion" from the south. Even though the numbers eventually achieving asylum had waxed and waned between 1996 and 2017, the average was only about 20–30 percent. Although some of those could fade into the undocumented ranks in the United States, the likelihood of acquiring legal status by this route is not that good (Gorman 2017; Tam and Caldwell 2018). As of 2019, the United States, one of the wealthiest and most powerful countries in the world, had only 0.85 refugees settled per 1,000 residents; 75th out of 175 countries with data (UNHCR 2019).

This would not seem like a propitious context for immigration across the southern border to emerge into political prominence in the United States. One source of this was undoubtedly Donald Trump's presidential campaign that began in 2015 with a rant against Mexican "rapists" and other "illegal" immigrants. His proclaimed ban on immigration from certain Muslim majority countries but not others further muddied the waters. Trump was careful never to be clear about whether he was concerned with illegality as such or more with immigration in general. This fit into his overall narrative of nationalists versus globalists with the latter, his target, in favor of "open borders." The failure of the US immigration system to provide a rational basis for sorting immigrants a priori and the fact that borders are invariably difficult to manage because of the need to keep them open for business and affluent travelers even as they must be policed was completely elided (Agnew 2008). The presumed impact of poor immigrants on the wages of people he was hoping might vote for him was part of the overall logic in his approach. His promise to build a wall along the southern border became central to his political performance. It both distanced him from his Republican rivals who were more circumspect about using immigration as a partisan wedge issue and served to attract support from those Americans concerned not so much about immigration per se as the fact that the immigrants in question were not predominantly white. Trump's views, as per usual with him, had been formed years earlier and did not reflect the fact that he was empirically out of date about the state of play at the southern border.

As a result of the centrality of immigration to Trump's political campaign, once in office he set about making it central to national policy. He became the "border president" (Hurd 2018). US law gives the president enormous leeway in policing the country's borders. This became clear in the US Supreme Court decision in *Trump v. Hawaii*, the so-called Muslim ban case, in which the majority let stand the ban Trump had imposed immediately on coming into office yet insisted that it was also at the same time overturning the infamous *Korematsu* decision of 1944 that declared the internment of Japanese Americans as constitutional. The decision turned specifically and entirely on questions of national citizenship and presidential authority over borders. At the same time it was engaging in the Muslim ban, the other wing of Trump immigration policy in early 2017, along with hiring more Immigration and Customs Agents (ICE) and carrying out increased numbers of raids on communities across the US housing undocumented immigrants, was devoted to devising and implementing a policy designed to discourage southern border crossing by deliberately separating children from their parents and throwing the onus for this onto the parents (on the illegality of deterrence actions in relation to refugees, see Ormsby 2017). As US Attorney General Sessions memorably put this, ignoring completely any US role in why refugees are coming, "if you don't want your child separated, then don't bring them across the border illegally. It's not our fault that somebody does that" (O'Reilly 2018, 7). Technically, because parents are arrested upon presenting themselves at border crossings or elsewhere, children are treated as "unaccompanied alien minors" and detained as such.

Initially declared in March 2017, this so-called zero-tolerance policy was publicly dropped after much complaint until spring 2018. Revived in secret in spring 2018, it then erupted into scandal only a couple of months or so later. In response to a perceived seasonal uptick in border arrivals, from April through June 2018, thousands of children were separated from parents and detained in makeshift shelters along the border and further afield (Miroff 2018; Domonoske and Gonzales 2018). Deflecting intense criticism, President Trump falsely claimed that "Democrats" were to blame for having introduced the practice (e.g., Rizzo 2018). But many of his aides, particularly Stephen Miller, defended what had been done. In 2014 the Obama administration had detained families but tried to keep mothers and children together in detention while their cases came to trial in court but dropped it after legal challenges. In 2005 the Bush administration had engaged in a quick deportation scheme along part of the Texas border but this did not include families with children. The big change with the Trump administration was in the explicit heartlessness of separating families as a deterrent to other potential asylum seekers and immigrants (Davis and Shear 2018).

Rather than directly addressing the deficiencies of inefficient immigration courts and a lack of decent public detention facilities, the idea was to overcome the system of releasing people to relatives or their own recognizance for later court dates by a deterrent system to discourage asylum seekers in the first place. Photographs of children in cages at detention facilities quickly turned the whole approach into a public relations disaster. Even though then–Attorney General Sessions, President Trump, and others tried to associate these border crossers with public order and criminal threats emanating from abroad, the "totalizing and binary language was vividly dehumanizing" (Heyer 2018, 150–51). The public outcry, even from political allies of the Trump administration, particularly right-wing Christian pastors, led to an abandonment of the child-separation policy. By late June 2018 Trump was in full retreat on the policy (Rubin 2018). Of course, he was not to blame nor was anyone else in his administration (Blitzer 2018b). The inefficiency of the border bureaucracy has been such, however, that as of late summer 2018 hundreds of children had not yet been reunited with their parents or parents had been deported without hearings and could not be found to have their children reunited with them (e.g., Dickerson 2018).

The entire "zero-tolerance" fiasco is revealing of two readings of the US southern border that have become common in contemporary US politics. The first is that the southern border has come to symbolize US openness to the world at large. In the popular mind it has become THE border. The news media have normalized this position and thus played into Trump's rhetoric (Gessen 2018). Even though most immigrants including refugees enter the United States at other ports of entry and come from countries other than those of Central America, it is the southern border that is given the most attention (Warren and Kerwin 2017; Mossaad and Baugh 2018). Trump's proposed wall is very much in line with this geopolitical imagination. It is easy to visualize in the mind's eye. But it is also largely irrelevant to the real questions of determining refugee status and managing overall immigration into the United States. Rhetorical appeal ("Build the Wall") trumps practical management. Militarizing the southern US border is no substitute for an immigration policy (Massey et al. 2016). At the same time, selling an idea is not the same as actually managing something. The US refugee panic of 2018 also followed on from the very real crisis of refugees entering Europe in massive numbers in 2015–2016. The slow slog of refugees through the Balkans in summer 2015 (around 1 million people on the move from Syria and elsewhere toward Germany) was recapitulated in the April 2018 obsession of Donald Trump with a caravan of fifty refugees "marching" through Mexico on its way to the US southern border (Solis 2018). His instruction to turn away the refugees at the border was a clear violation of international and US law governing refugees but paralleled the behavior of the Hungarian government in 2015 (UUSC 2018). But the televisuals from Europe were conjoined with those from the southern border to create an inflated sense of danger or threat coming from the south. Trump's electoral "base" was mollified. He continued this rhetorical approach in the fall of 2018 when a larger "caravan" of Hondurans set out from Guatemala and served as Trump's primary theme for the midterm congressional elections: this sad group of men, women, and children were portrayed as a looming menace to the national security of the United States

(Serwer 2018). When some of their number rushed a border fence in Tijuana on 25 November 2018, the US Border Patrol used tear gas across the fence to discourage further action (Webber 2018). Many Trump supporters cheered this unwarranted excessive use of force (Devega 2018).

The second is that "illegal" immigrants and refugees are not readily distinguished from one another in the way that southern border security is conceived. President Trump has never been heard to use the word "refugee." To do so would be to acknowledge that not all of those who arrive at US ports of entry or cross into the United States at the southern border are "criminals" in actual or potential violation of US law. Yet the United States seems increasingly reticent at recognizing its obligations to refugees under a number of international treaties. Not only has criminality become attached to any sort of uncertain immigration status, and this began well before Trump appeared on the political scene (Kerwin 2018), the actual reasons why so many Central Americans are arriving at the southern border requesting asylum elicits little or no interest from the US government. That these are often, if not always, people with some resources reflects the fact that they are fleeing for purposes other than simply looking for any old job (Alden 2017). They are on the run for their or their children's lives. This would require of course attending to the role of the United States and US governments in creating the conditions in Central America from which people are trying to escape (e.g., Garcia 2006; Frank 2018). As one commentator puts it: "There can be no common-sense immigration 'debate' that conveniently ignores the history of US intervention in Central America" (Tseng-Putterman 2018).

THE US IMMIGRATION "DEBATE"

Along with fear of government, immigration has long been one of the bugbears of far-right politics in the United States. Every wave of immigration from the 1830s to the present has brought with it intense hostility to the newcomers on the part of a segment of the "native" population (Bennett 1995). The irony in all this, of course, is that the complainants are themselves the offspring of previous groups of immigrants. The so-called second Ku Klux Klan of the early 1900s was as much anti-immigrant (particularly anti-Catholic and anti-Semitic) as it was anti-Black. The US Immigration Act of 1924, as with earlier legislation such as the Chinese Exclusion Act of 1882 and so on, was designed to limit immigration, particularly with regard to "national origin." This has been the continuing goal of American "nativism," as it has been termed by historians, to not only restrict immigration as such but to limit it as much as possible to people originating in NW Europe. Others bring pestilence, race mixing, crime, and cultural decline (e.g., Williams 2018).

Perhaps one of the most important shifts from the recent presidential administrations to that of Trump has been the open racialization of the immigration "debate." Immigration, specifically the ethnic origins of immigrants, had never before figured so centrally in a presidential election campaign as it did in Donald Trump's (Torres 2018). Trump's election campaign for the US presidency was openly based around identifying immigration as the biggest threat to his slogan of "Making America Great Again." In the Republican primaries it was Trump's focus on immigration from Mexico that was reportedly one of his main attractions compared to the other candidates. Not only has Trump himself engaged in all sorts of race baiting about immigrants, most notoriously in false claims about the high incidence of crime among undocumented immigrants (e.g., Moon 2018), he also has explicit praise for white supremacists and close association with assorted eugenicists and purveyors of "white extinction anxiety." His supporters, such as the far-right Judicial Watch, insist that Trump lost the popular vote in 2016 because of votes by undocumented immigrants for Hillary Clinton. They thus connect together immigration with efforts at voter suppression. This is quite a departure from recent times irrespective of what one might say about the negative features of previous models of immigration management at the US southern border (Heuman and González 2018). Two examples of this illustrate the overall point. With respect to the conduct of immigration policy, Trump has drawn his personnel overwhelmingly from organizations such as the Center for Immigration Studies, an alt-right enterprise deeply based in eugenic conceptions of racial difference and the role of immigration in American cultural "decline" (e.g., Beirich 2018). Trump supporters at Fox News likewise openly advertise the idea that the plight of the refugees/asylees in summer 2018 was secondary to the demographic danger facing white America. One of Fox host Laura Ingraham's guests Pat Buchanan, for example, openly described the refugee crisis as symptomatic not of the problems facing the refugees but of the collective "suicide" (his word) facing white America if immigration were to continue unhindered (Blow 2018).

The refugee panic of 2018 should be seen in this overall historical context. It was a type of "moral panic" set off by politicians seeking to use the topic to mobilize a segment of the electorate to identify immigrants as both a future threat and current source of job insecurity and crime (Lusk et al. 2012). The focus on the southern border to the exclusion of the wider geographical process of immigrant/refugee entry suggests how much the ethnic/racial status of the border crossers was important to the entire affair. Even though empirically it is easy to show that illegal immigration and overall refugee claims were on a downward trajectory and that immigrants do not commit crimes at anything like the rate of the established population and occupy jobs that are not in demand on the part of that self-same population, systematic disinformation and damaging anecdotes about all of this spread easily across new social media. Some of the success in creating the panic lies in the fact that immigrants from Latin America, including many undocumented ones, have spread across the United States in recent years beyond the places that traditionally housed them. Newcomers in town often inspire suspicion, particularly if they look different from the natives (Batalova and Alperin 2018).

But much of it also lies in the complexity of US immigration law and policies (see American Immigration Council 2016). Many Americans think that most immigrants are undocumented, for example (Bump 2018). Of course, the very concept of "illegal immigrant" is a recent one dating back only to the late twentieth century (Ngai 2014; Donato and Massey 2016). It reflects the breakdown of older temporary/permanent immigration schemes and the rise of the insistence that all immigrants are potential citizens. The documented/undocumented distinction was unknown when many of the ancestors of most current US citizens first set foot on US shores. Much political discussion, as in the 2016 presidential election campaign, has tended to focus on so-called illegal immigration and such ancillary issues as "sanctuary cities" (in which jurisdictions refuse to collaborate with federal immigration agencies) and establishing routes to citizenship for the undocumented, particularly those brought to the United States as children (the proposed "Dream Act"). Little or no attention is given specifically to the broader questions of immigration policy such as why legal immigration is next to impossible for certain groups particularly low-income workers (even though there is massive demand for their services in the US) and the fact that asylum seekers are a completely different class of immigrants from those simply crossing the border in search of a seasonal job.

Much evidence suggests that the United States needs immigrants, both skilled and unskilled, and that the US immigration system is broken (*Economist* 2018). Refugees need to be distinguished clearly because of the treaty obligations that apply in their case. The fact that the US refugee panic of 2018 was about refugees yet completely mixed up in a discourse about the pros and cons of immigration tout court is a measure of the low quality of the political debate about immigration. The complexities of US immigration law, then, contribute to the sense of crisis when politicians and government officials make none of the distinctions mentioned here. In other words, it has not been much of a debate. It has been more of an emotional rant in which any sort of rational discussion has gone by the board.

CONCLUSION

The US southern border is an asymmetric one but the US population and its recently dominant political discourse about immigration do not seem to recognize this fact. The United States is not and has not been for many years just any old state with borders that confine the geographic scope of its control and authority. Its spatial reach and grip beyond its borders is such that its effects at a distance transmit impacts back home. Arguably the refugee panic of summer 2018 in the United States is the outcome of decades of intervention and impact in Central America as much as a crisis of immigration management as it was largely presented to the domestic audience. It bears little or no connection to the empirical course of either cross-border immigration in general or refugee claims in particular. Its genesis as a panic lies almost entirely in the confused politics of immigration in the United States triggered most recently by the flagrant exploitation of it as a cultural and economic issue by Donald J. Trump. It fit neatly into the "globalist versus nationalist" opposition that was central to his presidential campaign but without much current empirical support relating to crossings at the southern border. But this outburst is only the latest in a long train of similar panics that have broken out episodically in the United States. It has taken the form it has this time because of the manifest failure to distinguish refugee claims from those of other potential immigrants and the overt racialization of the political debate compared to the recent past.

The fact is that the United States and Mexico, as well as the countries of Central America, are locked systemically into a common economic-demographic enterprise because of capital and trade flows as much as those of people whose migration has had and continues to have generally positive externality effects in the United States (e.g., Selee 2018). Recognizing this fact, as well as adhering to international treaty obligations, would have done much to minimize the damaging human effects of the 2018 panic. But, of course, that would require eliminating the demagoguery about immigrants and refugees that has recently tainted US politics to such an extent. There is little sign of that happening any time soon. Much of this ambiguity goes back to the geopolitical contradictions that have informed the US "project" from the outset. Can the United States have worldwide impacts that feed back to the national territory and at the same time pretend to be just another state? Until that is sorted out, not much progress can be expected in policing the southern or other borders in a more geopolitically self-conscious and as a result more humane manner.

5

Putting China in the World

The contemporary "rise" of China, historically outside of the golden circle of influential Great Powers in the modern era, provides an interesting case for examining the degree to which the hegemonic calculus at the basis to recent world politics can be expected to continue. Typically, China is viewed as either just another in a long succession of Great Powers rising to the top of the global hierarchy (e.g., Kennedy, P. 1986) or a completely new phenomenon because of its singular history associated with its imperial past, communist rejection of world capitalism, and cultural particularity (e.g., Keith 2009). In this chapter I take issue with both of these accounts to suggest that China's emerging position in world politics cannot be seen as just a process of "regular" hegemonic succession or as bringing a totally new script to the table. If the first view relies on the naturalized story about world politics typical of most understandings of "geopolitics," the second depends on a view of China as a completely separate "world" largely untainted by how world politics has operated over the past several hundred years.

From my perspective, however, Chinese elites have been in active confrontation and cooperation with the western-based world system since at least the nineteenth century and from this have developed a contradictory amalgam of western-style nationalism and a traditional totalistic conception of world order that remains reactive to and dependent on the ways in which world politics is currently organized. Like all modern states, China is an "invention" in the sense that it is a fusion of historic stories of its past, including its "humiliation" at the hands of foreign powers in the nineteenth and early twentieth centuries, and adjustment to and incorporation into the wider global order (e.g., Zarrow 2012; Hayton 2020; Perdue 2021). Thus, China does not currently provide some totally alternative scripting to world politics, although it could well contribute to a pluralization away from the recent hegemony of neoliberal capitalism associated with the post-1970s US global role (Agnew 2007a). Nevertheless, the various initiatives of Chinese government to claim a large part of the South China Sea (Rolf and Agnew 2016) and in the seemingly ambitious but ambiguously defined One Belt One Road infrastructure project designed as much to release investment for Chinese construction firms as to engage in any sort of global imperialism (Narins and Agnew 2020), tend to suggest a world moving beyond the US-sponsored globalization of the post-1970s era. Yet, at the same time, given that the 2020–2021 pandemic seemed to start in China and the government was less than forthcoming about what it knew and when it knew it, the reputational damage has contributed to the rise of an offensive nationalism on the part of many government officials that hardly bodes well for any chance of "China" easily shifting into the role as a global hegemon (as understood in chapter 2 in any of its modalities) any time soon (e.g., Khan 2021; Zakaria 2021). Still, within China, the course of the pandemic has been seen in many quarters as indicating the "success" of China as a model relative to the managerial failure in the United States (see chapter 7), at least during the time that Donald Trump was US President (Byun et al. 2021). This could lead to future popular dissonance if economic growth in China and China's global pretensions fail to materialize.

As a result of its rapid economic growth since the 1990s, China thus occupies a central place in what can be called "a prophetic culture"—the focus of classical geopolitics and the field of international relations on predicting future events rather than explaining current practice (Woodside 1998, 13). This requires applying a universal calculus to cases such as China in which empirical anomalies are viewed as minor particularities. In this vision, China is rising as either or both a miracle and a threat. As William Callahan (2010, 11) says: "China's experience lends itself to hyperbole—both positive and negative. The People's Republic of China has the world's largest population, largest portfolio of foreign exchange reserves, largest army, largest middle class, and the largest diaspora." The list of "largests" goes on. Much of this is usually put down to the recent success of the implementation of the East Asian developmental-state model as adapted and expanded from the practices of other states in the immediate region. Of course, it is based at least in part on export-oriented manufacturing and integration into the global financial system since the 1980s. The fateful decision made in the 1980s to open up the Chinese economy by price liberalization and invitations to foreign investment yet retain centralized regulatory control by the Communist Party led the country in a fundamentally different direction from what was to happen in the Soviet Union in the 1990s (Weber, I. 2021). But the transformation has older roots in the exotic allure and influence exercised by China in European and later American imaginative reconstructions of the country as a defining instance of "foreignness" (Porter 2001). So any Chinese foreign-policy decisions must be placed in this context. At the same time, because of US decline or retreat on economic and military fronts and the difficulties for a still relatively poor country in responding to this, according to a host of commentators, again in Callahan's (2010, 11) words, China is "either preparing to take over the world or is about to collapse" under the weight of its own political and economic contradictions. In this light, there is no possibility of any real agency resulting from political choices made by jockeying interests and competing identities within China itself with the inevitable involvement of external actors of various sorts (e.g., Leonard 2008).

In this chapter I attempt three tasks with the overall purpose of making a case for contextual theorizing. Each task in sequence helps to make the overall argument. The first task is to show that the making of "international relations" has been anything but universal. I rehearse the ways in which knowledge is made and circulates, arguing that there is never a "view from nowhere." Knowledge of human society is always "local, situated, and embedded" (Shapin 1998, 6). The main point is to understand that perspectives arise in distinctive geographical contexts. These then can "travel" and influence thinking and practice elsewhere but only if they have powerful sponsors. This is not to endorse a simple epistemic relativism but to insist that we need to know how knowledge is made and travels in order to judge how well it actually "works" (Agnew 2007a). Dominant perspectives are based on a radical separation of the domestic and international and reliance on European and American historical experience as a source of analogies for understanding the world tout court.

The second task is to examine recent discussions of "Chinese" versus "Western" approaches to world politics in terms of the geography of knowledge. I am particularly interested in how China's rising material significance is typically interpreted in terms of either/or thinking (historic repetition versus novelty, and so on) and how this can be interrogated to provide an alternative conception of "China in the world"—not just a repetition of other "cases" or the projection of Chinese exceptionalism but of the intersection between Chinese agency and the wider global environment including the diffusion of ideas about international relations. The rise of China particularly represents a crisis for the Eurocentric "modern geopolitical imagination" (Agnew 2003) that has become second nature in the conventional perspectives. This is a point repeatedly emphasized by some historians of Asia in drawing attention to alternative modernities to that of the West offered by mainstream accounts (e.g., Duara 2015; Woodside 2006).

The third task is to reflect something of the space-time crisis in the relationship of "China" to the world since its reopening to the world in the 1980s and the types of thinking about international relations that have emerged in China in this overall context. I suggest there are four currently popular international relations narratives in China whose provenance and jockeying for influence over China's foreign policy provide a better basis for understanding "China in the world" than simply importing a singular perspective from elsewhere. In brief compass, these are the Pacific Rim, Confucian–New Orientalist, *geopolitik*, and International Relations with Chinese characteristics narratives. It is the politics around these narratives that will determine what kind of knowledge about international relations and political practice China will contribute to the wider world. The making of Chinese foreign policy is currently the outcome of varied domestic and external contingencies partly because the geographical and historical limits of "China" are undergoing a fundamental redefinition as the Chinese government and other Chinese-based actors become more important in the world (e.g., Woon 2018; Foot and Goh 2019).

"FAMILIAR" ANALOGIES AND THE LIMITED GEOGRAPHIC ORIGINS OF THINKING ABOUT WORLD POLITICS

The strength of the conventional wisdom about international relations should not be underestimated. It draws from a pool of knowledge about an idealized European and North American history that gives it an authority well beyond the borders of the world in which it has developed (see chapter 2). Through the use of metaphor and analogy, international relations theory projects from a limited geographical experience onto the world at large a set of presumptions about the nature of statehood, empire, anarchy, and so on that make sense of the larger world in familiar terms (e.g., Acharya and Buzan 2017). So it is not so much a lack of knowledge or curiosity about the world beyond the confines of Euro-America that is at issue. It is the employment of terms of discourse that are rarely investigated for their particularity. They are simply presumed to be universal (chapter 3).

The familiar language of international relations theory is also hard to bypass even as it is imposed onto worlds for which it is possibly ill-suited or ill-matched. Most important is the case of an essential and undifferentiated "statehood" based on the model of a historic France or the United States, assuming that all other polities around the world conform more or less to the history and capacities of the ideal-type state. Full modern personhood has become attached to the image of the state, based in these examples, as its progenitor. Thus, imitating the originals such as France or the United States is the central moment of becoming modern for, for example, Russia, India, or China. This Western "culturism" underwrites the self-evident historical failure of such polities as China (Wang 2011, 21–2; also Wang 2014, 25–27). Failure to democratize in the same way as the United States, for example, is seen as an aberration, when the West itself has often failed to live up to its own lofty standards of democratic practice for long periods of time. "Illiberal tendencies" worldwide today suggest the need to rethink the easy association between the West and an essentially "democratic" modernity.

The historical geopolitics that brought Europe and North America to the fore globally from the sixteenth century to the present is seen as a simple "social fact" that can be taken for granted as animating world politics in its entirety. Whatever its precise economic and political roots, however, this global dominance has enabled the projection of a specific set of political norms onto the world at large. The "modern geopolitical imagination" refers to a way of thinking that privileges the idea of zero-sum conflicts between Great Powers in worldwide competition for "top dog" status and can be thought of as a "system" for visualizing the world with its most significant roots in the nature of the European encounter with the rest of the world in the sixteenth and seventeenth centuries.

The analogy to an essentially European statehood also feeds into the strong tendency to radically distinguish a worldwide modern state system without any history except for a sudden moment in seventeenth century Europe when it sprang to life: the myth of the Peace of Westphalia. Widely recognized now as a problematic starting point, it nevertheless still provides the term "Westphalian" to describe the essential nature of the modern state system. This reification of a seemingly timeless system, with new members acceding as they are recognized by existing ones, leaves little room to acknowledge let alone carefully consider how polities of various types have fared around the world with varying elements of empire, statehood as typically understood, and clan-tribal character about them (e.g., Halperin and Palen 2015). The world political map with its clearly defined borders imposes an image of geographical order on the world that is completely state-territorial (Agnew 1994).

In sum, and contradictory to the territorial understanding of statehood (as vested in juridical sovereignty), given that each state is presumed to provide equivalent sovereignty within its territory to all others, in geopolitical space sovereignty is up for grabs as states compete for global power and influence and weak states succumb to more powerful ones. This hierarchical and often imperialist geopolitical system is one that has come to be the byword of the political elites who occupy seats of power in the most important Great Powers, hitherto mainly in Europe and North America. They presume that Rising Powers, like China, will follow their example exactly (e.g., Mearsheimer 2006; Friedberg 2011; Allison 2017).

THE MAKING AND THE TRAVELS OF DOMINANT PERSPECTIVES ON WORLD POLITICS

Indeed, much of what today goes for "international relations theory" is the projection onto the world at large of US-originated academic ideas about the nature of statehood and the world economy (e.g., Kristensen 2015). This follows a mixture of largely mid-twentieth century European premises about states as unitary actors and American ones about economies as liberal and open (Inayatullah and Rupert 1994). The theory reflects the application of criteria about how best to model a presumably hostile world drawn from selected aspects of US experience and a US-based reading of world history.

My point is not that knowledge of world politics is simply a coercive imposition of the view from some places onto others. Rather, the dominant ways in which intellectuals and political elites around the world have come to think about world politics are not the result of either an open "search" for the best perspective or theory or a reflection of an essentially "local" perspective. More specifically, the most prestigious repertoires of thinking about world politics represent the historical emergence of theoretical genres intimately associated with specific times and places that circulate and adapt in association with the spheres of influence of schools and authors that have the best reputations and which in turn reflect the current geopolitical order. US universities have been particularly important in this process.

The presumption of my approach here is that global structures of political inequality underwrite whose imagination gets to dominate globally in theorizing about world politics. This is turn has obvious implications for any liberatory or democratic politics. In other words, thinking about world politics reflects the relative hierarchy of power within world politics. Yet much dominant thinking about international relations usually makes claims that either obscure or limit the degree to which the world to which it refers is seen as hierarchical. I first provide some premises upon which the argument is based and then use the case of Chinese examples of thinking about international relations to illustrate the argument.

The "marketplace of ideas" is never a level playing field. There is thus a geopolitics to knowledge production and circulation (e.g., Zhang and Kristensen 2017). That knowledge which becomes "normalized" or dominant and what is marginalized has something to do with who is doing the proposing and where they are located (Agnew 2005). In the context of world politics what is recognized as "serious" knowledge is socially conditioned by the rituals, routines, and recruitment practices of powerful educational and research institutions. At a world-scale, perhaps the outstanding feature of the past centuries has been the way most places have been incorporated into flows of knowledge dominated by Europeans and extensions of Europe overseas, such as the United States. This is the story, in Eric Wolf's evocative phrase, of *Europe and the People Without History* (1982). Consider, for example, how recent conceptions of "China" in the United States and elsewhere still rely to a degree on understandings established during the term that John Hay served as US Secretary of State at the turn of the twentieth century involving the Open Door policy and the recent Chinese Exclusion Act (Blanchard, 2013).

Of course, knowledge about world politics (or anything else) from one place is not necessarily incommensurable or unintelligible relative to knowledge produced elsewhere. Cross-cultural communication goes on all the time without everything being lost in translation. Cultures in the modern world never exist in isolation and are themselves assemblages of people with often crosscutting identities and commitments (Lukes 2000). From this viewpoint, culture is "an idiom or vehicle of inter-subjective life, but not its foundation or final cause" (Jackson 2002, 125). Be that as it may, knowledge creation and dissemination are never innocent of at least weak ontological commitments, be they national, class, gender, or something else. But the history of knowledge circulation suggests that rarely are ideas simply restricted within rigid cultural boundaries. This is a deficiency of postcolonial approaches that simply carve the world up into simple oppositional zones like Global North and Global South. Rather, with powerful sponsors, international and transnational networks arise to carry and embed ideas from place to place (e.g., Sapiro 2009).

The intellectually dominant realist tradition of US international relations theory (although even its opponents such as liberals and idealists share numerous assumptions with it) is based on a central assumption of "anarchy" beyond state borders (Agnew 1994). Realist theory was both a reaction against the behavioral trend in US political science in the 1940s and 1950s that presumed a science of politics could be founded entirely based on rational principles of individual behavior and the result of the desire to keep close connections between academic study of world politics and practitioners in a furthering of *Staatslehre* or the proffering of advice to political leaders on the basis of profound and presumably unchangeable truths about human nature and the state system (Guilhot 2008). It should be a "special field" separate from the other social sciences. Relative unease over whether or not "international relations" constituted or could constitute a separate "discipline" was never paralleled until recently by fears that it might well be a "science" based largely on projecting American views onto the world at large (e.g., Kripendorff 1989; Kahler 1993).

CHINA'S HIDDEN GEOPOLITICS

Given its changing material-geopolitical status, the situation of China in relation to international relations theory is no longer as simple as that of an importer of American International Relations theory. It would also be mistaken to see all of the many commentators and contributors to debate over Chinese foreign policy as working from exactly the same script. By examining the publications of numerous think tanks and universities as revealed by their websites and academic outlets, I identify four relatively distinctive streams of narrative that currently seem to inspire most constructions of "China" and its place in the world among Chinese policy entrepreneurs and intellectuals. After briefly identifying them, I turn to discussing each in more detail including its sponsors and their position within the current Chinese political-institutional constellation. At the close I suggest that the opening up of China since the 1980s and the fragmented authoritarianism of the regime tend to make a jockeying for influence among the narratives a real possibility. Future Chinese foreign policy will reflect this fact. This emphasis on the central importance of political agency in the face of divergent intellectual-policy influences would benefit IR theorizing in general well beyond Chinese shores.

In brief compass, the four streams of narrative are as follows. If the Pacific Rim story developed in the 1980s and 1990s is somewhat in eclipse, it still has considerable political-economic dynamism behind it and not a little Chinese history of its own, particularly in respect of the powerful diaspora influence of China around the world. The new Orientalism is the most invested in the revival of Confucianism as a guiding hand but relies on an idealized image of the Chinese past that also produces hostile as well as pacific postures toward neighboring states and the world at large. The "nationalist *geopolitik*" grouping is much less influential than the Orientalist, except perhaps among elements in the military, but is by far the most aggressive in finding much of its inspiration in the major revisionist powers of the twentieth century: Nazi Germany and Militarist Japan. Finally, the attempt at creating an international relations theory "with Chinese characteristics" represents the fourth type of international relations narrative as I have defined them. This is the seemingly most benign and as yet has had the least effect in terms of formulating perspectives that can feed into policy making. But that has long been a problem for international relations theory without Chinese characteristics as well.

What I wish to challenge most forcefully is the popular view that China's future "place in the world" can be either simply read off from a familiar story told by those oblivious to Chinese discussions about the "nature" of China and the effects that this will have on what will constitute Chinese foreign policy in the years ahead or by reproducing one of the Chinese accounts as "the" single truthful one. As William Callahan (2011, 12) says: "To take China seriously as an emerging world power, we need to understand how Chinese scholars and policymakers imagine their future on the international stage." Critical examination of what is being imagined and how it affects China's foreign relations then becomes the goal.

CHINESE NARRATIVES ON WORLD POLITICS

As China becomes a Great Power in the Western sense of the phrase, an economic and potentially military behemoth, its leaders and intellectual elites must struggle with how to respond. Given that "China" has had a centuries-long existence as some sort of polity, this task is made particularly difficult by the rich history of geographical forms and modes of rule that have characterized it down the years (Wang, H. 2014; Schuman 2020). Over the past thirty years, as modern China has opened up to the world and returned to mining its past for guidance in the present, its intellectuals and policy entrepreneurs have increasingly produced international relations narratives that rely heavily on past "experience" as a guide to the present. In universities, think tanks, party schools, the military, and among journalists a class of "public intellectuals" has grown up at least semi-independent of the ruling party-state (for the concept of Chinese public intellectuals see, e.g., Cheek 2006).

Such narratives are inevitably selective. It is what is selected that is of most interest. Some narratives emphasize martial and expansionist elements from the Chinese past, others pick up on more pacific strains in Chinese cultural history. A number of different refrains characterize the narratives about China's place in the world and its consequences. All of these invoke historical events and past geographies of China in their understandings of the present and their directions toward the future. Each has a distinctive geopolitical vision intrinsic to it. Different Chinese policy entrepreneurs and intellectuals and their foreign collaborators and influences have seen their narratives rise and fall in relative popularity over time. Of course, proponents see their narratives as the "best" ones in the sense of providing the truest accounts. They are associated with different intellectual venues across China having differing relationships to the Communist Party and to various governmental institutions. "China" is not the singular location that constant invocation of the country's name implies. Even with a powerful centralized state and the omnipresent Communist Party there is still a relative plurality of sites and settings across which interests jockey for influence and prestige (e.g., Duara 1995). In the end, however, it is which ones among the narratives that prove most influential to Chinese governments and in the wider world and what governments choose to do on that basis that really matters. But we should not simply leap to the end of the chain before establishing the range of positions in play.

As several commentators have noted, increased resort to historical events and philosophical concepts mined from deep in Chinese history has become de rigueur (e.g., Wang, H. 2014; Callahan 2011; Rozman 2012). At the same time, however, a deeply territorialized vision not only of China's past and present but also of its future inspires those narratives that are now most ascendant. This bias puts definite limits on the ability to break with the current global order by attracting allies and engaging in any sort of reorientation of global governance.

The idea of the Pacific Rim (or even that of Asia-Pacific) now seems somewhat dated. Yet in the 1990s it was central to much debate about the integration of the newly opened China into world politics inside as well as outside China. It is one-sided to see this narrative of China's place in the world as simply a US imposition (Connery 1994). The focus on China as part of a larger Pacific or Asian world, the terms vary, was designed to place China at the center of a web of connections around the massive Chinese diaspora in Southeast Asia and around the Pacific Ocean, paying particular attention to how a widespread network of nodes and territories had paid a disproportionate role in fostering the opening up and economic growth of China since the 1980s. This rendition of "China in the world" gives central place to trade and investment relations at the regional level. Unsurprisingly, the bureaucracy devoted to trade and opening China to foreign markets has tended to favor this narrative. Dubbed "Rimspeak" by Bruce Cumings (1998), rather than celebrating an essential Chinese identity locked into a historically given territory, this narrative sees China as a central geographical moment in a new geopolitical logic knitting together the Pacific Rim as an alternative global focus to the previously dominant North Atlantic core. Today some views of China in relation to Asian regionalism and plans for regional-level cooperation (such as the One Belt One Road and so on) continue to partake of this perspective (e.g., Pan and Lo 2015; Ye 2015). China's role as a center rather than as simply a periphery to globalization can also be played up under this schema (e.g., Hamilton, P. E. 2021; Labrosse 2022).

What was lacking in the older formulation, it now seems clear, was much to connect the contemporary vision to a positive rendering of the Chinese past. Its proponents seem to have thought that projecting what seemed to the dominant trend of the present into the future was sufficient justification. Yet the emphasis on the diaspora in particular always ran the risk of bringing to mind, implicitly if not explicitly, the years of Chinese "humiliation" at the hands of foreigners and the emigration of Chinese in search of greener pastures elsewhere than those left at home. The apparent postcolonial and post-territorial moorings of the Pacific Rim concept have also made it seem less attractive in China in the face of the country's seemingly self-sufficient economic growth, the crisis in global finance, and fears articulated in the United States of the military "threat" emanating reflex-like from an economically vibrant China.

It is the Orientalist vision that has probably been most visible among popular Chinese writers and government-oriented think tanks over the past ten years (e.g., McGann 2012; Zhu 2009). But this has older roots in the common insistence by many authorities, both Chinese and not, of Chinese history for most of its course down until the twentieth century as representing the workings of a Sinocentric world-system (e.g., Wang, F-L. 2017). In some accounts, Confucian adages often provide the sociopsychological basis to a Chinese exceptionalism that is completely different from anything to be found anywhere else. Prominent in certain popular works by Western writers (e.g., Fan 2011), this type of narrative based on an idealized image of China's past also has many Chinese proponents (e.g., Ye and Long 2013).

Such intellectuals and the policy makers who consume their ideas have been looking to venerable concepts such as *tianxia* (天下) to rethink empire and world order in a register drawn from Chinese intellectual history but applied to the contemporary world (e.g., Zhao Tingyang 2005, 2011). Thus, for example, Yan Xuetong (2011) borrows from the ancient Chinese philosopher Xunzi to construct a hierarchical-realist perspective predicting that a "balanced" economic-political-military approach to Chinese foreign relations will produce better outcomes all round than would a China emphasizing economic growth alone. Others look back not so much for philosophical inspiration as to identify popular "historical traditions" such as some variety of Confucianism or historical features such as the lack of a "balance-of-power" between polities in East Asia (see, e.g., Carlson 2011; Zhang, F. 2015) to underpin their prognostications about contemporary world politics.

Somewhat less publicly visible has been the discovery of pre–Second World War German and Japanese geopolitics reframed in Chinese terms. Termed "the *geopolitik* turn" by Christopher Hughes (2011), this type of narrative, epitomized by such books as *China Dream* (Liu M. 2010) and the immensely popular novel (and now film) *Wolf Totem* (Jiang Rong 2004), focuses on China's need to protect access to resources around the world through the projection of sea power. It is associated with the Chinese navy, other elements in the military, and Han nationalists. To one degree or another, all of these accounts recycle old geopolitical nostrums equivalent to lebensraum, organismic statehood, and racial categorization. They are characterized by the same "moral exceptionalism" as the older German model. China is sui generis. It is a Han Chinese enterprise in a Social Darwinian world. In this construction, China is awakening from its slumber to resurrect the martial values that in the past had led its dynasties to expand territorially across Asia. There is a particularly interesting parallel here with the strand of Japanese exceptionalism (the *Nihonjin ron* discourse) in the 1980s that emphasized climatic determinism: *shinfūdoron*. Indeed, the various narratives all have some parallel with the various strands of Japanese exceptionalist discourse. Perhaps all "emerging powers" are faced with similar dilemmas in establishing a strategic rationale for their foreign policies (e.g., Nau and Ollapally 2012)?

The message from the *geopolitik* posture for China's leaders is that every event in China's "neighborhood" involving other actors is a potential challenge to China's status and thus must be met with an immediate response. As a result, and among other things, "Ultimately no room is left for compromise in the contest with Japan, because control of the East China Sea is not just about energy reserves; it is about the bigger question of who controls Taiwan, access to the Pacific and ultimately to the world" (Hughes 2011, 620). The syncretism with foreign influences here is obvious, yet it now serves to justify totally Sinocentric ends.

Finally, by comparison significantly more anodyne, are those attempts mentioned earlier at configuring a political-science conception of international relations with Chinese characteristics (Qin 2011a; Kim 2016). Many studies are of this genre. As argued previously, much of what goes for international relations theory was invented in the United States. Sinicizing such an approach takes several forms. One involves "highlighting Chinese traditions as a partial explanation of Chinese diplomatic conduct" (Ming 2012, 105). In this way allusions to "harmony" and analogies to ancient dynastic wars take on deeper meaning as representing something fundamentally Chinese rather than as noble and arguably universal sentiments or historically contingent events of distant memory. Implicit here still is a potential celebration of an essential Chinese difference that remains unrelated to much actual Chinese history; the fact, for example, as Gilbert Rozman (2012, 122) puts it, "The hereditary family elite in China is steeped in family socialism, not Confucianism."

Rather more profoundly, however, the other narrative involves reorienting the entire field (inside and beyond China) around concepts drawn from the ancient philosopher Xunzi (and others), the benevolent nature of Chinese power, and a "normative hierarchical order." Reading across a number of writers, particularly Qin Yaqing (2011b), Yan Xuetong (2011), and Wang Yiwei (2007), Allen Carlson (2011, 101) sees evidence for "the development of a new vision of world order which supplements, if not replaces, Westphalia with newly resurrected, yet historically grounded, 'Chinese' concepts of how international politics might be reorganized." Much of this parallels the Orientalist narrative (second on the list) but using its explicit reference to Chinese history to engage with more universalist theoretical approaches rather than remaining a world apart, so to speak. For example, a rising China needs followers not just supplicants as in the hegemonic stability theory beloved of American exceptionalists.

Increasingly, however, these accounts appear more "realist" in their emphasis on China versus the rest than oriented to a "rationalist" view of relative gains among fellow states (Lynch 2009). Moreover, and ironically, that the reference point is Westphalia even as Chinese history is mined for concepts and crucial events to argue against it, is suggestive again of the degree to which this new narrative is of mixed and not simply Chinese origin. Yan, for example, writes of a "moral realism" to convey this hybridity (e.g., Larson 2020). Of course, this is by no means a new development. Chinese intellectuals and politicians have wrestled with Western influences, not least the now-increasingly forgotten borrowing from Marxism, for centuries (Callahan, 2015). Mining history, it seems, is as much about what is forgotten as what is remembered.

THE POLITICS OF THE NARRATIVES ABOUT WORLD POLITICS

To what extent can these narratives be seen as potentially leading to different possible foreign-policy positions significant beyond China's borders? In the first place, the possibility for jockeying among a range of positions inspired by different narratives has a contemporary historical basis. China's renewed opening to the world since the 1980s represents a "time-space crisis" in the sense that China can no longer be set in an eternally present and geographically contained world such as that of the Cold War but must be increasingly externally oriented and dynamic, drawing ideas both from abroad but also from what had been "lost" with the official disavowal of the past China from before the 1949 Revolution.

This introduces a fundamental instability into the making of Chinese foreign policy simply because the geographical and historical limits of "China" are undergoing a fundamental redefinition. Is it primarily a defensive territorial formation or does it aspire to cast a broader influence? Is it primarily reactive to external events or a molder of them? This helps to understand why perhaps so much contemporary debate in China involves recourse to prerevolutionary historical sources and analogies even as they must be adapted to a different world-geographical milieu than those historical ones from which they derive. China's new prominence demands looking back to when it had a perhaps similar destiny. This means, above all, that tropes derived from the Cold War between the United States and the Soviet Union like "containment" are fundamentally misleading (e.g., Rachman 2021). China is too much in and of the globalized world that the United States crafted, beginning during the Cold War, for this to make much sense at all (Christensen 2021a; Nexon 2021; Nye 2021; Wolf 2021a). It is currently the world's most successful "competition state" (Cerny 2010). Fashionable talk about "decoupling" between China and the world economy misses the extent to which businesses worldwide still see a real future in the country (e.g., *Economist* 2021g; Acemoglu 2021a).

Yet at the same time the Chinese economy relies on open trade, the government still exercises control over capital flows out of the country in the national currency and has massive investments in US government bonds. A rapidly aging population, massive internal income inequalities, a persisting development chasm between rural and urban areas, deep ethnic divisions, and the desire to develop technologically intensive industries likewise impose constraints for the foreseeable future on the possibilities of China creating an alternative to what currently goes for globalization, irrespective of what the leadership says (e.g., Rozelle and Hell 2020; McMorrow 2021; Cheng 2021; Economy 2021). Aggressive nationalist responses in the face of foreign criticism suggest how uncertainty and instability can feed into one another (Khan 2021; Zakaria 2021). Trying to play "both sides of the street" in supporting Russia yet not endorsing the invasion of Ukraine in 2022 suggests how much China's government under Xi Jinping is caught between the territorial-imperial geopolitical model represented by Russia and the globalist model it has been pursuing in a strange undeclared and inconsistent emulation of the United States (e.g., Hille 2022; Wang, Y-K. 2022; Campbell, C. 2022).

As yet, however, recognition of the fact that China is ensnared to a startling extent, for example, in the network-based logic of globalization (e.g., Pan 2009; Nolan 2012; Rolf 2020) has had only limited effects on most of the international relations visions so far in question (e.g., Hameiri and Jones 2015). This may change now that President Xi senses a role for China as a sponsor for the US-led globalization from which the United States itself may well now be in retreat. But contemporary theorizing remains largely captive to territorialized images of global politics with either a world of states or great swathes of the globe presumably always under some Great Power or other's sway. This focus has twin sources, not dissimilar to elsewhere but with Chinese characteristics. One is the centrality of bureaucratic politics with the jockeying for influence in higher circles between ministries and political factions (Zhang 2016). The other is the emphasis on centralized diplomacy and the presentation of a Chinese "face" to the world (Ho 2016). Together these certainly encourage a degree of pragmatism in the approach to strategic policy (e.g., Stenslie 2014). The "experimental" character of policy innovation in China down the years since the 1949 Revolution suggests the extent to which this attribute permeates China's governance notwithstanding the attribution of a presumed "baked in" fixed outlook to the party-state (e.g., Lim 2019).

It is also important to emphasize that although Chinese government remains authoritarian, policy making is relatively open to a variety of influences including that of intellectuals, military officers, journalists, and others. The literature on Chinese politics sometimes refers to such people as "policy entrepreneurs" suggesting that they compete with one another for the ear of political leaders and an increasingly vibrant public opinion (e.g., Lieberthal and Oksenberg 1988; Murtha 2009; Jakobson and Manuel 2016; Wong, C. H. 2021). This "fragmented authoritarianism" offers a useful heuristic for considering the wide range of IR narratives that have emerged into prominence in recent years. The Chinese party-state is no longer if it ever was best thought of as a singularly monolithic entity (*pace* Doshi 2021). Nevertheless, capitalist entrepreneurs, most notably Jack Ma, of Alibaba and Ant fame, risk business and personal independence if seen as too powerful (Anderlini 2021). Yet, at the same time, the mixed economy that has brought China much of its recent growth is easily undermined by closing it off from the world in the face of the demands of an aging and still on average relatively poor population, the need for innovative risk taking to fuel an economy increasingly dependent on technology, popular protests that are not invariably zero-sum in outcomes, and, contrary to some opinion, the declining overall importance of the state in China's economy—which all point toward much greater ambiguity than the confident predictions of the conventional geopolitical wisdom (e.g., Huang and Levy 2021; Lee and Zhang 2013; Roberts 2020; Rosen 2021).

Not only do not-too-distant fissures within the party elite over promotions to top-tier leadership positions reveal distinctive ideological, policy, and personalized factions, different factions are clearly recruiting support from within the ranks of the burgeoning intelligentsia to provide them with rationales and justifications for their policy positions. There is simply not a singular grand strategy unifying the Chinese central government but a frequently chaotic struggle between factions contending for influence (Jones and Hameiri 2021b). This said, it is important not to overstate the degree to which opinions can be freely expressed outside fairly narrow and officially prescribed limits. China may be a post-totalitarian society but it is hardly an open one. The elevation of the princeling Xi Jinping to head the party and the state, only the second leader of post-1949 China chosen by his peers (Mao Zedong was the other), seems to represent the beginning of a clampdown (McGregor 2019). The decision in 2018 to abolish term limits for this president suggests an increasingly personalized, centralized rule (Wong and Zhai 2021).

This centralizing process has been on full display in the mass imprisonment of Uighurs in Xinjiang for suspected separatism, the rejection of even partial democracy in Hong Kong, and the lack of transparency about the origins of the COVID-19 pandemic in the "wet markets" of Wuhan followed by a massively restrictive if seemingly successful approach to its management. The example of what happened to the former Soviet Union when the Communist Party lost its control haunts the memory of the contemporary Chinese Communist Party. Surreal as it often appears in a country no longer based on centralized plans but on capitalist enterprises, knowledge of Leninist doctrine is still necessary for getting ahead politically and within many putatively independent social organizations (Mitter and Johnson 2021). But it was not centralization but relative regional autonomy that brought about the dynamic expansion of the Chinese economy from the 1990s to the present (Delong 2021; Lim 2019; Rosen 2021; Wong, A. 2021). Good Leninists should see a contradiction when there is one.

But as Roderick MacFarquhar (2015, 6) remarks with respect to Xi's lack of an appealing if incoherent ideology such as Mao Zedong Thought to guide him: "Without a substantive positive ideology to grip the Chinese people, Xi has been forced to go negative, listing alien doctrines to be extirpated" with only his anti-corruption campaign to possibly transform the party he leads and to prevent the collapse of single-party rule. A mélange of Marxist-Leninist slogans, state capitalism, and Confucian adages, Xi Thought seems unlikely in itself to ever provide a coherent guide to Chinese foreign policy (Wong and Zhai 2021). To the extent that it does, one can see a certain rendering of the sort of view expressed by Zhao Tingyang (2005) about a "balanced" approach to China's foreign relations drawing explicitly on examples from Chinese imperial history even as China still remains officially attached to the Principles of Peaceful Coexistence premised on a classical or Westphalian view of territorial sovereignty. Implicit in it is also the strategic vision of a figure such as Yan Xuetong (e.g., 2014). Interestingly, both Zhao and Yan frequently write op-ed articles in leading Chinese and foreign newspapers and magazines (e.g., Yan 2018; Zhao 2018). As a result, and at least for the near future, as the Chinese proverb says: "The gun shoots the bird with its head up" (*qiang da chutou niao*) (quoted in Esarey and Qiang 2008, 755–6). In other words, there would seem to be strict limits to political-intellectual pluralism in the face of renewed political centralization. Xi is in a rush to establish China as a major player in world politics but this is risky given the domestic challenges he must also confront (Blanchette 2021). The perception of US decline, wildly popular in nationalist Chinese circles, is not enough in itself to do the job (e.g., Che 2022). At the same time, events in the wider world, however, may well mandate significant shifts in the balance of power between the various narrative streams in the years to come. Attachment to the Principles of Peaceful Coexistence may be stretched to the limit.

CONCLUSION

In brief compass, I have tried to outline and tie together three general themes. The first is the importance of considering the geographies of knowledge about international relations theory rather than simply accepting its self-evident universality. Its very familiarity then informs how we look at the world. Yet it is the result of a very specific contextual rather than universal historical experience. The second is how China represents a clear challenge to the conventional wisdom in IR theory but in a way that opens up the possibility of thinking about theory in different terms than we usually think: that of contextual theorizing based on understanding the contingencies between global pressures and local/national agency. The third theme brings these two together by examining recent efforts within China at articulating that country's relationship to the wider world (putting China in the world) and how this focus can help us understand international relations in a more contextualized manner paying close attention to the intersection between Sinocentric elements on the one hand and borrowed elements and influences on the other. From this perspective, and as illustrated by the case of contemporary China, actual international relations are best theorized in terms of the politics of choice between alternative framings that influence foreign policy rather than as the invariable outcome of some general theory that stands above and beyond the world and is the projection of a current hegemony and its understandings of that world. It is at the conjuncture between what is happening in China and influences from the wider world that answers are to be found as to the possible impact of a "rising China" on that wider world.

III

GEOPOLITICS OF DEVELOPMENT

6

Territorial Politics after the Financial Crisis

One fundamental feature of the global capitalist economy is its cyclical character. Notwithstanding the efforts of national central banks using monetary policies and national governments using fiscal policies, shocks to the world economy occur both regularly and episodically. Some of these are systemically more challenging than others because they are intrinsic to the economy, being related to production or financial cycles, rather being exogenous, like pandemics or many civil wars. Even as macroeconomics claims to come up with the perfect answer to economic cycles, the crises keep on coming as they have since the onset of the modern world economy in the seventeenth century (Reinhart and Rogoff 2009).

Thus, although the 2020–2021 global pandemic had worldwide effects with dramatically different impacts across the world, with the world's poorer countries much more negatively affected economically than the richer ones, the financial crisis of 2007–2008 was much more of a threat to the richest countries and the world economy on the whole, not least because it was banks and other agencies in the richest countries involved in the sale and purchase of the financial products whose collapse produced the crisis. Arguably, the rich country governments had also learned from the previous crisis that massive fiscal and monetary measures would be necessary to soften the economic and social blows from the pandemic and they, along with China, were capable of doing this in ways that most of the poorer countries could not (Wolf 2021b). National development is thus hostage to the ways in which crises play out differentially across the world and which agencies, national, supranational, and regional, can and cannot manage them to a satisfactory outcome (figure 6.1).

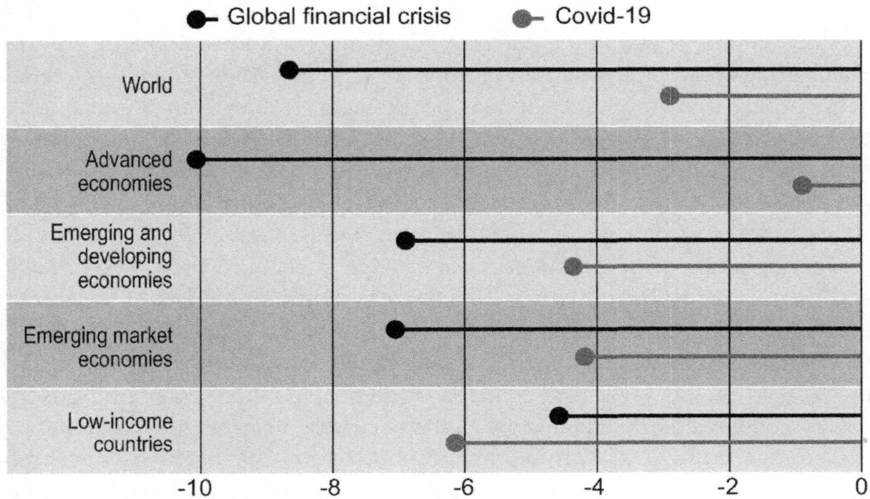

Figure 6.1. How the 2007–2008 Financial Crisis and the Pandemic Compare in Terms of Economic Impacts, "Advanced" versus "Emerging" and "Low Income" Countries. GDP change four years after crisis, percentage difference from pre-crisis forecast. (Redrawn from M. Wolf, 2021b)

A second, less-noted feature of the world economy as we experience it today is its lack of conformity to a straightforward country-by-country pattern of development, as we are used to thinking about economic trends. Although, of course, intra-country differences in economic growth and income inequality are long-standing, during the period following World War II in the world's most developed countries at least, there was increased convergence in economic outcomes across regions. Since the 1970s with the boost to globalization from all the forces identified in the introduction concerning trade and investment flows, this pattern has gone into reverse. Particularly in some countries, most notably the United States and United Kingdom, significant new gaps in employment prospects and incomes have opened up between regions and localities. If the financial crisis produced an even further boost to spatial inequality within countries, the pandemic crisis has been one in which the management of quarantines and sanitation measures was effectively territorial in relying on limiting movement and then delivering vaccines. This was how countries have been judged in their responses even if there have been major regional and local differences in infections, hospitalizations, and deaths. Though often lacking managerially, in the rich countries national governments seem to have muddled through without the long-term damage to their economies that happened after 2007–2008 and, so far at least, without the major subnational differences in economic impact of that crisis.

Much discussion of the 2007–2008 global financial crisis followed the familiar country-by-country narrative. Yet the putative nationality of the main protagonists was much less important than how they actually operated across space and time and national governments were given prime billing as the resolvers of the crisis when they often turned out to be impotent or ineffective. In this chapter I want to redefine the financial crisis as a crisis of governance rather than as a primarily economic one conforming to the typical statist framing of macroeconomics. In other words, the 2007–2008 financial crisis, beginning with the subprime mortgage debacle in the United States and transmitted through the world banking system into a crisis of sovereign bonds following government bailouts of banks and the calling-in of bad loans to sovereign borrowers by the self-same banks, was the direct result of the breakdown of the very state-centered system of political-economic governance so many commentators saw as the necessary instrument of regulation.

The chapter begins with a brief account of the mismatch between the geographical activities of major financial actors, on the one hand, and the geographical scope of state regulators, on the other. I then address three geographical dimensions of the mismatch and their consequences for territorial politics: what I term the spatial uncertainties of contemporary governance because of the way globalization favors the development of some places and the underdevelopment of others; the consequences of this for the increased political tensions between so-called world cities, on the one hand, and their surrounding hinterlands, on the other, particularly when national government policies favor the biggest cities over the rest of their territories; and the difficulties of "devolution" to local and regional governments when expenditures are devolved but revenue-raising and regulatory powers are not. I wish to question two of the main narratives about territorial politics in the aftermath of the financial crisis: that which saw an "inevitable" return to a state-based world of finance and associated regulation and that which saw a decline in the possibilities of devolution as a result of the crisis.

THE GEOGRAPHY OF THE 2007–2008 FINANCIAL CRISIS

A commonplace of contemporary economic geography is that dramatically lowered transport costs and the revolution in information and communications technologies have been dual catalysts in the growth of supply chains within large firms or between those firms and subcontractors that are increasingly stretched over space and across international borders. Businesses have found that they could build factories in locations with lower costs, ship parts to be assembled there, and then export finished products to consumers everywhere. Of course, distance has not been entirely vanquished. Regional trade agreements, time costs, and agglomeration economies encourage clustering or supply chains among neighboring countries. What is clear, however, is that the world economy is now connected transactionally across borders in ways for which country-by-country models of economic growth cannot account.

The financial sector has also become increasingly diffuse in its reliance on funds and borrowers spread across the world. From the 1970s until 2008 the big multipurpose banks, such as Citibank, Deutsche Bank, and HSBC, for example, became both much less focused on their home-country markets and more engaged with financial products attracting investments from across a wider range of places. Yet, at the same time, these banks have also centralized their market-making activities in a limited number of global centers, particularly London, New York, Singapore, and Hong Kong. In these cities they enjoy agglomeration economies and political favoritism that they cannot find elsewhere. They benefited from "light touch" regulation in such places even as their investments were increasingly at work elsewhere beyond the borders of their "home" states. Describing many banks as "German" or "British" missed the extent to which their main activities were well beyond home shores.

By the early 2000s a global system of financial capitalism was firmly in place. It was this system that exploded beginning in August 2007 and that took years to reach its final denouement. The vast expansion of credit following the East Asian crisis of 1997–1998 allowed consumption to grow faster than incomes and fueled the vast expansion of production in China and elsewhere through export growth. The collateral offered by a massive boom in residential real estate in the United States and in some European countries underwrote the increase in borrowing. Effectively, the savings of low-wage earners in China paid for the consumption binge of western middle-classes whose own incomes had stalled since the 1970s. When the mortgage products that were the Achilles' heel of the arrangement were no longer sustainable as buyers reneged on contracts and houses went into foreclosure, the entire system unraveled. The large banks that had organized and securitized the mortgages faced massive losses that were either bailed out by national governments or nationalized. The banks, particularly those active in the Eurozone, loaded up on public debt by borrowing at low interest rates and buying government bonds paying 3–4 percent interest in 2009. So as the overall recession deepened, the weaker economies of the Eurozone not only became more indebted in the sovereign bond market as they borrowed to make up for revenue decreases and increased expenditures (on unemployment benefits, etc.), the banks were faced with huge losses on their bond investments. Bailing out the banks is essentially the leitmotif for this second round of the crisis: the sovereign debt crisis is in truth a continuation of the banking crisis (see chapter 9).

Three geographical features of what happened are worth identifying to show why a simple country-by-country account is problematic. First, the US-originated subprime mortgage-backed securities were purchased by banks and hedge funds all over the world. Indeed, new financial products of all kinds were marketed worldwide. The precise origins of and collateral associated with a given mortgage were lost. Second, long-distance hierarchical financial contagion was built into the system. In putatively spreading investment risk across a wide range of banks and places, the possibility of impacts from little understood products emanating from unknown sources was magnified enormously. In turning derivatives and credit-default swaps into financial products in their own right (as opposed to seeing them as insurance against losses), betting against the profitability of other investments further increased the volatility of the system as a whole. Finally, governments themselves became active participants in financial markets above all through their vastly expanded use of bonds to finance their activities in the face of reticence to increase and/or collect taxes yet not rein in expenditures. This made them prisoners to fortune, both in relation to other market participants (particularly hedge funds betting on their relative prospects) and private regulators, in particular credit-rating agencies, whose downgrades could potentially sink future borrowing.

In the immediate aftermath of the crisis, banks and governments began to circle the wagons, so to speak. In many countries domestic banking assets came to exceed GDP by anywhere from 100 (US) to 450 percent (UK). In response, governments proposed redividing the retail and investment operations of universal banks, restricting bank employee earnings, reining in the capacity to exploit offshore tax havens, and prosecuting what increasingly appeared as widespread malfeasance. National governments also began to coordinate their financial surveillance systems (Van Hulten 2012). According to some commentators (e.g., Jessop 2010), the overall effect of these changes is to re-empower the central states that had seemed to cede so many of their powers to "the markets" under the sway of neoliberalism. Who else could bail out the banks and socialize the costs of the financial excesses that produced the recent financial crisis and attendant recession? Yet businesses well beyond the financial sector (from clothing and car making to legal services) were tied in increasingly complex ways into the global financial system with the reliance of national governments on the sovereign bond markets and the dependence of pension funds and infrastructure projects on geographically diversified sources of finance strongly suggesting that the genie could not and will not so easily be squeezed back into territorialized bottles.

SPATIAL UNCERTAINTIES OF CONTEMPORARY GOVERNANCE

The rising importance of non-state actors in world politics since the 1970s, licensed by states but increasingly exercising separate authority because of informational leverage and specialist knowledge, means that global politics can no longer be seen in purely state-centered terms. I do not see that this trend as yet has undergone any sort of permanent body blow from the financial or the pandemic crises. Arguably, for example, the Big Three credit-rating agencies represent the emergence of one set of transnational actors whose practices have fundamental effects on the well-being of people within the borders of self-defined sovereign states (see chapter 8). They exercise "fields" of power, and I would claim, authority, acceptance of their decisions as at least quasi-legitimate in the eyes of investors, political elites, and segments of mass publics, that can be seen as displacing the authority of public agencies with democratic or governmental accountability.

From this viewpoint, it is not that globalization or some other supranational process is eroding state sovereignty but that states have outsourced authority to a variety of other agencies including private as well as supranational and global interstate ones. Many existing state functions are delegated and potential new ones accrue to novel private and public but not single-state centered ones. Since the 1980s, national government budgets, such as those in the United States and United Kingdom, have not shrunk but actually grown with much of the expansion in spending going as payments to private contractors in providing public services and massive subsidies to businesses even as corporate and high-earner taxes, particularly in the United States, have been cut (Sharma 2021). Multinational corporations and various regulatory bodies, both public and private, now directly intervene within national territories in distributing investment and providing tax bases to local governments. Some of this is down to the retreat of many national governments from industrial policy as it was practiced in the 1960s and 1970s. But more is due to the increased openness of national economies to external capital since the 1980s. States are increasingly "competition states" (Cerny 2010) engaged in attracting outside capital on the best terms possible rather than simply agents of their own embedded businesses looking out into the world on their behalf, as much conventional wisdom would have it.

Rather than stimulating coherent national-state level responses, financial and other shocks, such as the 2020–2021 pandemic, also lead to pressures to try and manage outcomes regionally and locally because of the differential connections that different places have with the world economy (see chapter 7). Territorial politics within countries is a particular aspect of this. Thus, during the financial crisis of 2007–2008, British and US governments could favor either London or New York and their major financial institutions, respectively, on the one hand, or their national taxpaying publics living elsewhere with different economic interests, on the other. They chose the former and imposed austerity measures on the latter. Arguably, the financial crisis and the pandemic have also served to reinforce pressures for territorial devolution to subnational governments. The specificity of regional interests and identities have been highlighted by these crisis events (e.g., Agnew 2013; Mance 2021).

Following the logic about globalizing governance laid out in chapter 1, it has become clear that the contemporary world economy is not one in which entire national territories serve as its singular and homogeneous building blocks. Regulation of money and finance has become increasingly driven by private and quasi-private actors rather than by states per se. Government agencies of various types follow different agendas, such as central banks versus finance departments, etc. Governance has been reconstructed to meet the needs of increasingly globalized private actors such as banks and industrial corporations rather the needs of the territorialized populations of states across the length and breadth of countries. Increasingly, these populations have very different experiences as a result depending on the places in which they live within their respective countries. Local and regional differences in relative prosperity have all increased in Europe and the United States over the past fifty years after diminishing in the 1950s and 1960s (e.g., Robertson 1994; Lussault 2017).

Second, and as a consequence, no longer can "the political" be seen as uniquely deriving from states or from societies entirely defined in national-state forms. The spatial boundaries governing political interests and identities run through countries as much as around them. They are profoundly the boundaries defined by the investment and regulatory activities of private/public businesses, pension funds, banks, international law firms, standard setting, and credit-rating agencies. From 2007–2008 onward, national taxpayers paid off the creditors of loans issued by "their" banks well beyond their national borders. In return they were subjected to austerity measures that cut back on spending for the general welfare that had particularly deleterious effects in regions with relatively poorer populations.

Third, and finally, in this context, the idea that territory and its partitions across multiple levels of governance closely match the spatiality of power associated with the current spatial logic of finance and economic development is put into question. Classically, European sovereignty was intimately associated first with the body of the monarch and then with a people occupying a territory, but this no longer makes sense when the very basis to sovereign decision lies in the interstices between states in the capacities and identities of non-state actors rather than in states and "their" non-state actors (business and so on) acting solely in domestic interests and then knocking into one another. Spaces of flows now challenge the rule of territorial places in the making of economic development.

The geography of governance has never been as stable as we have pretended, with the colored blocs of territory on our maps telling us everything we need to know about the realities on the ground (Agnew 2018). In *Tom Sawyer Abroad* (1894), Mark Twain alerted us to the fact that the colors on the map—in this case designating the US states of Illinois and Indiana—were not much of a guide to the location of the protagonists in their hot-air balloon over the

American Midwest. This is not simply to recognize that the map is not the territory but also to question the adequacy of the claimed functions associated with the particular territories for understanding their governance. It has long been established that the recent (post-1980s) official version of US federalism—with a strict division of powers between the tiers of government—is in fact a poor guide to the reality of shared and parallel jurisdictions exercised in relation to functions from criminal investigations to immigration management and public education. The pattern is even more variegated in that the governments of some states, Mississippi, for example, do much less in terms of even exercising their own powers never mind challenging federal authority compared with states such as California and Massachusetts (Agnew 2013).

Spatial uncertainty—the unpredictability of finding exactly the same disposition of governmental powers across a given territory—in this case about the relative powers of governments under a federal system, is not new. In the United States, events have produced a host of legislative and regulatory measures that have made governance infinitely more dynamic and uncertain than a simple recitation of constitutional niceties about the role of state and federal tiers might lead you to expect. These events include the Civil War, Supreme Court decisions in the late nineteenth century that encouraged a national market, two World Wars, the New Deal of the 1930s, the War on Poverty of the late 1960s, and the attack on the federal government from the far right since the 1980s and 1990s. Other countries offer similar litanies. The problem also repeats at other geographical scales of governance, from the interstate to the supranational and the international, with various institutions having and deploying powers in complex and overlapping ways that defy the straightforward correlation of discrete powers with specific scales of governance (Agnew 2018; Jessop 2016). If anything, the trend has increased exponentially in recent years, even if there are now signs of "push back" from populist-nationalists and separatists who wish to return to a status quo ante of singular territories without overlapping powers that is often more imagined than real.

Perhaps two empirical trends have been given particular attention in this context and their relevance was nothing but enhanced by the 2007–2008 financial crisis. The first is the notion of an emerging system of world cities dependent on flows between them challenging the territorialized political map typically privileged in geopolitics. The second is the rising demand for regional devolution or independence in a wide range of countries.

WORLD CITIES VERSUS STATE TERRITORIES

The 2012 Olympic Games in London could be seen as a celebration of the seamless continuity between the capital city and its hinterland in the rest of the United Kingdom. The Opening Ceremony was a national tableau, of sorts.

Yet, as has become increasingly apparent in the aftermath of the financial crisis, what is good for London is not necessarily good for the rest of the country. National government policies that have effectively turned the City in London into an offshore financial center do not clearly redound to the favor of the rest of the country. A political-economic tension exists therefore between the trend to "hidden geopolitics" associated above all with networks of world cities, on the one hand, and the continuing claim of states to represent the identity and interests of their entire populations wherever they live, on the other.

The British-London case may be an extreme one but it is by no means singular. Similar tensions exist between New York and the United States, Frankfurt and Germany, Dublin and Ireland, and wherever a single city has global ties that supersede those to its geographical hinterland. Global elites flock to the great financial centers to make their fortunes, live the good life, protect what they have got, and sue one another in court. Other smaller cities with manufacturing and other bases suffer decline and lose population to the new supersized cities. World cities have distinctive economies based around agglomeration effects that cannot be reproduced at will. These reflect historic imperial and commercial linkages (e.g., Scott 2001; Taylor 2004, 2013). Pools of bankers, traders, and lawyers provide the centerpiece to these connections. The cities in which they cluster allow for reductions in transaction costs, cooperation between specialized parties, and the governance of long-distance networks. Think of the reinsurance business and how central London has long been to it. Increasingly, a new *Lex Mercatoria*, or legal system devoted to transnational transactions, has grown up across such centers (Sweet 2004). This is largely autonomous from national and public international law. It symbolizes the degree to which some world cities are becoming politically, economically, and legally separate from their putative national jurisdictions.

Beyond the difficulties of taxing finance, because of its informational advantages over governments when it comes to tax avoidance, and thus geographically spreading the proceeds of finance throughout the national territory, government policies privileging finance can wreak havoc in the rest of the national economy. For one thing, by pushing up overall price levels in the economy and making the local currency higher than it otherwise would be against others (the so-called Dutch disease problem), an overemphasis on finance makes it harder for other sectors such as manufacturing and agriculture to compete with foreign goods at home and abroad (Shaxson 2011, 277). It also seems responsible for a large component of the increase in income inequality in countries such as the United Kingdom and United States since the 1970s (e.g., Piketty 2013; Wodtke 2016). As of 2019, predictions suggest that the relative income and quality-of-life gaps between London and its hinterland will widen rather than narrow beyond their already large size (e.g., Burton 2021; Pidd 2019) (see figure 6.2 on population growth predicted from

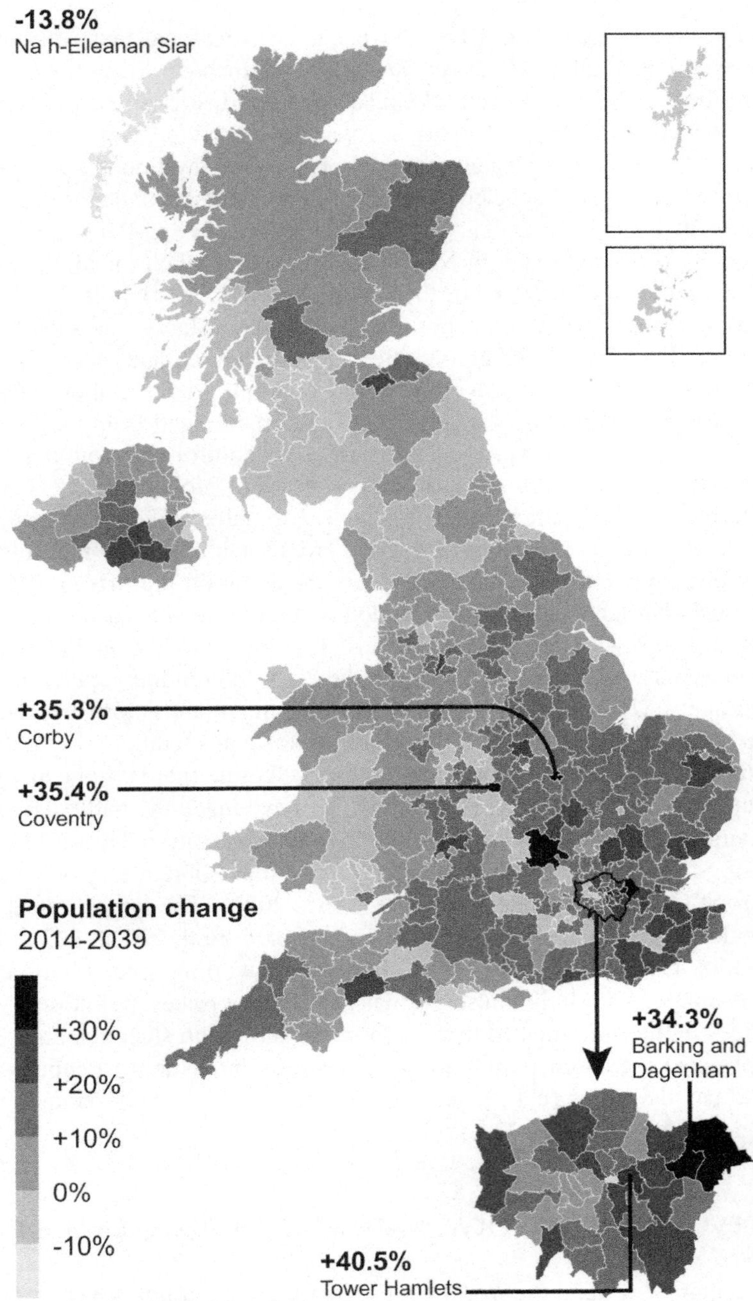

Figure 6.2. Estimated Rates of Population Growth by Electoral Districts in the United Kingdom 2014–2039. Population growth as a surrogate for economic development. (Redrawn from UK Office of National Statistics, Overview of UK Population, January 2021)

economic trends across the UK). Yet it has been national taxpayers on the whole who have bailed out the banks and other financial institutions for the bad bets they made on assets circulating across world cities and tax havens. As Nicholas Shaxson (2011, 278) puts it, referring to London's financial center, the City: "Under the City's new imperial project, money floods into London, then is repackaged and recycled out again, often via offshore satellites, to build glittering skyscrapers in Dubai, giant condominiums in Sao Paulo and games of financial bait and switch in New York." Not that much makes it into the broader hinterland of England or the United Kingdom as a whole.

The tension between world cities and their national states seems likely only to deepen. The promise of competition from financial centers in Asia and elsewhere will encourage governments to continue to favor their financial sectors. Empirical evidence suggests that London emerged from the financial crisis in a particularly weakened position as a "control and command center" given its overall dominance in certain areas of global finance (Csomós and Derudder 2012). Brexit likewise has led to shifts in some of London's most lucrative financial activities to Amsterdam, Dublin, and Frankfurt. Yet British governments seem intent on doubling down on the offshore finance advantages that could accrue to a United Kingdom outside of the European Union and this will undoubtedly benefit London notwithstanding the fact that London's own population voted in the 2016 referendum against leaving the European Union (Agnew 2019b). Beyond this there is also tremendous inertia built into the system, so I would look for considerably more political conflict over the benefits of privileging finance before there will be any resolution (Mirowski 2013). Brexit, though, may have made the battle harder for maintaining let alone enhancing London's financial position. Howard Davies, chair of NatWest Bank, said in mid-May 2021 that London's "Golden Age" as Europe's financial capital was over (Jones 2021). The largest cities such as London and New York have also been battered by the 2020–2021 global pandemic, leading many to suggest that remote working and the diseconomies associated with living in such cities (high house prices, pollution, visible income equalities manifested in homelessness and rough sleeping, and so on) may produce increased population and business movement to suburbs and even to smaller cities (e.g., Kolko 2020; Edsall 2021a). This remains to be seen (e.g., Levy 2021).

DEVOLUTION TO LOCAL AND REGIONAL GOVERNMENTS

Many countries around the world have recently gone through several decades of calls for and examples of significant devolution of powers to lower from higher tier governments. This is most apparent in Spain and Britain but is also evident in countries as divergent in other cultural and institutional respects as China, Italy, and Canada. Some of this has reflected a "fashion for federalism" or the desire to acquire separate powers locally and regionally to defend cultural difference, localize more governmental powers to match local concerns, limit wealth redistribution by central governments, or serve as incubators for economic development. A strongly dualist image of federalism as a "line-drawing exercise" inspires much of the rhetoric about federalism even when practical examples around the world (such as the US, Australia, and Switzerland) suggest much more by way of concurrent administrative practice and redundancy than the rhetoric allows (Schapiro 2005–2006) (see chapter 7). In Europe, much of the rhetoric and politics of devolution is put down to the role of the European Union in enabling a new multitier political geography (Murphy, A. D. 2008). Be that as it may, some research suggests that between 1970 and 2004 only two states among forty-two in the OECD became more centralized, while almost three-quarters saw an increase in regional powers (Henderson 2010, 439).

Globalization, along with the growth of supranational entities such as the European Union, is often seen as encouraging this trend. The overall effect of increased trade on *fiscal* decentralization, however, is not that great. Both Garrett and Rodden (2003) and Treisman (2007), for example, find little to support the idea that devolution actually does what it is cracked up to do in the face of globalization. With the onset of the financial crisis, central governments became increasingly aware of the debt loads built up by devolved units, whether they be Spanish regions or American states (e.g., Gardner 2012b; Whitney 2011). This suggests quite strongly that devolution has not been without its fiscal effects. In some cases this is because regional governments have floated their own bonds in the absence of local taxation powers or lower-than-anticipated central government subventions (Gardner 2012a)—in others because they have spent without responsibility, knowing that they would be backstopped by central governments if all else failed (Harter 2012). The redesign of devolution, therefore, was thought to be one of the most important consequences of the crisis, if in some cases there was also something of a rebalancing back to the center (Greer 2010).

Notwithstanding its questionable fiscal impact, devolution has had other effects that are likely to persist or even increase. In some places, for example China, it is closely associated with the entire engine of localized economic growth beginning in the late 1980s. It certainly encouraged the emergence of various "experiments" in private-state partnerships out of which a number of enduring models came about (Heilmann 2011; Lim, K. F. 2019). Yet central political leaders also retained much power and influence over provincial officials (Sheng 2010). The same could not be said, however, for the Italian industrial-district model as it evolved from the 1950s down to the early 2000s. There, local entrepreneurs and politicians have been on their own without much if any help or positive influence from the central government

(Ricolfi 2010). Between-region income inequalities within countries have certainly begun to increase again after convergence in the post–World War II period (OECD 2016). With the financial crisis striking differentially across different places (with their different industry mixes and economic profiles), this is likely to continue, absent some mechanism for utilizing a true federal system to redistribute regional incomes around an agreed national norm. Even then, as with contemporary Germany and the United States, richer regions can resent the redistribution of revenues to poorer ones and political parties can use this resentment to mobilize popular support. In the United States, it is many of the poorer states that have relied on low or no income taxes and heavy subsidies/anti-union measures to incoming investors that are the most hostile to federal government redistributive measures largely in terms of either a long-standing commitment to so-called states' rights where slavery was once central to local economies or in terms of a sense of being "left behind" culturally and economically elsewhere but without much of a sense that government can do much of anything about it (Agnew and Shin 2019). The recent populist trends in US and UK electoral politics—and the calls for regional "leveling up" they have entailed—owe much to the geographical polarization of public opinion within the countries between the metropolitan states in the northeast and on the west coast and the rest of the country in the United States and between metropolitan areas, particularly London, and the deindustrialized north of England in the United Kingdom (Agnew and Shin 2019; Payne 2021; Broz et al. 2021).

Devolution can also encourage a trend toward secession by regions if, for example, austerity measures pushed by central governments have particularly negative impacts in such regions (Béland and Lecours 2021). This seems to be what has happened in Scotland where the combination of UK-wide austerity policies introduced after 2007–2008 and Brexit in 2016 have produced significant shifts in public opinion to the Scottish National Party and its goal of Scottish independence, albeit within the European Union. Anti-London sentiment and pro–European Union positions have thus produced a trend so far toward separation rather than more devolution of hitherto centralized powers (Wellings 2020). Scotland itself, however, is not completely unified across its own regions in its political predilections, so it is difficult to say what the final verdict would be in a future referendum (Agnew 2017b). The economic costs of hardening the border with England may loom larger in such a contest than in the previous 2014 one, prior to Brexit, when a majority voted to remain within the United Kingdom.

Finally, devolution can sometimes take the poison out of intergroup conflicts such as those of recent vintage in Northern Ireland and the former Yugoslavia. This does not mean that everyone is happy with the outcome or that the causes of the conflicts in question have been adequately addressed. Brexit has made the compromise in Northern Ireland increasingly fraught even if most people there do not see it as necessarily leading to unification with the rest of Ireland or reimposition of direct rule from London (Murphy and Evershed 2021; McKay 2022). Many more people express "mixed identities" to pollsters than was once the case even as the so-called nationalist population grows and the so-called unionist one shrinks in size (Devine 2021; McKay 2021). The region's hybrid status because of the Brexit agreement, inside the European Union for goods trade but out of it for everything else, could also give the region the competitive advantage it has hitherto lacked (O'Toole 2021). Of course, this could be merely wishful thinking. At the same time, Irish governments in Dublin, for their own reasons relating to managing a potentially hostile minority, now "dread a vote on a united Ireland" as much as the northern Unionists favoring continued partition do (Tóibin 2021). But there has been a retreat from the violence that previously characterized these places through either consociationalism (power sharing) or partition. These effects will not be readily undermined even in the face of continuing financial crisis and its more general economic effects as the forms of governance adapt to changing circumstances.

CONCLUSION

The financial crisis did not lead to a simple "return of the state." Nor did it lead to an abandonment of devolution to local and regional tiers of government. The global financial system that imploded beginning in 2007–2008 shows few signs of being replaced by anything more stable or equitable. There is no sign yet of a global New Deal, as it would now have to be (Fraser 2013). Indeed, the system has shown great resilience. The two trends toward increased separation between world cities and their surrounding territorial states and the struggle for increased devolution to capture mobile global capital for regional and local purposes seem set to deepen in the aftermath of the 2007–2008 crisis and subsequent shocks such as Brexit and the COVID-19 pandemic. These have been my two main claims. The hidden geopolitics ripping at the seams of established territorial states needs to be related clearly to what often begins well beyond their borders.

7

Anti-Federalist Federalism

Pandemics are by definition global in character and spread from place to place through travel and community spread. They are a test for different governmental systems and the geopolitical-territorial arrangements upon which they rest (Horton 2020). Absent much in the way of effective global governance, national-level governments typically have the best resources and expertise to limit spread and manage healthcare as the disease spreads across their territories. Simply leaving management to lower tiers of government can create major problems when they adopt different testing and mitigation strategies and do not have adequate resources and expertise to institute them. But centralization is also problematic insofar as it presupposes a one-size-fits-all strategy that fails to account for regional and local specificities in susceptibility and resources to manage a major health emergency. Viruses do not spread or succumb to suppression solely on a territorial basis. That also goes for a host of other things that require regulation and management. Given that we are stuck with multitier territorial governance, how best can that be put to work on our collective behalf?

In the United States there has been much controversy over the problematic role of the federal government in the COVID-19 pandemic. The United States has had one of the highest death rates relative to population size worldwide and one of the most incoherent and inconsistent national governmental responses in terms of public health policies and financial support to the tiers of government (state and local) at which "policy" has been administered (e.g., Beaubien 2020; Lerner et al. 2020; *NY Times* 2021). The lack of any national plan for dealing with the pandemic was particularly obvious from the outset (e.g., Haffajee and Mello 2020). Much of the critique has focused on the performance of president Donald Trump; from his months-long dismissal of the dangers posed by the pandemic to his chaotic administrative approach to the challenges posed by the spread of the virus and his politicization of the pandemic for electoral purposes (e.g., Kristof 2020). Trump was certainly more part of the problem than any sort of cure. But the pandemic exposed rather deeper structural flaws in the US system of government than just the managerial, psychological, and intellectual flaws displayed by the person who just happened to occupy the office of President at a trying time. So much of what has gone for political debate in the United States since the 1980s has been over the *size of government* when it should have been over the *quality of governance* with respect to what the federal government should and can do. The question is what the federal government must do that other actors cannot, and also how one can coordinate between them and across tiers of government from the federal to the local. This hidden geopolitics of US governance has been exposed to view during the pandemic.

The major danger inherent in any federalism lies in not allocating "sufficient powers to their general governments to deal with modern economic [and other] crises" (Wheare 1963, 244). Crucially in the United States, a federal Senate biased to favor low-density rural parts of the country and an Electoral College that reinforces this bias in presidential elections have led to a mobilization against the sort of relatively powerful and redistributive central government that Founding Father Alexander Hamilton favored (Rodden 2019; Deaton 2020). A minority of the population has thus come to have a major influence in reviving the radically dualist (states *versus* federal) vision of US federalism (Millhiser 2021). This vision was the one that had defined the so-called Philadelphian system of weak federal government and strong states that prevailed before the Civil War (Deudney 1995). It was fully revived beginning in the 1980s. This has led to the present impasse where the federal government and its proper functions have been systematically neglected or actively undermined to the detriment of the system as a whole (Mishra 2020). In December 2021 an abortion law in Texas brought before the US Supreme Court raised fundamental legal questions about whether individual states can nullify constitutional rights previously decided for the country as a whole. In allowing this law to stand, the majority on the Court opened the door to further cases on gun ownership, voting rights, and so on, that would essentially undermine the role of the Supreme Court as a national arbiter laid down early in the history of the United States (Budowsky 2021). So not only the legitimacy of the administrative agencies at the heart of the federal government but that of the US Supreme Court itself would fall victim to a dualist vision with a very limited conception of the place of US-wide institutions.

More specifically, there is a fundamental contradiction between a president like Donald Trump elected on a national-populist basis and the reality of a US governmental system that since the 1980s has been increasingly anti-federalist in its legislative and executive preferences for privatization.

It has also favored "small government" and is thus immune to any sort of forward-looking role for the federal government in domestic policy. That this has not involved trimming government budgets as much as redistributing largesse from the population at large to businesses in outsourcing government functions to private businesses and massively subsiding businesses (such as the banks following the 2007–2008 financial crisis) has rarely been noted (Sharma 2021). The manifest federal-government failures in managing the COVID-19 pandemic in the United States are the outcome of this contradiction between the advance of anti-federalism and the desire for national solutions (at least for certain groups such as white people). But it is the federal-state-local nexus that has been more central to the mismanagement than the bureaucratic failures of the federal government per se, even though they have long played a role in skepticism about the performance of the US federal government (e.g., Schuck 2014). To the extent that discussion of the federal failure in the pandemic has extended beyond Trump and his coterie it has been to the specific failings of such federal agencies as the CDC, NIH, and the FDA (e.g., Bandler et al. 2020; Piller 2020). Notwithstanding their importance, I want to argue that the bigger problem has been a geographical one: the revival of a dualist model of federalism that does not match the multiple geographies of power at work in the world and across the United States.

"Revival " of dualism is the operative phrase. A New Deal coalition dominated by the Democrats but subsequently supported also by many Republicans prevailed from the 1930s down until the 1970s. It knitted the country together across a number of significant economic and cultural divides. In the early 1960s the United States was widely viewed, inside and outside the country, as having an exemplary "civic culture" compared to many other countries in terms of trust in government at all levels and in a sense of popular collective political efficacy (e.g., Almond and Verba 1963). But it unraveled beginning in the 1980s through the 1990s with the emergence of major urban-rural and sectional differences on a range of policy issues, not least the role of the federal government in the American economy and society (Mellow 2008). Rather than acting as partners, the states and the federal government were increasingly seen as opponents. During the Progressive era in the early twentieth century and following the 1930s New Deal down until the early 1970s, a federalist rebalancing as a result of social mobilizations had led to a more efficient and redistributive national government. Given the ambiguities surrounding the US constitutional compact, disputes between federalists and anti-federalists, originalists and proponents of a living constitution, and so on, the relative legitimacy of the powers of the various tiers of government (and delegation of executive powers) is ideologically forever up for grabs (e.g., Balkin and Siegel 2009; Mortenson and Bagley 2020). But Trump's rhetorical dictatorial style with support from minions like Attorney General William Barr devoted to a "powerful" executive vis-à-vis the legislative and judicial branches should not be confused with an empowered and effective federal government tout court (e.g., Schwartz 2020). Indeed, the "unitary executive theory" expounded by far-right justices on the US Supreme Court (and by right-wing legal organizations like the Federalist Society) seems to be more about limiting the discretion of federal administrative agencies than empowering the president as such (Skowronek et al. 2021). This was central to the paradox of Trump's presidency.

Arguably, testing is crucial in managing a pandemic. The highest tier of government could be expected to take a leading role in coordinating across all lower-level jurisdictions in this respect at least. But as late as September 2020 the federal government was acting as if the pandemic were past and still leaving the states and municipalities to cope largely on their own (e.g., Weiner and Helderman 2020). There was still no national testing program by 12 June 2020, five months into the pandemic. Things came together tentatively on testing nationwide only on 22 June. But testing then became a topic that Trump could use to underplay the seriousness of the pandemic. Too much testing, according to Trump, was painting too dire a picture. As a result, in late June 2020, Trump even suggested that testing ought to be slowed down to make the pandemic look better than it was (Cohen 2020). In late June federal funding was pulled from testing sites in five states undergoing major spurts in cases and hospitalizations (*LA Times* Editorial 2020). At the same time, national testing capacity was still much less than needed to respond to the spread of the pandemic across the country (Madrigal and Meyer 2020). Even as Trump continued to boast about "our great testing program," as of early July many cities still could not test all those they needed to in order to trace and isolate spreaders, suggesting how deluded the president was about the empirical reality the country faced (Weiner 2020). Contact tracing, absolutely key to suppressing the spread of infection, turned out to be a total debacle, despite the best efforts of some state governments (Steinhauer and Goodnough 2020; Khazan 2020; Molteni 2021). In early August 2020 a group of seven states (Maryland, Virginia, Michigan, Ohio, Louisiana, Massachusetts, and North Carolina) *abandoned* the federal government for their own consortium in quickening the pace and scope of testing (Baker and Court 2020). Trump's delusion about the unconstrained course of the pandemic fed into his inability to see that *sustainably* opening up the economy depended on dealing with the pandemic, not denying its existence (Bassett and Linos 2020). The US strategy, if that word is appropriate, was exactly backward: instead of conquering the virus first and then opening up, opening up was seen as the priority much too early and then the virus rebounded. As the *Economist* (2020a) wrote: it was like a hospital investing "in palliative care while abolishing the oncology department."

After Trump failed at reelection in 2020, notwithstanding his outlandish claims that the election was "fixed" against him in crucial states, and a president with a much more activist view of the federal role in the pandemic was elected, the governmental system still failed to respond adequately. The baked-in anti-federalism of many state governors, the federal courts, and the posing of mask and vaccine mandates as assaults on the "sovereignty" of individuals undermined the national response producing particularly negative outcomes in hospitalizations and deaths in states and localities with the strongest association with the politics of anti-federalism (e.g., Fernandes et al. 2021; Cochrane 2021; Hsu 2021; Wood, D. 2021; Chalfant 2021; Holpuch 2021).

After providing an overview of the spatial uncertainties of multitier governance revealed by the pandemic both in the United States and elsewhere, I turn first to the case for a putatively national-populist leader such as Trump, how he has campaigned and ruled, and then briefly to the paradox of the geopolitical framing at the center of Trump's appeal: the opposition between the national and the global. Suggesting that Trump's performance during the pandemic cannot be understood entirely in these terms at all, I turn to the longer-term institutional imbalances in the US federal system that have hobbled response to the pandemic. Of particular importance I claim has been the lack of coordination across the tiers of government from the federal through the state to the local that is a by-product of the anti-federalist perspective on US federalism that has become dominant politically in the United States since the 1980s. The dualistic view of federalism (federalist versus anti-federalist) has undermined the possibility of a more polyphonic practice that would have led to better management of the pandemic. Just blaming Trump, therefore, has been to miss noting a more systematic institutional failure.

DUALISM VERSUS POLYPHONY IN FEDERAL GOVERNANCE

In Europe regional-level politicians and big-city mayors have been at odds with national governments over what policies to follow in order to suppress and/or mitigate the COVID-19 pandemic (e.g., Hall, B. et al. 2020). In the United States state governors have clashed with the president and his administration and local officials with state and federal ones over public health measures such as face masks, physical distancing, and quarantine rules. At one point the president even encouraged armed supporters of his to "liberate" states such as Michigan run by Democratic governors that he considered his adversaries (e.g., Cook and Diamond 2020; Edelman 2020). In this context there has been widespread disagreement about the relative merits of more or less decentralization in managing a crisis of such proportions as the COVID-19 pandemic. After an initial disastrous response to the first outbreak in Wuhan, the highly centralized authoritarian Chinese government brought the pandemic under control in its territory relatively quickly and effectively. At first, but with later problems, the federal German system produced a relatively positive outcome (Studemann 2020). The asymmetric devolution in the

United Kingdom and the US federal system both produced relatively poor outcomes in terms of cases, hospitalizations, and deaths. Cherry-picking your cases, however, can lead to whatever conclusion you wish.

Political debates in many countries about the relative balance of powers between different tiers of government tend to discuss them in terms of neat divisions between competencies and autonomies exercised at different levels: national, regional, and municipal (see Treisman 2007). From this viewpoint, a technical process of matching functions to levels on the basis of externality effects from and popular demands for different public goods and services will lead automatically to a clear and demonstrable geographical separation of powers. Historically, however, different jurisdictional levels have large areas of joint or concurrent powers or what can be termed "polyphony." In the United States, for example, federal and state laws frequently regulate the very same goods and conduct, from drug trafficking to education, gun control, and bond trading. There is no tight combination of territorial level of governance and particular good or service for a wide range of goods and services. There is a constant *practical* struggle between tiers of government over powers in relation to numerous issue-areas. Even what might seem to be areas "settled" at one level, say immigration regulation and foreign policy actions, have become subject to cross-jurisdictional dispute and coordination. Witness popular attempts in California and Texas, respectively, to impose immigration regulations and to police migrants crossing the US-Mexico border (usually defined in a dualist perspective as a purely "federal" function) and Massachusetts's so-called Burma Law banning all state agencies from signing contracts with companies active in Burma (Myanmar) because of the Burmese government's history of human rights violations (e.g., Guay 2000; Goodman 2021; Paul 2002). That the US federal courts have tended to turn these measures back is only an indication of how extreme any "sharing" of functions of this type would be. Many other functions, however, cannot be limited solely to one tier of government yet are typically viewed these days as if they should be.

In practice, therefore, governance is rarely if ever about exclusive and non-overlapping spheres of authority neatly divided between geographic scales or tiers of government. The term "polyphony," coined in this context by the American constitutional lawyer Robert Schapiro (2005–2006; 2009) to refer to the interaction, competition, and coordination between state and federal powers in the United States, captures much better the actual practices of fuzzy definition, competition, and antagonism that typically inform all attempts at managing power within multitier governance. The word comes from music where it refers to two or more independent lines of simultaneous composition rather than single lines such as a chant or simple and parallel dual ones like a duet. Schapiro sees the dualist vision that has come to dominate both legal philosophy and much popular discussion of federalism in the United

States as having had twin roots. One is the economic argument of the state as a "firm" or private corporation within a system in which the federal government then operates as an agent of antitrust. In this market model, popular with conservative lawyers and with conservative-dominated US Supreme Courts since the late nineteenth century, federalism is essentially an exercise in line drawing between two tiers of government. Gerald Frug (Frug 2001; Barron and Frug 2006) has pointed to problems with the historical accuracy of this account and specifically to the analogy that inspires it, not least to the fact that local government in the United States is increasingly "defensive" rather than reflective of "true" autonomy, and this is so largely because US federal courts have consistently favored private corporations (i.e., businesses) and their expansive operations over public ones such as municipalities.

The other root of dualism lies in the normative republican model that is often held to have motivated the founders of the United States and, more particularly, inspired the writing of the US Constitution. From this perspective, a rigid specification and separation of functions between tiers is held to promote various vague but rhetorically powerful goals: "efficient and responsive government, participatory self-government, and protection against tyranny" (Schapiro 2005–2006, 248). The dualist view's continuing ideological attraction, therefore, is long-standing and continues to draw adherence because it is deeply connected to common narratives about US history and US constitutional exceptionalism (Lim, E. T. 2014). Obviously, the US federal experience sets it apart from countries such as France, Spain, Italy, and Britain, to name just a few, with very different governmental histories and dominant regime ideologies on the continuum from unitary to federal systems. But the distinction that Schapiro draws between dualist and polyphonic perspectives on multitier governance is a useful one that can be applied more widely. The tension between them reflects a more realistic grasp of contemporary geographies of power than simply accepting the older dualistic one as an inevitable fait accompli.

Why does the polyphonic perspective make more sense? There are at least three ways of thinking about how power is related to space with respect to political institutions: bounded territories, networked flows, and topological ties (Allen 2009). Typically, we think of governance almost entirely in terms of the first and arguably, for much of human history, this has made considerable sense. Territories contain power in the sense of being "tiered" units of space in which services, for example, are supposedly provided on an equal basis within the unit as a whole or differentially as a result of conscious political decisions within the various parts. The "scaling up" of power and the workings of power more generally, however, often, and increasingly, involves networked flows across territories including across their borders. The need for higher tiers of government can reflect the sense that only at a larger territorial scale can networked flows be managed or regulated. Relations of connection, though, are not always simply topographical, reaching across or bounding concrete spaces. They are also topological: gaps between "here" and "there" are increasingly temporal moments (across the internet, for example) rather than distanced connectivities. Indeed, powers of reach are potentially beyond territorial containment.

It is important to identify these multiple spatialities of power because at least part of the issue with contemporary questions of territorial governance is the degree to which the externalities emanating from the second two spatial modalities can be captured or entrained within any sort of territorial framework (Agnew 2018). As yet, means of managing flows and more diffuse relations of connection outside of any sort of territorial reference remain radically underdeveloped. Plausibly, the financial products at the heart of the financial/economic collapse of 2008–2009 flowed in real time between networked nodes around the world but were increasingly free of territorial regulation simply because the products and their agents defied the territorial imagination upon which regulation has been largely based. Likewise, our conventional thinking about how to challenge shadowy terrorist networks remains to a high degree trapped within a territorial imagination that can only work on a state-by-state basis rather than directly adapting to the modus operandi of the groups in question. Pandemics and how they spread are not all that different either (Horton 2020).

So governance is no longer simply a question of matching "functions" to the most appropriate level of territorial resolution (local, metropolitan, regional, national, etc.), as for example in Mann's (1984) classic account of the territorial origins of state autonomy, but also of adapting territorial modes of governance to more complex spatial modalities of power. Arguably, the contemporary world is more pluralistic in its spatialities of power than are available means for managing them politically. But this is also a contributory factor to why any sort of strict division of powers territorially is increasingly problematic in a world where power is not even contingently always divisible territorially. The pandemic has been exhibit A in showing how much practice of a coordinated and overlapping rather than mutually exclusive and divided territorial model of governance would favor better management. Arguably, for all their problems, the cases of Germany and Australia suggest how much a polyphonic federalism can serve to mitigate the disastrous effects of a pandemic as opposed to the either/or opposition between decentralization and centralization that has tended to prevail latterly in the United States.

DONALD TRUMP AND NATIONAL-POPULISM

Donald Trump campaigned for the US presidency in 2016, unlike previous Republican candidates for that office, on an openly populist platform (Agnew and Shin 2019). His central claim, emblazoned on the baseball hats of his supporters, was to "Make America Great Again." Following on a two-term first-time African American president, whom Trump had personally insulted and run down from before the 2008 election, including being the primary source of the charge that Obama was an illegitimate president because he had not been born in the United States, this slogan was not hard to decode. Indeed, since his election much of what Trump had done was to undo what Obama had done with respect to social, healthcare, and environmental regulation (John 2020). Apart from that, Trump followed recent Republican orthodoxy on slashing the federal income tax on high-payers and appointing ultraconservative judges to the federal courts. In the 2016 election campaign, however, more than these initiatives, Trump emphasized "toughness" in "bringing back" jobs in manufacturing that had somehow been stolen by "China" (not a word about the role of US multinational businesses or technology in this) and building a wall with Mexico (that Mexico would pay for) to keep out the "illegals" that he spent much energy on the campaign trail decrying for their presumed criminality and threat to the racial composition of the country (see chapter 4). The entire thrust of Trump's public persona was to present himself as a national savior with a very clear sense that those he desires to see exalted after the Obama years were the largely elderly/southern white demographic that he appealed to support him in 2016. Since arriving in office he made no attempt to portray himself as a president of the entire country, *only* of those who display loyalty to him (Wehner 2020; Edsall 2021b).

Attacking the "mainstream media" (particularly so-called quality newspapers and television news that report in a fact-driven rather than ideological way) played a vital part in establishing Trump in his prophetic role as leader. The media must be discredited to undermine the empirical truth in which they claim to trade. Steve Bannon, Trump's house theoretician, insisted that the imperative is to dominate the conversation, not to engage in a battle of ideas: "The Democrats don't matter," he says. "The real opposition is the media, and the way to deal with them is to flood the zone with shit" (quoted in Thornhill 2018). Trump has thus appealed to a cultural vein in American society that is suspicious of specialist scientific knowledge and the notion of objective truth (see, e.g., Knight 2002; Hofstadter 2008; Du Mez 2020). His most important stock-in-trade is to accuse all and sundry who are not loyal to the lies and fabrications he espouses of trading in "fake news" (Serwer 2021; Luke 2021). This is how he appeals above all to "his people" or "base."

Say what you will about him, but Trump has been a political genius in managing to conquer a Republican Party that initially was allergic to his appeal, particularly on economic issues such as trade barriers, and in his consistently receiving since his 2016 election support in opinion polls of around 80 percent or so of self-identified Republicans polled through October 2020. In the 2020 presidential election, even while losing nationally and in the

Electoral College, he still received around 74 million votes. So, even in the face of a dismal record of mismanaging the early warnings of the coronavirus pandemic, Trump still retained significant popular support (Gabriel and Lerer 2020). This lasted well into 2022 and promised the possibility that even if he could not be back as a candidate for the presidency in 2024, his populist agenda would live on (Andrews and Collins 2022). His reservoir of support among Republican Party voters is based on a "fealty, a visceral and emotional attachment" that is still triggered by his open displays of nativism and attachment to a nostalgic vision of an America that had been "lost" (quoted in Waldmeir 2020). Indeed, in parts of rural/small town America, his supporters were already prepared to blame their globalist conationals who travel abroad for the virus coming into their America (Kilgore 2020). That he rhetorically continued by and large to demonize his political opponents and rewrite his own history in relation to the pandemic shows how much he had not changed operationally even as the challenges he faced were no longer those of his own invention, like the Ukraine imbroglio over denying military aid to that country as blackmail for its government providing "dirt" on his likely presidential opponent in 2020 (Joe Biden) that led to his first impeachment, but something that would test even the best of leaders (e.g., Baker 2020; Bump 2020; Parker and Rucker 2020).

Even in the face of the most significant challenge facing a US president in a generation, he remained focused on his reelection in November 2020 rather than dealing with the crisis at hand. Populism always seems to privilege campaigning over governing, not least because its main tenets, beyond claiming "the people" as its leitmotif, are riling up anger and resentments rather than pursuing rational policy goals or good governance per se (Agnew and Shin 2019). Trump's performance in a prime-time speech about the pandemic on 11 March 2020 as he struck a "starkly militaristic and nationalistic tone" while the country was being radically upended by what he termed a "foreign virus," as if it were not already abroad in the land, was widely panned by critics (Glasser 2020). But it probably resonated positively with those he wished to mobilize for the November 2020 presidential election. Because the pandemic had started in China, even as their favorite son was off playing golf at one of his own resorts, and rallying his base in rambling soliloquies rather than preparing administratively for the pandemic no longer just on the horizon, he was not held responsible.

Key to the entire geopolitical framing that brought Trump to the White House was the discursive opposition between globalism (and globalists) on the one hand and nationalists favoring the people and its national state on the other. The fusion of an idealized people with the national state is by no means alien to American political development (Peel 2018). Since the early 2000s national populism has also become a worldwide phenomenon, partly in response to the blame put on globalization for cultural change and employment losses, notwithstanding the more complex realities of technological and demographic change. This partly explains Trump's affinity for other national-populist demagogues like Putin in Russia, Modi in India, and Orbán in Hungary. The Russian intervention on his behalf in the 2016 election points perhaps to a somewhat stronger tie to Putin (Unger 2021). The nationalist versus globalist framing was one suggested to Trump by Steve Bannon in which, rather than pitching himself as the agent of Wall Street and as a business-as-usual Republican, the only way Trump could win in 2016 was by bringing into national electoral politics people alienated from both of the dominant parties by the lackluster performance of the US domestic manufacturing sector and slumping median household incomes since the 1990s. In turn, the best way to do this was to criticize the liberal global order and talk about reestablishing a territorial sovereignty over borders and the economy that had been lost with the latest round of globalization since the 1980s. Imposing tariffs and opposing international trade agreements were the main strategies used to pursue these goals, even as massive tax cuts widened the federal government fiscal deficit that could only be financed by foreign sales of US treasury bonds.

At the same time, of course, Trump was himself very clearly a globalizer with his foreign investments in hotels and golf courses. His cover on this was to paint himself as an American everyman down to how he spoke and what he ate. This is a typical move on the part of right-wing populists everywhere. His business "successes" therefore (notwithstanding a long history of bankruptcies and questionable loans) could be viewed as evidence of his managerial intelligence even as he had to overcome the disability of being just another everyman. As a neo-patrimonial figure dispensing favors to his subjects/people, Trump would reward his supporters through punishing foreign interests and by channeling federal resources and tax-favored capitalist investment to their benighted communities (Riley 2017). This self-presentation met with enormous success among a significant portion of the electorate concentrated largely in southern and western states but with enough strength in what turned out to be the crucial states (given the indirect nature of US presidential elections through the Electoral College) of Michigan, Pennsylvania, and Wisconsin to give him a victory in 2016 even as he failed to achieve a majority of the national vote. As a caveat, I should note that both he and his opponent, Hillary Clinton, had the largest negative approval ratings of any presidential candidates since polls had asked the question (Agnew and Shin 2019).

The claim to a national people as the primary constituency, even though we know that Trump supporters tend to be a very particular demographic-cultural grouping, is central to the entire populist rationale (e.g., Hibbing 2020; Rosenthal 2020). In the US case this rests first and foremost on ideas about the founding groups and their racial-ethnic profiles. These, of course, are people of primarily Western European ancestry like Trump himself. When

Trump first declared his presidential candidacy, as he descended the escalator at Trump Tower in New York City in 2015, he made his case centrally by declaring what he was *against*, in the case at hand, Mexican immigrants crossing the southern border of the United States and defiling the national space by their very presence, to which his answer would be to build a wall and otherwise close off the United States from the rest of the world as best he could. This was Trump's national-populist promise.

THE RETREAT OF THE FEDERAL GOVERNMENT SINCE THE 1980s

While representing "his" people, presumably a national constituency at least in theory, Donald Trump has also been heir to a set of ideological positions that have been to a considerable extent contradictory to his national-populist claim. These were apparent in his 2016 campaign but became glaringly obvious in the years in office. Certainly, hostility to professional expertise and science and disdain for disinterested journalism are often fundamental components of right-wing populism (e.g., Gerson 2020). But in the contemporary United States they are frequently connected popularly to government. President Ronald Reagan famously announced in his inaugural address as President of the United States that "Government is not the solution to our problem, government is the problem." Reagan did not so much have professional expertise in mind. But he certainly wished to trim and limit the role of the federal government. He opened the door to doubts about the very idea of the "public interest" and disinterested pursuit of objective knowledge. This reflected a long-standing political current in the United States increasingly dominant since the 1960s in the Republican Party suspicious of the expanded role of the federal government in enforcing regulations on business and civil rights on the population at large. At the same time, however, as noted by Janen Ganesh (2020): "Republicans seem to mistake the public's cynicism about 'government' in the abstract with indifference to actual services and fiscal transfers."

The very term Federalist was redefined to mean the exact opposite of what it meant to the writers of the US Constitution (e.g., Agnew 2005, 102–18; Edling 2003). Thus the right-wing Federalist Society is in fact largely anti-federalist in orientation, belittling and undermining the roles of the federal government that Madison and Hamilton had championed (see, e.g., Hamilton et al. 2014 [1788]; Ketcham 1986). Trump has picked up on this truly anti-federalist viewpoint in his attacks on the purpose and expertise of the federal government tout court and in relation to the experts in government agencies such as the EPA, the Department of the Interior, the Department of State, the FBI and the Department of Justice, and the Department of Defense. Shrinking the role of the federal government thus fulfilled the view that markets and maybe local governments were always better than central government and that there is no such thing as the public interest (e.g., Frank, T. 2008; Brown 2019).

The Reagan years marked the beginning of what has been called the neoliberal assault on the role of the federal government in managing the US economy and providing for the expansion and protection of fundamental civil rights. From the neoliberal perspective, the best government is that which does least, except insofar as it favors privatized solutions and capitalist interests over public institutions. In practice this was to declare an open season "to strip-mine public assets for the benefit of private interests" (Packer 2020). It certainly did not require the shrinking of the size of government budgets. It was a question of who would be beneficiaries: business or the general population (Sharma 2021). But it was an organized reaction against the so-called liberal-Keynesian view that governments should use fiscal policy, government spending, and tax increases to stimulate consumer demand during economic downturns (Cohen and DeLong 2016). In its place neoliberalism variously encouraged monetary as opposed to fiscal policy and tax cuts, particularly on the wealthy and business, as supply-side stimulus. It also preferred private to public provision even of goods, such as healthcare, that most people might reasonably regard as better made available on a public basis. Trump certainly governed in this neoliberal vein (Packer 2020).

At the same time, Trump inherited and cultivated the anti-federalist vote that came out of the civil rights struggles of the 1960s and led to the Republican strategy since Richard Nixon of hunting for white voters in the US South (Miller 2015; Maxwell and Shields 2019). From this viewpoint, the federal government represents both the hated "Union" that won the Civil War and the imposition on the South of norms and regulations that do not fit their "heritage." This heritage, as Maxwell and Shields (2019) brilliantly deconstruct, consists of an amalgam of white racism, patriarchy, and religious zealotry used to justify the other two. In this construction, the "Deep State" to which Trump frequently refers, typically associated with right-wing conspiracy theories, is not the bugaboo that libertarians might associate with limiting access to certain calibers of guns or imposing vaccinations, although these can be present too, but more the sense of a national-level government that imposes rules such as affirmative action, restricts local law enforcement, enforces environmental regulations, and insists on the basic equality of all citizens in the eyes of the law. With more than a nod to a Confederate imaginary of the United States, Reagan in his day often used the locution "these" United States to emphasize the sovereignty of the states against that of the federal government. Trump's recourse to the rhetoric of culture war over abortion, gay rights, immigrant undermining of American "culture" and so on all are designed to appeal to a constituency that sees the federal government (particularly the federal judiciary) as useful only in the negative sense of restricting its enforcement powers in the jurisdictions where they live rather in terms of an affirmative role in providing public goods and services on an equal basis nationwide.

The net effect of these two trends toward an anti-federalist conception of the federal government has been to produce an increasingly paralyzed and ineffective national government apparatus. Beyond this, however, the impact has also been to invest in a sort of "Darwinian" federalism in which the states are essentially left to their own devices without the necessary support and leadership of the federal government (Cook and Diamond 2020). This federal failure was on full display in relation to the crisis spawned by the spread of COVID-19. Trump judicial appointees resisted federal mandates of all sorts even after Trump himself was out of office (Chalfant 2021; Hsu 2021). The so-called conservative-originalist reading of the US Constitution, resting on a dystopian view of the modern centralized administrative state (and its executive agencies) and a preference for "states' rights" (never expressed as such anywhere in the US Constitution) and a wildly individualist understanding of certain constitutional rights (such as on gun ownership and the personhood of a fetus from the moment of coitus) but not others (such as a woman's right to privacy in relation to abortion), ruled what now went for federalism (e.g., Dodson 2003; Ablavsky 2019; Mortenson and Bagley 2020; Goldstone 2021). If rather than the either/or logic of the dualist vision a practical polyphony had been at work, the states and the federal government would have operated as alternative and coordinating power centers. So rather than asking if some function, like public health or pandemic management, "belongs" to one tier or another, we should ask how overlapping and coordinating power operates and can actually improve how some issues are addressed. What is of most use in the distinction between dualism and polyphony that Schapiro (2005–2006) makes is that it draws attention to values of plurality, dialogue, and redundancy in the latter over against those of uniformity, finality, and hierarchical accountability associated with the dualist vision. The point is not to ennoble the polyphonic alternative conception normatively so much as see it as methodologically more useful in terms of the workings of multitier governance in practice, for example in relation to managing a pandemic. In the crunch, Australian and German federalism seemed to exhibit more of this polyphony than did that of the United States.

THE SPATIAL PARADOX OF TRUMP'S "POPULISM" AND THE COVID-19 PANDEMIC

So at the same time Donald Trump has appealed to a conception of a tightly walled and contained national-territorial homeland, he is also heir to a weakened federal government and federal system that is the outcome of years of systematic degradation at the hands of anti-federalists of several types. On the first count there have been the years of systematic underfunding of national agencies devoted to health and welfare (e.g., Himmelstein and Woolhandler 2016). This reflects a bias against public funding (and federal taxation) and a preference for private initiatives with limited regulatory controls. On the second count there has been a trend to leave all sorts of issues, such as healthcare finance and provision, entirely to the states and localities (Kettl 2020). This reflects in part the view of the federal government as a usurper of local "heritage" and traditions, and the dangerous enforcer of equal citizenship and rights. It is not so much that a case cannot be made for effective local and regional democracy but that the federal role as a coordinator and manager has been systematically sidelined because of an anti-federalist ideology that has completely vitiated Trump's claim to represent an idealized national-people walled off from the rest of the world.

Trump himself weakened the federal government in very specific ways since arriving in office in 2017, not least in relation to public health management. Trump's neo-patrimonial promises referred to previously as important to his 2016 campaign for president were largely forgotten. The promised investments in national infrastructure and in replanting manufacturing industry came to little or nothing. Would these have finally mattered to his reelection? Perhaps not, but more importantly he made numerous promises to address the COVID-19 crisis *practically* rather than just rhetorically but without much delivery that may well have come back to haunt him in November 2020 (Drezner 2020). His main achievements in office were a giant income tax cut for the wealthy and business in 2017 and the appointment of numerous ultraconservative judges to the federal courts. Even as he continued with his populist-nationalist rhetoric, Trump systematically degraded the functioning of the US federal government (e.g., Bergen 2019; Rucker and Leonnig 2020). Federal government departments had thin or acting leadership for long periods. Many of the political appointees running their agencies were utterly incompetent for or opposed to the charges they received. Regulations and rules were rolled back across the board from education to the environment, transportation, and healthcare. Anti-corruption measures and procedures were undermined and unenforced (Shaub 2020). Trump even left the US Postal Service, the oldest existing federal agency, out of the massive public financing package addressing the economic effects of the pandemic. This is symbolic of the entire attitude to the utility, or from the anti-federalist perspective, the futility, of the federal government.

Crucially in the context of the COVID-19 pandemic, the federal pandemic warning system was dismantled as a leftover from Obama; the CDC, the main federal government agency charged with preparing for and managing disease outbreaks, had its budget gutted; and Trump left the states and their governors to fend for themselves without much of any real federal policy or plan to speak of (Haffajee and Mello 2020). Simultaneously, Trump also exhibited a complete disinterest in collaborating with other countries, including longtime allies, in addressing the pandemic. This would have been to resurrect the dreadful global international order that he consistently decried. He attacked and then withdrew the United States from the World Health Organization for being too pro-China and as if it were to blame for his own months' long passivity. On the positive side, the US Army Corps of Engineers and the vaccine development program, Operation Warp Speed, provided the basis for excellent responses, respectively, in helping hospitals deal with tenting hospitalized patients and promising a conclusion to the pandemic though mass immunity by way of vaccination. Made possible only because of federal government action in both cases, the latter, however, then fell foul of the continuing lack of proper coordination between the federal government and the states in rolling out the vaccines beginning in December 2020 (e.g., Smith and Choi 2021).

Repeatedly, Trump returned again and again in 2020 to the populist idea that the pandemic was the product of travelers, particularly foreign ones. He substituted this for the idea that once the virus was present within the country, it was tracing and isolating people (as in "community spread") who test positive that should take center stage rather than simply restricting international travel. Returning to his obsession with immigrants, he obscured his mismanagement of the pandemic by announcing a total ban on immigration as if immigrants were the continuing source of infection (*NY Times* 2020). Yet as time went by the federal government seemed less rather than more effective in testing for the virus (Lim, D. 2020). The states were left carrying the can, so to speak. Finally, in his daily press conferences early in the pandemic Trump was in full populist mode: accusing hospital staff of pilfering face masks and other Personal Protective Equipment, contradicting the public health experts, peddling his own doubtful cures like a snake-oil salesman, and instead of showing any grasp of the managerial issues facing his government, verbally assaulting the media representatives present and dispensing advice that was the opposite of that he had given the day before (e.g., Wright and Campbell 2020; Rucker and Costa 2020; Lipton et al. 2020).

CONCLUSION

In the end, therefore, President Trump's populist potential in addressing a national problem like the pandemic through coordination between federal and state governments proved impossible to realize. This was not simply because the populism he represents is inherently oppositional and rhetorical rather than practical. It was more because a constituency committed to limiting rather than empowering the federal government elected Trump. At the same time, and reflecting this anti-federalist electorate, he was also the prisoner of a long-standing set of ideological-institutional trends in the United States that have systematically weakened the role of the federal government in managing *across* other tiers of government and thus laid the groundwork for the failures manifest in the US response to the COVID-19 pandemic of 2020. The displacement of a polyphonic version of federalism by a rigidly dualist one since the 1980s arguably undermined the possibility of an adequate federal response, notwithstanding Trump's own problematic approach to the pandemic crisis. In this context his national-populism could only ever be a fake version of the real thing. The dualist vision of US federalism that Donald Trump inherited finally proved fatal for a large number of Americans.

IV

GEOPOLITICS OF GLOBAL REGULATION

8

Global Regulation

Conventional geopolitical wisdom can be faulted for an excessive focus on the "high" geopolitics of foreign-policy making and for slighting what lies beneath and around it, both the reproduction of geopolitical images and practices in everyday life and the roles of non-state actors in the making of world politics. The 2007–2008 global economic meltdown serves as a salutary reminder of the ways in which the world has become hostage to the activities of a range of agents—from bankers and mortgage brokers to transactional lawyers and credit raters—whose activities have rarely figured in discussions about global geopolitics. One of the most controversial aspects of the 2007–2008 global financial meltdown was the role of the Big Three credit-rating agencies (Moody's Investors Service, Standard and Poor's (S&P), and Fitch Ratings) in both rating bank credit portfolios and government (sovereign) debt and the bonds servicing that debt. These private organizations are an important aspect of the privatization of authority in the world economy since the 1970s. This chapter asks: How did this happen (particularly in relation to sovereign debt), how do these organizations work, and what are the implications for contemporary hidden geopolitics?

The credit-rating agencies are an example, albeit a controversial one given their role in the 2007–2008 financial crisis and subsequent Eurozone crisis (see chapter 9), of a genre of regulatory bodies that have emerged down the years beyond the borders of states and intergovernmental organizations (such as the WHO, WTO, IMF, and so on). Their existence and efficacy remind us that authority, the legitimate exercise of power, is not singularly in the hands of states or public agencies with some sort of popular base (such as nongovernmental organizations like Human Rights Watch or Greenpeace). Chapter 1 presented a typology of all of these "global rulers" (table 1.2) (Büthe and

Mattli 2011). This chapter is concerned with the genre of standard-setting and regulatory bodies that are private and, in the case of the credit-rating agencies, also profit making. These have cropped up historically to serve purposes for private actors underserved through the channels provided by territorialized entities such as states. These could be construed as public goods provided privately, in this case bond ratings, but standards for a wide range of products and engineering rules can also be thought of in similar terms (e.g., Yates and Murphy 2019), as can the certification of forest, coffee, and seafood products of various types (e.g., Auld 2014). The product/engineering category goes back to the nineteenth century and reflects the need to establish technical standards for trading products globally and serving infrastructure needs with universal definitions of appropriate standards for building bridges and making electrical machinery conform to minimum safety rules, to name a couple of examples. What they all suggest is a set of authoritative powers operating to create the very possibility for many of the market-based transactions that constitute the capitalist world economy. They reflect the fact that states are economically interdependent in all sorts of respects but that the regulatory reach of each is limited given that many firms operate transnationally and there is no central authority to resolve differences among competing businesses and states (Murphy, D. D. 2004). But, as we shall see, the various private regulatory bodies illustrate path dependence in their history. In other words, many of the bodies at hand sprang up first in Europe and/or the United States and have extended their spatial scope into the rest of the world only subsequently.

Two brief vignettes help to orient the chapter to its subject matter of the three main credit-rating agencies: (1) In August 2011 S&P downgraded US long-term debt; the first time this had ever happened. This was a controversial decision, not least because France, for example, in the midst of the Eurozone crisis, was not downgraded until much later, but the downgrade hasn't had much effect. The US economy as a "safe haven" and home of the US$ has other assets beyond its bond ratings. This suggests the limited impact of bond ratings, at least as far as the United States is concerned. (2) Elsewhere, however, the story is different. Since the mid-1970s when the whole business of sovereign debt credit rating took off, ratings have been a good indicator of sovereign-default risk. All countries that have defaulted on their bonds since then have had their grade cut to "junk" (highly speculative grade) at least a year before it happened.

Why have ratings agencies become so important in relation to sovereign debt? Briefly, this reflects the demand for private regulation as a result of the massive financial liberalization of the world economy that has occurred since the 1970s. States have had to concur with judgments made by these organizations because they possess information about corporations, banks, and countries that no one else does as stock, money, and bond markets have effectively internationalized with the ending of the Bretton Woods era. Thus, in raising funds through bonds, governments have become as dependent on rating-agencies as have private businesses. Bonds have become pivotal to the world financial system not least in the United States where the dollar's global role encourages all types of businesses, pension funds, and banks irrespective of nominal nationality to invest in them. The stock of US tradable sovereign bonds amounted to $20.5 trillion in 2020, about 100 percent of US GDP and about double the share in the 1990s (*Economist* 2020b). Funding the exploding US federal deficit in the aftermath of the 2020–2021 pandemic will undoubtedly increase the demand for US sovereign bonds and enhance the authority of the credit-rating agencies in governing the terms on which the bonds are sold. The credit-rating agencies' geographic scope has also increased with that of the number of states requiring ratings in order to raise funds to pay for infrastructure and other projects. Banks used to serve this function but increasingly rather than bank loans it is bonds and tradable securities (mortgage-backed securities, loans, derivatives, etc.) that circulate in capital markets without bank intermediation. Informational leverage, therefore, is the way in which credit-rating agencies have come to exercise authority, not simply coercive power within the world economy in general (particularly in relation to corporate debt) and over state sovereign debt in particular.

THE RISE OF CREDIT-RATING AGENCIES IN RATING SOVEREIGN DEBT

Rating agencies have grown from beginnings as "market surveillance mechanisms" in the mid-1850s largely in the United States. This is an aspect of the prototype world economy within the borders of the United States that later became the template for the hegemony associated with American "marketplace society" in the world at large (Agnew 2005; Quinn 2019). In the United States the role of the agencies reflected the lack of a single clustering of banks and businesses around a single financial center such as characterized most European economies at the time until New York finally acquired this role. Information was so diffuse spatially that agencies were needed to collect it and provide it to potential investors. Henry Poor and John Moody were pioneers.

In the 1920s foreign governments sought ratings by the US-based (and other) agencies for their bonds but defaults in the 1930s led to retreat of the agencies into rating the stocks and bonds of municipal and large industrial firms. From the 1930s until the 1960s only a few creditworthy countries had rating coverage. Fees derived from issuers were widely introduced only in the 1960s. Of course, this brings about a conflict of interest when the rating agencies are paid by those whose bonds/stocks they are rating. It is only since the 1970s that the major rating agencies have internationalized on a massive scale with offices now scattered around all of the world's major financial centers and tax havens. This has reinforced the role of the Big Three (although

S&P and Moody's are really the most important globally). Fitch has its most profitable niches in the municipal bond market and in rating banks.

All three agencies are headquartered in Manhattan (New York City) with a major overseas presence. Fitch, like the others, was founded in the United States, but from the 1990s until 2018 had partial French ownership. It has about forty offices worldwide. There are over 100 other credit-rating agencies worldwide but most have primarily domestic markets. China has struggled to develop its own credit-rating industry even as many ambitious private Chinese firms still rely on the Big Three (e.g., Kennedy, D. W. 2008; Bloomberg 2021). The Chinese rating firms tend to issue inflated grades for much corporate debt and have not yet been able to break into the lucrative sovereign-debt rating business. Indeed, none of the credit-rating agencies outside the Big Three has yet acquired the "global reputation" to challenge their sovereign-debt ratings (e.g., European CEO 2020). Moody's and S&P are both parts of larger corporations (Moody's of Moody's Corporation, S&P of McGraw Hill). Those rated by them can thus also own shares in them. This self-evident conflict of interest was behind much of the concerns raised after 2007–2008 when products that had been highly rated suddenly imploded.

Arguably, the authority that the Big Three wield over debt markets results from their designation as "nationally recognized" ratings firms (licensed in the US by the SEC since 1975). This gives them quasi-regulatory status when their judgments are seen as elements of the rules governing banks, insurers, funds, and state bond issuers. Since the 1990s, ratings have been used in setting capital standards for banks and in central bank collateral eligibility rules. Ratings are also embedded in private contracts for derivatives and pension fund investments. They have become "hard-wired" into the global financial system. They do seem to generate positive information externalities whether in relation to downgrades or upgrades, though there is some controversy about the latter (e.g., Binici et al. 2018). In this context, questions have arisen about rating quality in the absence of much competition between agencies, conflicts of interests, and "cliff effects" as sudden rating shifts cause massive disinvestments. The consistency of criteria for judging bonds across the agencies is also problematic as illustrated from the period before and during the 2007–2008 crisis. S&P has been far more likely to downgrade sovereign debt than the others (figure 8.1). Yet even as it downgraded US federal debt in August 2011, S&P announced that some states and local governments could preserve their top-notch ratings if they showed how they might cope with reduced federal benefits!

HOW ARE RATINGS DONE?

Ratings can be initiated by issuers or by the agencies themselves. This is irrespective of the financial product involved: bonds, stocks, or sovereign debt.

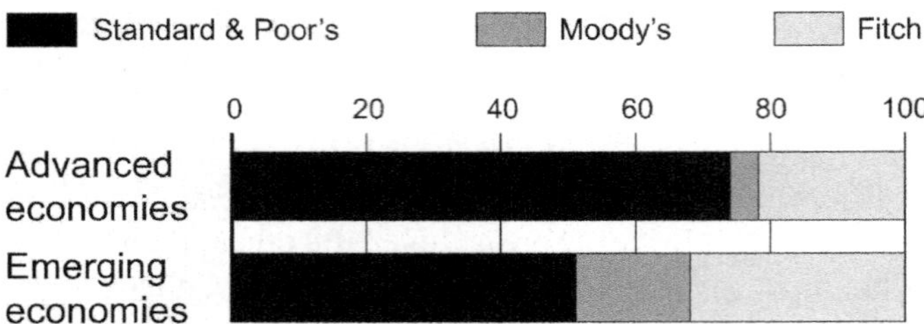

Figure 8.1. The Big Three Credit-Rating Agencies during the Time of the 2007–2008 Global Financial Crisis: Which Acted First to Downgrade Sovereign Bonds? Percentage of first-mover negative rating actions.
***Note*: Out of a total of 66 negative rating actions, January 2005–July 2010. IMF staff estimates from the Big Three Credit-Rating Agencies.**

Analytical teams undertake research, meet with issuers, and write reports proposing ratings and their rationales. What then happens is shrouded in much mystery. Moody's is infamous as the most conservative agency and until the 1990s did not publish rating criteria. A 2012 cartoon in the *Financial Times* shows two men leaving a building named "MOODY'S" with one saying to the other: "I had a bad dream about the UK's credit rating." The other agencies have been more forthcoming about the criteria they use to rate and rank different countries bonds and the relative danger of default in different cases. Typically, financial ratios of revenues/expenditures or debt-burden versus debt-bearing capacity are used to decide which "grades" to award. Rating committees, at S&P typically of eight people, make the final determinations. A major distinction is drawn by all agencies between "investment" and "speculative" grades of bonds, reflecting the language of US securities legislation from the 1930s. AAA for S&P and Aaa for Moody's are the highest investment grades. The move to speculative grades begins at BB+ for S&P and Ba1 for Moody's. For both agencies there are ten levels of investment grade and eleven of speculative grade. D is default for both of them (see Sinclair 2005, chapter 2).

In practice the letter symbol takes on a totemic quality. The clarity it offers also reflects the selection and suppression of various types of information that a more complex narrative or statistical indicator might better avoid. Monitoring of the bond and its context then becomes the next step in the agencies' task. Discipline operates through the possibility of appearing on a "Watchlist" (Moody's) or "CreditWatch" (S&P) signaling a possible regrade is in the works for a country's bond rating.

The opacity of the rating process has become a major political issue since the US bond downgrade of August 2011. The companies defend themselves by saying that the process remains secret to "maintain analytical independence" (Creswell et al. 2011). From available sources, it seems that three people were the most involved of all employees in the S&P decision to downgrade US federal bonds from AAA to AA+: David Beers, head of the company's entire sovereign ratings division, his deputy John Chambers, and Nikola Swann, an analyst responsible for the ratings of the United States, Canada, and Bermuda. All have spent most of their careers at S&P rating countries around the world. Rumor has it that "being first" in a re-rating has been important to Mr. Beers. He declines to comment. S&P certainly is usually the quickest of the agencies in downgrading. The US Treasury noted that S&P made a $2 billion error in its draft report on the downgrading. Moody's and Fitch left well enough alone. In September 2011, the SEC, the regulator of much of the US financial sector, reported that S&P's pending downgrade had been leaked and the information traded on before the official announcement (Wyatt 2011). But the SEC failed to do anything about this. This has been par for the course. Regulation of the credit-rating agencies has been notoriously loose. All of them rated the subprime mortgage-backed securities that were the immediate cause of the 2008 great recession at the highest grade until the markets actually said otherwise. In the same report, the SEC failed to say anything very specific about any credit-rating agency in particular while criticizing them en masse for giving priority to their revenues over analysis, for feeble controls over employee ownership of rated products, and for conflicts of interest (e.g., Council on Foreign Relations 2015).

There is little then except some gossip from former analysts and defenses of the agencies by PR spokespersons to go on about how the agencies actually work. The possibility of a "fly-on-the-wall" sort of ethnography within the corridors and offices of the Big Three is beyond the realm of possibility. Trading in information is their business. They don't share it with outsiders. What we await is the sort of personal/institutional biography of Stephen Axilrod (2009) describing his years working at the Fed. Until then, there's not much to go on. In part because of the opaqueness of the process, the entire rating process is now under a cloud. Reliance on ratings for a wide range of financial products including sovereign bonds is now under attack. The agencies are fighting back by lobbying hard in Washington to keep their various roles (Eggen 2011). The Dodd-Frank Act has made it illegal for US regulators to use ratings for regulatory purposes. The problem is that the simplicity of the ratings for potential investors makes them hard to replace. Having more raters is one alternative, particularly ones less tied into the Washington–Wall Street axis. The other side of the problem is that sovereign bond ratings have come to be treated as an "emblem of national virility" (Stephens 2012). This is what happened to President Sarkozy in 2012 when he said that a downgrade of France's AAA rating by S&P would kill his presidency. Belief in the magical powers of the ratings has become part of their power . . . and a major problem.

PRIVATE AUTHORITY AND STATE SOVEREIGNTY

Arguably, the Big Three credit-rating agencies represent the emergence of transnational actors whose practices have fundamental effects on the well-being of people within the borders of self-defined sovereign states. They exercise "fields" of power, and I would claim, authority, acceptance of their decisions as at least quasi-legitimate in the eyes of investors, political elites, and segments of mass publics, that can be seen as displacing the authority of public agencies with democratic or governmental accountability. The "game" of sovereignty has changed and thus has the "practical" basis on which it rests (Bigo 2011). From this viewpoint, it is not that globalization or some other supranational process is eroding state sovereignty but states have outsourced authority to a variety of other agencies including private as well as supranational and global interstate ones. This is what Sakellaropoulos (2007) has interestingly termed the "rise of the headquarters state." Many existing state functions are delegated and potential new ones accrue to novel private and public but not single-state centered ones. Cities such as New York and London are where these regulatory authorities tend to be located, at least for now. The transversality of the contemporary global economy lies in processes such as these (see introduction and chapter 1).

Credit-rating agencies are one among a range of new transnational actors exercising such authority today. They may not be "The New Global Rulers" that Büthe and Mattli (2011) write of—that study focuses on standard-setting organizations for high-tech products and accounting rules such as the International Electrotechnical Commission (IEC) and the International Accounting Standards Board (IASB), respectively. Some transnational organizations, however, can sometimes lay claim to emerging democratic bona fides particularly in the areas of human rights and law (Erman and Uhlin 2010). Most, however, conform to one of four "types" of regulatory organizations that are technocratic or expert and representative of industry groups rather than based on transparent democratic rule making in the interest of people(s). First are public rule making but nonmarket agencies such as the Universal Postal Union, the Kyoto Protocol, the IMF, and the Basel Committee on Banking Supervision. The second group covers public but market-based organizations such as the US Federal Trade Commission and the EU Directorate General for Competition. Third are private nonmarket bodies such as those establishing accounting and electronic product rules previously mentioned. Fourth, and finally, are private market-based entities such as the Forest Stewardship Council and Microsoft (an international standard setter with the Windows computer operating system). The credit-rating agencies fit best into the private market-based category of transnational organizations. They are privately owned and claim to base their judgments on market criteria rather than technical standards as such. But they are arguably much more influential in relation to conventional notions of state sovereignty than most of the other so-called new global rulers put together.

Crucial to the entire question of private authority and its relation to state sovereignty is what we understand authority to mean. As Katsikas (2010, 116) has usefully pointed out, we need to distinguish between "non-state governance schemes that generate formal legal results and those that do not, since the former are clearly associated with institutional, political, and symbolic transformations that the latter do not necessarily invoke." In this regard, credit-rating agencies of the scope of the Big Three have exactly the sort of legitimate power to be "in authority," rather than being "authorities," in the sense of simply having knowledge, private power, or influence. This distinction suggests that we can no longer (if we ever *should have* is a different question) pretend empirically that states monopolize sovereign authority without engaging and enrolling other private and public actors of various types and vintages (Agnew 2018).

Even while licensed to operate without any consciousness of the effects they could have on the sovereignty of states, it seems to me that the Big Three, if not other credit-rating agencies, currently have an authority remarkably akin to what we conventionally label as sovereignty or sovereign power. Of course, whether we should want this to be the case is one of the big political questions of the moment. The lack of accountability except to investors leaves them open to the charge of conflict of interest. Yet it is their very lack of connection to conventional centers of power than endows them with the image of "autonomy" that is crucial to their authority.

GEOPOLITICAL CONSEQUENCES

In what ways does a focus on and analysis of the Big Three credit-rating agencies lead to a reconstituting of our understanding of contemporary global geopolitics? First of all, and increasingly, in the same epoch in which the Big Three have come to exercise such authority as they do, central banks, for example, have also become independent of their respective governments. Regulation of money and finance has thus become increasingly driven by private and quasi-private actors rather than by national governments per se. Governance has been reconstructed to meet the needs of increasingly globalized private actors such as banks and industrial corporations rather than the needs of the territorialized populations of states. State sovereign bonds underwrite this system and socialize risk onto domestic populations in return for back stopping the speculative activities of private banks, hedge funds, and other investors (Kirshner 2014). Looming in the background, the differentials of bond revenues between countries determined in international financial markets and evaluated by the credit-rating agencies determine the fiscal and monetary prospects of the many states who rely on bond revenues to fund their outlays.

Second, the agencies represent the workings of a historical path dependence in which what began as domestic actors entirely in the United States have become significant global actors in their own right beyond the purview of official US regulatory agencies (such as the SEC), except in the most perfunctory manner (Lavelle 2013). The story of their initial and continuing success lies in their association with the historic role of the United States in the world economy. Yet, at the same time, they have increasingly justified their authority by their seeming autonomy from their origins and any sort of raison d'état. This contradiction may become more obviously evident in the face of US retreat or decline relative to other actors both state and non-state related in the years to come. If competitors emerge elsewhere, in Europe or China for example, then the whole model may have to change depending on how the newcomers operate. So far, at least, this shows little sign of happening.

Third, the spatial boundaries governing states themselves are no longer the national ones. They are profoundly the boundaries defined by the investment and regulatory activities of private/public businesses, pension funds, banks, international law firms, standard setting, and credit-rating agencies. Even as the economic crisis of 2007–2008 and the subsequent Eurozone crisis could be seen as calling the roles of all of these into question, they have, if anything, emerged from the crisis more strongly entrenched than they entered it. The credit-rating agencies in particular, although seemingly discredited by their many "bad calls" before and during the 2007–2008 crisis, have become more important than ever given the reluctance of governments to raise corporate taxes in a world of competitive investment and thus increased reliance on bond sales to fund everyday government. States compete for the highest bond ratings to maintain their edge in a neoliberal world where lower corporate tax rates have become de rigueur for attracting mobile capital, both domestic and foreign (Cerny 2010). If there is some international agreement on minimum global corporate tax rates then perhaps there will be a possibility of reducing the reliance of governments on sovereign bonds to fund themselves.

CONCLUSION

I have used the important role of credit-rating agencies, private transnational organizations with recognized authority, to make the case for one aspect of a different understanding of geopolitics in the contemporary world. This perspective on hidden geopolitics draws attention to the differences between the present and the past by being attentive to the vital roles of new non-state actors. Little is known about how credit-rating agencies operate. What is known is that they have been heavily involved in the ranking and management of the financial products that are at the center of the world's financial economy today. They represent a specifically privatized source of authority. Yet they also illuminate several aspects of an emerging geopolitical order in which states can no longer be seriously regarded as single unified actors ("the United States does this" etc.); key concepts such as market and state, private and public have taken on distinctively novel meanings, and the expropriation of land no longer lies at the center of geopolitical relations but is being replaced by control over financial products and flows (see the introduction and chapters 1 and 6). As the world changes so should our attempts to account for its geopolitics.

9

Managing the Eurozone Crisis

The debt crisis afflicting the Eurozone in the aftermath of the 2007–2008 global financial crisis was not simply the outcome of an absolute imbalance in debt between weaker (e.g., Greece) and stronger (e.g., Germany) national economies with the former mortally injured by proportionally larger government bailouts of insolvent banks. It was primarily a geopolitical crisis reflecting the mismatch between the normative model of a "successful" national economy based largely in the German experience of an export-oriented economy projected onto a larger and much more heterogeneous Eurozone economy. In other words, it was a geopolitical crisis based in the practical conflict between the *political* demands of a historically German institutionalized conception of political economy (*Ordnungspolitik* or "ordering policies") that has come to dominate Eurozone monetary policy, on the one hand, and the fact that the crisis was in its origins a political-*economic* crisis of the territorial form (the national economy) that the German experience of political economy takes, on the other.

The crisis was the result of the fact that the global economy out of which the financial crisis emerged works according to neoliberal capitalist practices that are at significant odds with the German model including, increasingly, within Germany itself. If the German model simply cannot suddenly replace the more diverse national political economies of the Eurozone, its own placement within a "variegated capitalism" (Jessop 2012) makes its application as a standard of excellence to the peripheral economies anachronistic in the extreme. The expectation on the part of German political leaders, with European Union and IMF leaders in broad concordance, that the application of an idealized German model could magically reform the heavily indebted public economies such as that of Greece was the major factor in the persistence and deepening of the Eurozone crisis over the years 2010–2015 and its continuing effects since then in light of the differential economic impact of the 2020–2021 pandemic across the Eurozone.

The chapter begins with a brief overview of the two broadly dominant views of the crisis. Attention then turns to the practical course of the crisis and the role of the German perspective on economic policy in its perpetuation, particularly in relation to the case of Greece. The paper lays out the argument for the history of German *Ordnungspolitik* and its limits as an approach to economic policy today at both home and abroad. Finally, the territorial mismatch thesis suggests that widening public recognition of the territorial limits of the application of an idealized German policy model is necessary for the future of the Eurozone and thus for the European Union to move toward permanent resolution of the roots of the Eurozone crisis in particular and furthering the possibility of European integration in the long term more generally.

POPULAR ACCOUNTS OF THE EUROZONE CRISIS

The Eurozone crisis appears in most contemporary popular discourse as anything but a conflict between distinctive institutionalized policy outlooks and governmental practices. It is usually portrayed as either the result of government profligacy and/or weak economies on the part of the highly indebted countries or the parallel outcome of patterns of lending to cover up bank debt intrinsic to the neoliberal capitalism at the root of globalized finance that triggered the financial crisis in 2008 and after. In this section, broad portraits of these perspectives are drawn using a range of sources from academic and media representations of the Eurozone crisis. In the first case national behavioral stereotypes tend to prevail, harking back to historical slights and resentments long before the onset of the crisis. In the second case the crisis is "naturalized" as a by-product of the machinations of a Capital inflicting its spatial fix on the weakest links in the global chain of capital accumulation or the poor design of the Eurozone institutionally that concentrated its negative effects on already fiscally weak economies. The politics of economic-policy making reflecting both the cross-national incidence of institutional practices and the economic ideologies they embody is missing from both of these accounts.

The first perspective comes down to the total opposition between prudence versus profligacy. This is conventionally a morality tale about the absolute incidence of patronage politics, tax avoidance, and political corruption between Germany, on the one hand, and Greece and the others, on the other hand. Simply put, the peripheral countries have consumed more than they can afford by borrowing excessively at the low-interest rates that the euro has afforded them. Those low-interest rates reflect market judgments about the overall economic health of the Eurozone which is due to the efforts of its more productive members not to the peripheral slackers. Often, particularly in the media, the opposition involves a recycling of national stereotypes: on the one side, for example, Greeks are portrayed as children unable to control their impulses and, on the other side, Germans are imagined as penny-pinching housewives. Opinion leaders of various types have characterized the crisis in three different ways. One is in terms of collective psychology. Thus Jürgen Stark (a member of the European Central Bank Board from Germany) in the *Financial Times* (11 February 2015) said of the peripheral countries that "the real deficit is the failure of the political elite in many countries and the lack of credible institutions." Chris Giles (the economics editor of the *Financial Times*) on 19 April 2015 went further in comparing Greece to a "child" in need of parental discipline. John Dizard writing in the same newspaper on 17 April 2015 claimed that this was a very old story indeed by quoting an 1826 book to the effect that "The majority of Greeks do not rightly comprehend the meaning of a [foreign] loan, but simply conclude that it is some European method of making a present." Francesco Giavazzi, a well-known Italian economist, announced in the *Financial Times* (9 June 2015) that the Greeks had chosen poverty by refusing to "modernize" their economy. Apparently, the austerity policies imposed from outside have had no role in helping them realize their "choice."

A second approach is in terms of mutual incomprehension. Thus the Spanish film *Perdiendo el Norte* (Losing the North or Losing One's Bearings) is a comedy about two desperate Spaniards who go to Berlin in search of work but it fails to live up to expectations. One of the duo, Hugo, complains that he is part of the "best-prepared generation Spain has ever had" but he has ended up working in a kebab-shop kitchen. All of the Germans are portrayed as cold, strict, unsmiling, and, of course, blond (Buck 2015). Finally, and most notoriously, the opposition is one of mutual resentment and antagonism. The best example of this is the controversy that erupted in March 2015 over the positioning of the left finger of Yanis Varoufakis, finance minister in the left-populist Syriza-led government of Greece after January 2015. Did he raise his offending digit in an obscene gesture directed at Berlin as he called for Greece to default on its debts? He denies that he flashed what in German is called the "*Stinkefinger*" and claimed that the video from the 2013 conference in Croatia had been doctored (Wagstyl 2015). For much of March 2015, the German press, particularly the tabloid *Bild* owned by the Springer publishing group, was obsessed by whether he did or did not. For their part, Greeks have made a claim for reparations from Germany based on the costs incurred on them when occupied by the German Nazi regime during the Second World War.

More rarely, if more seriously, the Eurozone crisis is put down entirely in academic circles either to a continuation of the financial crisis by other means or to the poor design of the Eurozone. The first of these sees crisis as endemic to capitalism (e.g., Harvey 2011). Declining profit rates for business since the

1960s have required constant restructuring to facilitate recovery. But none has proved durable. They never do. Problems are moved around geographically rather than resolved. Consequently, in the face of the global financial crisis, the state interventions of 2008 boosted fiscal deficits massively around the world. The Eurozone response, which is typically explained by this perspective in terms of simply being "different" from that of the United States and China, was to tighten both fiscal and monetary policy. The United States followed a very loose monetary policy and an expansionary fiscal one. China followed an expansionary fiscal policy but a relatively tight monetary one. The heterogeneity of the Eurozone economies, above all the absence of a common bond rating, meant that the countries more exposed to the bond markets through borrowing to maintain consumption levels and bail out their banks were also more open to attack to provide what is effectively a "sinicization" of their labor standards and public goods. As a result, a new round of uneven development within the Eurozone, and new possibilities of profit for multinational capital, are the likely outcomes and not the spatial balancing of incomes and wealth across the Eurozone promised by membership in the common currency area.

Of course, and this is the second account under this heading, the Eurozone is not and never was an optimum currency area by any stretch of the imagination. Simply put, the national economies subsumed under the Eurozone with their distinctive fiscal histories, disproportionalities in industrial structure and trading patterns, and asymmetries in flows of capital are a poor fit with one another (e.g., Piris 2011; Polito and Wickens 2013; Eichengreen 2014). Beyond this, measures that could have increased complementarities such as fiscal redistribution between richer and poorer countries and a common sovereign bond were entirely off limits at the time that the Eurozone design was being put in place. These were widely viewed, particularly in Germany, as steps too far. The Eurozone crisis, therefore, is a direct outcome of the fact that whereas national governments were faced with primary responsibility for bailing out their banks in the aftermath of the financial crash of 2008, this came back to haunt those governments that had to raise funds externally through the bond market to finance the public deficits they now had because of the bailout and the declining revenues they faced because of decreased economic growth. The central institutions of the Eurozone, such as the European Central Bank and the Commission, simply did not have the proper tools available to respond for the Eurozone as a whole. Consequently, the crisis became one of the stronger economies setting the terms under which the weaker ones could stay in the Eurozone, notwithstanding the fact that the stronger ones had often previously violated the criteria of monetary responsibility that they were now imposing on the weaker ones. The Eurozone crisis is thus one of an institutional deficit that could be fixed politically rather than a symptom of the immutable crisis of capitalism that is ultimately beyond repair.

ANALYZING THE EUROZONE CRISIS

There is little doubt, however, that the Eurozone sovereign debt crisis is a direct outcome of the banking/financial crisis of 2008 (see, e.g., Bordo and James 2013). Its continuation is something else entirely. How this is so is the primary focus of this chapter. To make the case, it is worth briefly reviewing the course of the Eurozone crisis and its geopolitical roots.

The 2008 financial crisis began with the collapse of the so-called subprime mortgage market in the United States in which many European banks had invested heavily. It derives from the conversion of bank debt into government debt as national governments bailed out banks and borrowed in the bond market to cover the tremendous loss of revenues from dramatic decreases in economic growth. The biggest relative debt loads were those of southern European countries and Ireland whose economies were either more open to the transmission of external bond shocks because of their own inflated mortgage markets (as in Ireland and Spain) or already overextended public debt loads from borrowing to expand public goods without adequate expansion of revenues (as in Greece and Italy). The banks that extended the credit to the peripheral economies were overwhelmingly from Germany, France, Switzerland, and the United Kingdom. By 2010, Eurozone member-country banks were exposed to the equivalent of $727 billion in Spain, $402 billion in Ireland, and $206 billion in Greece. It has been the conversion of this private debt into public debt that has been at the center of the crisis. Thus, and for the case of Greece, for example, what was in December 2009 entirely bank-held debt was translated by the actions of national governments, the European Central Bank, and the IMF into debt held by states and owed to the troika of ECB, EU, and IMF (figure 9.1). At least for the case of Greece, there was something of a shift between "whose" banks held the debt in December 2009, on the one hand, and which governments held the now public debt in September 2014. What is clear is that banks were no longer the holders of most Greek debt. Eurozone member governments had taken on the debt. The crisis lay in the impossibility of Greece paying back its debts to other national governments beyond further borrowing from the troika in the face of the imposition of austerity policies by the Eurozone authorities (and the IMF) designed to restrict continuing public-sector borrowing but which in turn also prevented government spending to encourage the economic growth that would (potentially) increase government revenues and reduce private borrowing costs in the bond market.

Four points arise in relation to the course of this crisis. The first is that with the exception of Italy, the debt loads of the peripheral countries in fact were relatively small (all under $500 billion) compared to the absolute public debts of such Eurozone members as Germany and France (between $2500 billion and $3000 billion, respectively) and even in terms of debt-to-GDP

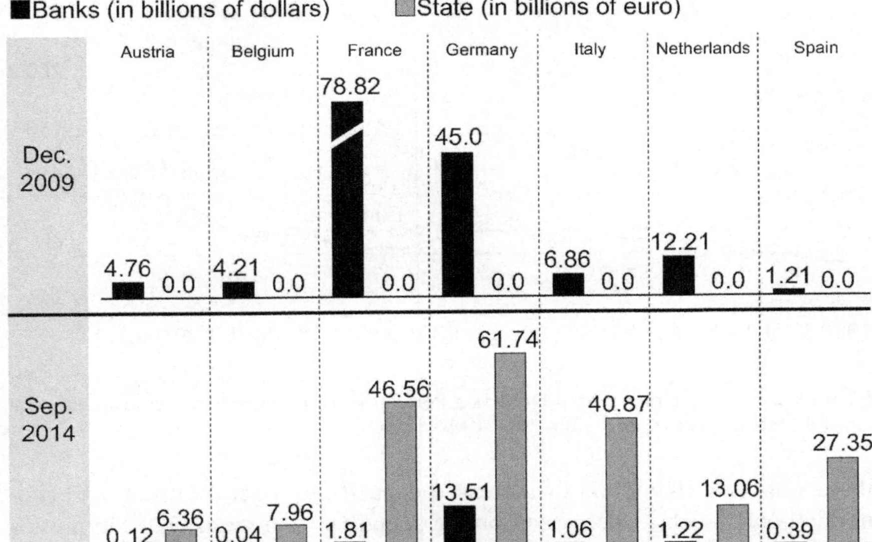

Figure 9.1. Exposure of Banks and Other European States to Greece, 2009–2014 (European Central Bank data)

ratios, Ireland, Portugal, and Spain (at 80–95%) were much the same as the presumably "stronger" core countries (Germany and France both at 83%) as of 2014. In this latter respect, Greece was the outlier. The second is that the overall Eurozone government debt problem was very similar to that of the United States and the United Kingdom but much less than, for example, that of Japan (figure 9.2). It looks as if the Eurozone crisis then had some basis other than the size of the public debt or the overall "threat" to the currency from public-sector indebtedness.

This leads to the third point. In 2008–2009, at the very outset of the financial crisis, many governments around the world, from the United States to China, intervened to use government spending to stimulate an economic rebound. This worked to various degrees. But in the Eurozone as a whole, fiscal stimulus was not considered at all. Rather, fiscal consolidation and structural reform became the rallying cries. Over the period 2010–2014 fiscal austerity was rewarded with loans from the troika to pay off old debts with new ones. For example, in 2010 Greece received $110 billion in return for a 20 percent cut in public-sector pay and pension cuts; Ireland received $60 billion in return for a 24 percent cut in public spending. The impact of these cuts and associated austerity policies has been devastating for the economies in question, none more so than Greece. There over the period 2009–2014 aggregate real GDP fell by 27 percent with real spending collapsing by a third. The unemployment rate reached 28 percent in 2013, while government spending fell by 30 percent between 2009 and 2014. Under such conditions

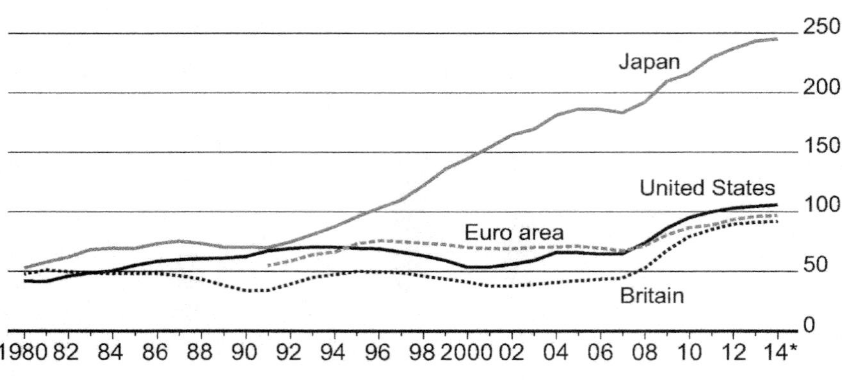

Figure 9.2. Gross Government Debt as a Percent of GDP, Eurozone versus Japan, the United States, and Britain, 1980–2014 (IMF data)

there was little likelihood of increased capacity to meet the fiscal and economic goals (such as decreased public spending relative to GDP, improved labor market flexibility, and so on) mandated by the troika. Ironically, given that it was ordinary Greeks who had to bear most of the burden of "adjustment," as Martin Wolf (2015) has pointed out, "the vast bulk of the official loans to Greece were not made for its benefit at all, but for that of its feckless private creditors. Creditors, too, have a duty to take care. If they are careless, they risk big losses. If governments want to save them, their own taxpayers should be told to pay up."

The fourth point is crucial to why the austerity course was taken. The institutional decision-making process in the Eurozone was central. It reflected in its workings the monetarist origins of the Eurozone and the German model of the European Central Bank as a technocratic entity both beyond "political influence" and geared toward a rules-based modus operandi. Monetary policy mandated a very limited economic-policy menu in which fiscal stimulus was strictly taboo. This was not just because fiscal policy remained in the hands of member governments but because a German model of "good practice" blocked its use as a way to potentially exit from the crisis. The choice of fiscal austerity was therefore absolutely central to the Eurozone model, not simply an ad hoc feature that just "happened" and set the Eurozone apart from, for example, the United States and China.

The austerity approach was premised on two flawed assumptions that the roots of the 2008 financial crisis in Europe suggest no longer make much sense under global capitalism, even if they may have previously. One is that it assumed a bank/country matching that the way the crisis evolved suggests is no longer operative. Banking has been internationalized, yet the Eurozone remains without any mechanisms in place to regulate this except at the national level. So, even if banking debts are incurred somewhere else, home countries are presumed to be the lenders who would save them from collapse. Eurozone-level banking regulation backed up by a Eurozone bond would have prevented the crisis from escalating into the bilateral set of crises—Ireland and the Eurozone, Greece and the Eurozone, and so on—that required country-by-country austerity in the sense assumed by the German model of good monetary and fiscal practice. The second flawed assumption is that rapid labor market and welfare reforms (in response to which new credit to repay old debts would be released) are fundamental to correct what went wrong after 2008. As we have seen this was undoubtedly a banking/capital mobility crisis before it was a bond crisis, so the focus on public-sector spending is wrongheaded. It was not public spending that was the primary driver behind the Eurozone bond/debt crisis. It was also not primarily a crisis about overall national economic competitiveness, although the single-minded focus on austerity has helped to turn it into that. Globalization had been having negative impacts on such Eurozone economies as Italy long before the 2008 financial crisis. This has continued. At the same time, national differences across the Eurozone in relative labor-market efficiency are not as great as the economic folklore about countries such as Italy, Spain, and Greece would lead one to believe. Although there are real inefficiencies in, for example, registering companies and in protecting certain job categories, these reflect differences in degree rather than kind between the peripheral and the core Eurozone countries (figure 9.3).

In one perspective, this outcome can be seen as the clash between different "varieties" of capitalism, with the dominant one, that of the German model directing the Eurozone, maladapted to both the times and to the scale

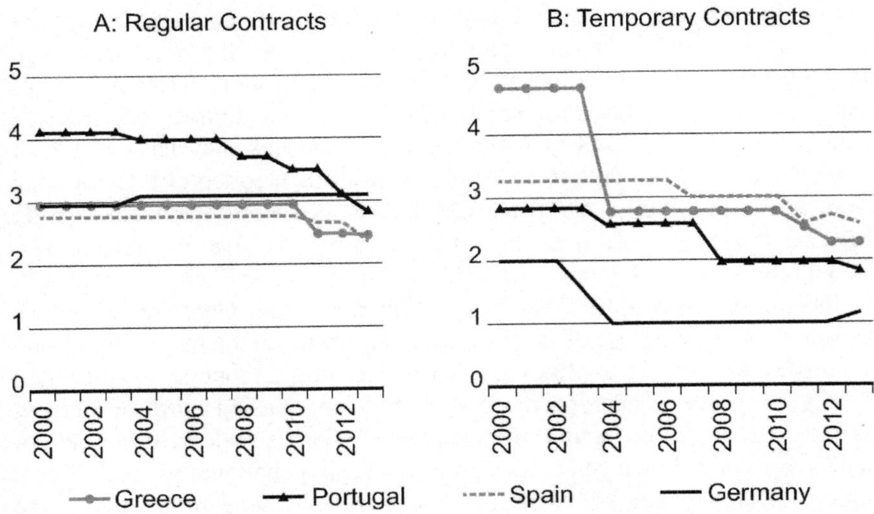

Figure 9.3. Employment Contracts in Various Eurozone Countries, 2000–2014 (the lower the index, the greater the flexibility) (OECD data)

of the Eurozone as a whole. Certainly, as Peter A. Hall (2014, 1225) argues, the design of the Eurozone "ignored durable differences across the political economies of the EU in favor of the ideal economy as one built on classically competitive markets operated by highly informed actors whose management would require only the minimal institutions with which the new union was endowed." But there was more to the problem of the Eurozone than this. It has been the projection of one idealized national model onto the others in a global context in which national borders have limited effects in shaping flows of capital, goods, and people that is more a propos. More specifically, and here Jessop (2012, 102) is a useful theoretical guide, the "shadow of finance-dominated neoliberalism" emanating from beyond European shores, but increasingly interpellated with European financial practices, fell over a Eurozone bringing together economies with a variety of models of capitalism (coordinated market economies such as Germany, dirigiste ones such as France, and clientelist/corporatist such as Italy and Greece) but integrated, if that is the correct term, through "the assumptions and operations of the European Central Bank, which largely derived its policy paradigm from the German model and placed undue faith in the capacity of market forces to produce upward convergence in economic performance."

The potentially problematic character of this "variegated capitalism" within the design of the Eurozone was noted early on in its history (e.g., Grahl 2001). Perhaps the experience since the 1980s of Germany's largest private bank, Deutsche Bank, is illustrative of the devastating impact of the muddled multiscalar combination of global activities and idealized national economic model that is variegated capitalism in the Eurozone mold. Beginning in 1989, the bank's management concentrated on transforming the bank from a corporate and retail bank focused on Germany into a global corporate and investment bank (e.g., Gapper 2015). But it remains caught between the two imperatives. At the heart of Germany's industrial base, with its name as a reminder of its roots, recent leaders have aspired to divest the retail division and become a global rival to the likes of Goldman Sachs. On this they have met with much resistance from within the bank and from its German clients. German newspapers from the left-of-center *Süddeutsche Zeitung* to the business daily *Handelsblatt* have urged a return to the "boring"—and national-territorial—model of lending to German households and firms. Yet the bank is faced with an incredibly competitive retail banking market within Germany. It is thus trapped between the logic of specializing and globalizing, on the one hand, and of remaining within the confines of a German territorial economy, on the other. This speaks to the broader macroeconomic problem of using a historic German model of territorial economic management at a larger scale across a heterogeneous set of political economies all now deeply penetrated by a neoliberal logic by which capital knows no boundaries. This is both the tragedy of the Eurozone and the basis for its particular crisis (e.g., Atkins 2011; Beck 2013).

WHAT IS *ORDNUNGSPOLITIK*?

In design, the Eurozone was the result of compromises over the relative roles of national and new Eurozone institutions. But the main Eurozone institution, the European Central Bank, and the monetary policies that informed the workings of the Eurozone from the outset were modeled on those of Germany. The particular justification for austerity in the face of the Eurozone crisis likewise comes out of the German model and is not the same as that, for example, at work in Britain or inspiring small-government conservatives in the United States. In the latter cases it is all about shrinking or rolling back the state; in the former case it is all about the proper role of the state in relation to markets (Blyth 2013, 133). The crisis raised the fear in some quarters in Germany that with the European Central Bank under the direction of an Italian, Mario Draghi, that "instead of exporting the *Stabilitätskultur* of the Bundesbank to the rest of Europe as they had hoped . . ." Germany's "geo-economic encirclement" will lead to its "importing others' weak currency culture into Germany" (Kundnani 2015, 112). The roots of this fear are not difficult to trace. The concern with monetary stability comes out of the bitter experience of modern German history. More specifically, in the aftermath of Nazism in the 1950s, a particular view of the relationship between state and markets came to prevail among the German political elite, particularly in the dominant Christian Democratic Party, that is distinct from that operative historically in, for example, Britain or the United States. So-called ordoliberalism has dominated economic thinking and practice in Germany since the 1950s in the way that Keynesianism did in Britain and the United States after the Second World War down until the 1980s. The key difference is that:

> ordoliberals see the role of the state as setting the framework conditions necessary for markets to operate effectively in the first instance. The state they are happy to live with is not, however, the macroeconomic manager focused on the demand side of the economy that emerged out of British New Liberalism. Rather, the ordoliberal state is a rule setter that enables competition and aids market adjustments through the development of specific economy-wide mechanisms and institutions. (Blyth 2013, 133)

It is this distinctive view of the role of the state that prevented the easy resolution of the crisis through debt forgiveness or mutual fiscal stimulus on the part of the member countries of the Eurozone. Yet, of course, and as noted previously, Germany itself is no longer the isolated territorial economy directing its own fortunes that that this model presumes. Be that as it may, the powerful image of an economy built around "*Ordnungspolitik*" or a rule-based constitutional framework to shape markets but not intervene directly in them guided the development of the Eurozone and to a degree directed economic policy over the course of the Eurozone crisis. The latter can be exaggerated. As various authors have demonstrated, while shaped by ordoliberalism, the policies guiding the handling of the Eurozone crisis have also exhibited pragmatism and variation in terms of which aspects of the *Ordnungspolitik* framework to emphasize (Jacoby 2014; Feld et al. 2015).

Nevertheless, the overall focus of this framework on an appeal to order as the road to stability is worth underlining. This involves, inter alia, imposing strict budgetary discipline on governmental entities, ensuring that business cartels do not develop, providing social safety nets, and ensuring a politics of order and stability. Though often simply associated with a school of economic thinking that, with origins in the early 1930s, came to capture the imagination of political leaders and filtered into German society at large in the 1950s, real historical experience has also entered into strengthening the grip and persistence of this overall perspective even as its relevance to the prospects of the Eurozone has been increasingly in question. Two periods of disastrous monetary inflation in 1923–1924 and immediately after the Second World War led to a search for an alternative to both laissez-faire capitalism and the state-based industrial capitalism of the Nazi period. The popular collective imagination in Germany about the hyperinflation of the Weimar period has been welded to the memory of mass unemployment in the Great Depression (1929–1934) to argue against loose monetary policies as morally dubious as well as threatening to monetary stability and to see anti-inflationary policies as good for growth (Haffert et al. 2021). As an occupying power after 1945, the US government also encouraged an active focus on competition or antitrust policy as an important feature of government policy that was more readily adopted in Germany than, for example, in Italy where there was no such conjuncture with a homegrown stress on limiting cartels (Segreto and Wubs 2014). The resulting "social market economy" of West Germany in the 1950s was thus based on a social contract in which government set rules that privileged price stability, freedom of private contracts, competition between firms and not consumption as the key to stimulating economic growth, and the scaling up from the household as a model for the national economy. The remarkable economic success of West Germany over the course of the next fifty years has been popularly associated with this political-economic recipe.

The argument from a historical experience as more significant for the perpetuation of this framework than just the inertial continuation of a particular academic economic model adopted by policy makers is worth emphasizing. For one thing, this accounts for the general popularity among ordinary Germans of the austerity option for the peripheral countries. A "habit memory" passed on by families and in official discourse has made the threat of inflation, as experienced particularly in the 1920s, the central gauge of monetary policy. Even with no evidence of inflationary tendencies (indeed the opposite trend has been marked), the rhetoric of price stability has dominated popular German discourse (O'Callaghan 2012). This conclusion is reinforced by the fact that the initial design of the Eurozone was popularly associated in Germany with the export of German monetary order to the rest of Europe (Kaelberer 2005). Ordered development is good for others as well as for Germany (e.g., Sinn 2014; Hillebrand 2015).

For another thing, recent German experience in relation to the stagflation turn of the 1970s, reunification in the 1990s, and economic reforms in the early 2000s all suggest how much others might benefit if only they shared the German approach. In the 1970s, German governments strove to commit US governments and others into ending stagflation through increased interest rates and austerity policies. Arguably, then, the turn to neoliberalism and away from Keynesianism in Britain and the United States owes something to German evangelism for strict budgetary rules (Germann 2014). The process of German reunification in the 1990s, judged as being largely successful by West Germans, if not always by the ones from the East being integrated into the new economy, has also reinforced attachment to a focus on order and stability. Yet, as Gerhard Ritter (2011) has shown in considerable detail, the costs of reunification were systematically underestimated and led to much more direct state involvement in achieving some degree of socioeconomic convergence than the conventional "model" would lead one to expect. In response to some of the economic problems arising from reunification and the challenges of globalization, in the early 2000s the German government of the day reformed labor markets to make them more flexible and German firms more competitive in export markets (Kundnani 2015). This successful adaptation while still keeping a close eye on public sector spending is seen as the main reason why the German economy survived the financial crisis relatively unscathed compared to those elsewhere in the Eurozone, particularly those in the southern periphery. *Ordnungspolitik* may have been made in Germany but it is available for export. In the end, however, satisfying the domestic German audience was more important over the course of the Eurozone crisis than shifting ground to enable its resolution (Bulmer 2014).

THE LIMITS OF *ORDNUNGSPOLITIK* IN VARIEGATED CAPITALISM

The idealized German model reflects the social-market economy that did develop successfully in Germany from the 1950s onward. The problem is that it no longer adequately describes the actual workings of the German economy and its relations to the broader global capitalism in which it is now embedded. The point here is not that the German model has "converged" with or been subsumed under some alternative national model, as the varieties of capitalism literature (e.g., Hall and Soskice 2001) would suggest is the only viable substitute, even while skeptical that this is likely. What has happened is that the German economy has been subject to "creeping liberalization" (Streeck and Yamamura 2001, 36). This has happened because of the breakdown of the social consensus upon which the social-market economy relied (cooperative labor relations and so on) and the rising significance of a financial sector in a country in which an industrial bourgeoisie was long dominant politically. Simply focusing on the persistence of institutional arrangements that seemingly distinguish Germany historically can mean missing the slow breakdown of the political settlements underpinning them (Coates 2000). The joint weakening of labor unions and increased mobility of capital across national borders has characterized Germany as much as anywhere else over the past forty years. This is because the German economy is not an "isolated state" but subject to institutional regulation at other levels of governance (including the EU and the Eurozone) and to the same pressures on economic performance from global capital increasingly common worldwide (see the introduction and chapters 1 and 8).

Germany's recent experience, therefore, suggests that *Ordnungspolitik* is as problematic at home as much as it is for foreigners. In the first place, Germany's current economic position is unsustainable. Its large trade surplus has been earned at the expense of corresponding current account deficits of the peripheral countries in crisis (Tooze 2012). Having others adopt its export-based manufacturing economy as a model for growth (implicit in the emphasis on labor market reform as a key to improving productivity) is simply ridiculous when Germany's own growth depends on their not doing so. Even though German firms have diversified their exports to China and elsewhere, they are still heavily dependent on European trading partners including many in the Eurozone. It was German exporters who were the strongest voices behind the Euro project in the 1990s when skepticism prevailed among the most ordoliberal sectors of German public opinion. Beyond the prospect of global stagnation over the next few years, perhaps the major challenge facing the German economy is a demographic one. Over the next fifteen years, Germany is faced with one of the largest increases in old-age dependency ratio of any European country because of a very low fertility rate. This means there will be far fewer people in the working-age bracket to pay taxes for those retired as the increased number of retirees puts increased demands on pensions and healthcare. An influx of younger migrants can temper this shortfall but not that much, since the native population is still much larger than the number of new arrivals (*Economist* 2015).

Second, recent German governments have failed to take advantage of incredibly low interest rates to borrow to pay for improvements in infrastructure, energy, wages, and pensions. Austerity has been damaging at home (e.g., *Economist* 2014). Not only have median wages stagnated since 2000 but spending on public goods such as highways and industrial research and development has grown at a lower rate than in Britain and France. One recent German commentator says that Germany is now a country with outdated infrastructure whose total factor productivity is about one-half what it was in the 1990s (Fratzscher 2014). One indicator that things are not so well at home is the large increase in strikes in the period 2010–2018. Most of these have affected the service sector where most jobs are now concentrated. Export-oriented manufacturing has been much less involved. This has been the thriving sector for the past several years. But progressive privatization of former public services, rising under- and precarious employment, and rising wage differentials and income inequality have contributed to increased labor militancy in other sectors of the economy (Streeck 2015).

Third, and by way of conclusion, the strength of the German economy under the variegated capitalism that has prevailed since the 1970s has long lain in its export-oriented manufacturing (figure 9.4). Alone among the large industrial capitalist countries, it has not only maintained but has actually expanded its prowess globally in this sector. Whether or not this orientation is sustainable in the face of declining research and development, increased foreign competition, and the high probability that the world economy is facing stagnation for the next few years is open to doubt. Yet it has been this success, which does not seem to have much to do with any facet of *Ordnungspolitik* in particular, that has set Germany apart from the rest of the Eurozone. But as mentioned previously, emulating Germany on this score might not only damage the German economy, it would also potentially remove those markets that currently account for some two-thirds of German manufactured exports. Therein lays the real limit to *Ordnungspolitik* at the level of the Eurozone as a whole.

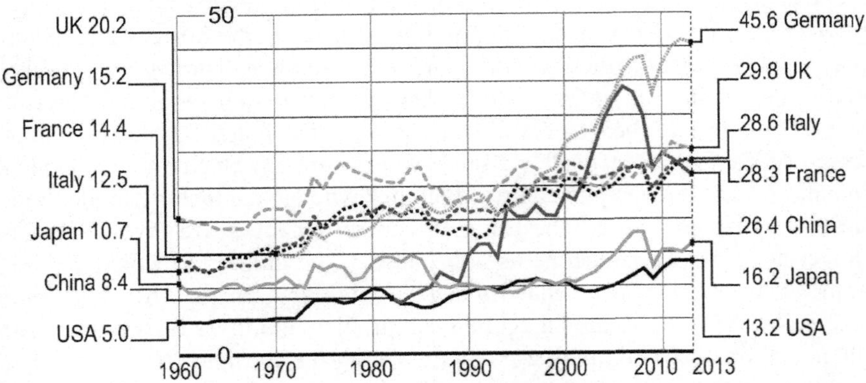

Figure 9.4. Exports as a Percent of GDP for Various Eurozone Countries, the United Kingdom, the United States, Japan, and China, 1960–2013 (World Bank data)

THE TERRITORIAL MISMATCH THESIS AND THE EUROZONE CRISIS

The Eurozone crisis was a crisis based on the application of an idealized model to the construction and management of a currency area that developed in a specific national context, which is no longer useful in describing the economic dilemmas facing that context, and that was absolutely disabling in resolving the crisis. It is clear that acquiring membership in the Eurozone did not require conforming to basic macroeconomic standards (including data reporting) and there were no believable institutional mechanisms to ensure common fiscal goals, coordinate crisis management, or compensate for cyclical differences in boom and bust across the member states. In place of such institutions, practices and norms was the "policy paradigm" (Jessop 2012) based in the German model. Convergence among members would occur if they followed in its footsteps. The gap between the historic precursor for this model, Germany, and other member states was greatest with the peripheral economies of southern Europe. No attention was paid to the "rescaling" of this model from German experience to the Eurozone as a whole. As we have seen, the German economy required that these countries run balance-of-trade deficits with Germany for the German export machine to function. Beyond that, the various peripheral economies had diverse economic strengths and weaknesses, only some of which were complementary to Germany and other northern European countries. The form of governance in the Eurozone developed initially on giving priority to the technocratic anti-inflationary purpose of the European Central Bank was antithetical to the long-standing use of currency devaluations to achieve export competitiveness by governments such as that of Italy.

Together, therefore, the heterogeneity of the economic structures of the member countries and the modeling of the Eurozone regime after the priorities of *Ordnungspolitik* made it impossible to match at the Eurozone level the purported benefits of the German model as it had once operated within Germany. The scaling-up of the model in this way also of course ignored the fact that a "transfer" of the successful German model to failed economies on the fringe of the Eurozone made no sense when Germany itself was embedded in a more variegated capitalism to which its own vaunted historic model bore little or no resemblance. The Eurozone crisis remained irresolvable within the terms set by the Eurozone itself because of the failure to recognize these realities: the territorial mismatch between Germany, on the one hand, as a role model for other national economies, problematic in its own right given the actual character of and the problems facing the German economy today, and the absolute impossibility of establishing at a Eurozone level the terms and conditions for a satisfactory imposition of *Ordnungspolitik* in any shape or form. Though the 2020–2021 pandemic saw some evidence of greater collaboration in creating a common "bailout" fund, questions remain as to how resolved the German government and courts are in making this the model for the future (e.g., *Economist* 2021b, *Financial Times* 2021; Cachia 2021).

CONCLUSION

"German macroeconomic exceptionalism," as Wolfgang Münchau (2014) terms it, needed to figure more centrally in discussions of the Eurozone crisis. Indeed, the real reason it was a crisis was because of the imposition of an austerity model that did not fit the parameters of the crisis itself. This crisis was a crisis of government lending to bail out banks, not primarily one about government overspending. It has not been resolved because the dominant narrative guiding Eurozone management has derived directly from the German tradition of *Ordnungspolitik*. As I hope I have shown, the political-economic model that has derived from this is a terrible guide to policy for exiting from the crisis. First of all, it cannot be applied to such a heterogeneous set of economies as those in the Eurozone. It will not magically suddenly do so through spontaneous action. The Eurozone managers must recognize the "polyphony" at the heart of the enterprise (e.g., Zielonka 2014). Second, *Ordnungspolitik* no longer really represents the variegated character of the German economy itself, which is also today suffering from policies based on its strictures. Third, and finally, the Eurozone crisis is not a crisis of Capital, as such, nor is it simply about the mismatch between monetary policy at one scale (the Eurozone) and fiscal policy at another (the national). It was a crisis brought on by the poor design of the Eurozone founded on a historically anachronistic model of the German economy in the face of global neoliberalism and the competition-state model on which it is based. Until it is recognized as such, no progress will be made in truly resolving the crisis or in rebuilding a Eurozone that matches the real nature of the economies of its member countries including, not least, Germany itself.

V

HIDDEN NO MORE?

10

Conclusion

Who is "Us"? is no longer easily answered, if it ever really was. All sorts of ties bind and govern all of us worldwide without a singular territorial home to report back to. The world is organized on a transversal rather than on a singularly territorial basis with all manner of transnational and global networks and flows drawing distant locations into topological proximity. This has been the main argument of this book as laid out in the introduction and chapter 1 and then developed in various ways in subsequent chapters.

The first three chapters were devoted to how this has happened, with the foundations laid in the historical geography of the United States in the early nineteenth century projected into the world at large as a result of US global prominence and the shadow cast across contemporary world politics by metaphors imported from prior geopolitical epochs (chapters 1–3). The second part of the book addressed the important global roles played historically and potentially by, respectively, the governments of the United States and China (chapters 4 and 5). The third section traced the ways in which (a) the 2007–2008 financial crisis played out in territorial politics within countries around the world particularly in Western Europe and the United States, and (b) in the way the 2020–2021 pandemic was mismanaged under US federalism (chapters 6 and 7). The fourth section explored the emergence of global regulatory agencies with respective chapters examining, first, the regulatory role of the Big Three credit-rating agencies and, second, the regulatory contradictions of the Eurozone in responding to the fallout from the 2007–2008 global financial crisis (chapters 8 and 9). All told, then, the later chapters use the leitmotif of crises to examine the ways in which the current geopolitical order based around globalization grew out of previous eras and adopted varied forms of regulation and management to match the current reality.

Yet much thinking about the world, and thus political action, still rests on understandings that do not reflect the complexity of this contemporary reality but more the projection into the present of the world described in the first part of chapter 2 and the rhetorical conventions described in chapter 3. So, by way of example, and first, reports of declining population sizes among the Great Powers now elicit much concern (e.g., Eberstadt 2019). Some of this is put down to fears of being unable to provide for the increased numbers of elderly dependents as working-age populations shrink. But much of it is seen as undermining the geopolitical potency of the countries in question. The idea of a large population available for sacrifice on the battlefield informs this perspective. Yet, in the twenty-first century, this is enormously backward looking. Will mass armies ever be in vogue again? The main lesson of recent efforts at military interventions by Great Powers, from the United States in Afghanistan and Iraq to Russia in Ukraine, is that they do not turn out as intended. Defense increasingly trumps offense. Indeed, such wars can also have major negative domestic effects, from increased emigration of talented people (as in Russia in 2022) to collapse of trust in government because of the disinformation often accompanying foreign interventions (as in the US since 2007) (Cocco and Ivanova 2022; Luce 2021; Taylor, A. 2022). Investing in human capital in the face of global economic competition and trying to rein in the power of behemoth companies with vast assets and revenue streams beyond their nominal homelands would seem to be better emphases rather than worrying about relative population sizes.

Secondly, in 2021 the US and Chinese governments sparred over the apportionment of blame for the 2020–2021 COVID-19 pandemic, as if they were alone in the world and could score points in a zero-sum game (Christensen 2021b). This completely obscured the geographical complexities about whether the virus came from bats traded in a market that could originally have come from Southeast Asia to whether it was a release from a laboratory that was partly funded by a grant from a US government agency. As they sparred, US-based investors were pouring investment into China (Hale et al. 2021). The rest of the world worried more about the global mismanagement and problematic responses of their own national governments to the pandemic than about who was totally to blame for how it started (e.g., on India see *Economist* 2021c). There was more than enough blame to go around.

We are as yet stuck in an in-between world where Great Powers joust over their relative superiority but at the same time all sorts of hidden geopolitics is actually what is driving much of how the world works. Some of this confusion is down to what Hannah Arendt called "the tragedy of the nation-state" which is the overinvestment in a political form that usually fails to live up to promise in practice. The provision of public goods has long been seen as entirely under the purview of states. Increasingly the logic of interdependence in relation to environment, financial stability, peace, access to water, and knowledge mandates that the spatial scope of provision be extended beyond national borders (Innerarity 2016). The mismanagement of the pandemic by most of the world's national governments is a good example of the failure to do this (e.g., Jones and Hameiri 2021a). But it is not the first nor will it be the last. The hypocritical pretense that all states are equal yet at the same time one or a few necessarily really rule the roost is at the root of the problem. The ways history and other subjects are taught on a country-by-country basis has been particularly important in perpetuating this make-believe (e.g., Manela 2020).

An emphasis on hidden geopolitics is one way of countering this conceit. Three of its features are worth explicit mention. The first is that the world is not nor has ever been neatly divided into territorial silos even if some identities and interests are still highly territorialized. For example, the current world is one in which citizenship is often for sale to the highest bidders and increased immigration, the obvious solution to population decline, is politically problematic across the world if it involves poorer people. Money is increasingly digital and potentially denationalized (Coy 2021). The internet is up for grabs in terms of whether it will be open worldwide or subject to serious territorial closures and thereby lose much of its innovative power to link the world topologically (Khanna and Srinivasan 2021). Yet computer code can potentially provide a noninstitutional basis to regulation (e.g., Livni 2021). But control over the satellite and other services on which the internet depends for planetary-scale delivery are becoming increasingly privatized and beyond much national regulatory authority. Current international regulation is inadequate to the task at hand (e.g., Weber, R. H. 2021). Frequently it is worries about the presumed local and regional impacts of increased global interdependence that inspire most contemporary political concern as manifested, for example, in national populism (Agnew and Shin 2019). In terms of a sound bite: if capital is increasingly global, labor is still predominantly local. Regional and broader national income inequalities have been increasing even as global income inequalities have decreased (Firebaugh 2003; OECD 2016; Milanovic 2018). This excites status anxiety and a sense of being left behind in the places most affected.

Yet the national scale is often increasingly irrelevant or secondary in a world in which flows of goods and investment are placed in terms of the nexus between global business goals and local conditions (Knox et al. 2015; Robinson 2018). So, even as the world's largest companies still come overwhelmingly from the United States, and other parts of the world, particularly Western Europe, Japan, and China also participate massively in terms of shares of total global business activity (*Economist* 2021e), much of the revenues of US multinationals and many of their assets now come from or are located in specific places well beyond their nominal homeland (AEI 2018). Indeed, even as US-headquartered businesses dominate the top ranks of the world's largest firms by revenues, assets, and stock prices, the US territorial economy itself is increasingly less engaged with the global economy to the net detriment of the US population as a whole in terms of investment, trade, and jobs (Djankov et al. 2021). Yet this is much less true for the major metropolitan areas and the specialized industrial zones still intimately tied into the wider world economy. This internal division within the United States shows itself in recent presidential election results with Biden in 2020, for example, winning majorities in counties that account for 70 percent of total US GDP (Muro et al. 2020). Concurrently, it was the national-populist candidate, Donald Trump, who dominated in the "left behind" regions.

Second, there is much contemporary global governance of all sorts, as detailed in previous chapters (particularly chapters 1, 8, and 9). The main problem with this is not only that it is frequently utterly unaccountable to publics at large, it is also not place conscious in acknowledging the different conditions relating to regulation characteristic of different regions and localities (e.g., Brousseau et al. 2012). It is also often both dispersed and fragile (Bulkeley and Schroeder 2012). If states could reorient themselves toward integrative global governance rather than the pretense of total autonomy mentioned above then this would be a real improvement over the current situation (Bartley 2018; Pagden 2021). Even so, there would still be a need for arbitration and regulation beyond the geographic scope of states that have enough difficulty coping with their domestic problems (e.g., Hale 2015; Lake 2021; Wolf 2021c). As more states have drifted toward strongman rule (think of Putin in Russia, Orbán in Hungary, Modi in India, and Trump in the United States as exemplary, to mention just a few) and away from democratic accountability (Guriev and Treisman 2022), it seems churlish to complain that specific organizations such as the European Union and international organizations more broadly are singularly guilty of increasingly personalized and informal governance as opposed to institutionalized accountability (e.g., White 2022). We should challenge the presumption of territorial-state accountability and efficiency against the inequities of all other forms of governance. This was the basic fallacy behind the Brexit fiasco (Agnew 2019b). Reforming and reinvigorating international organizations specializing in functional areas such as the WTO (in trade), WHO (in health), and Interpol (in law enforcement) would be one place to start. Revamping the IMF and the World Bank to create and enforce a truly rules-based order of trade security, environmental sustainability, shorter more durable manufacturing-supply chains, and labor rights rather than allowing the use of resources and monetary privilege for geopolitical leverage and massive income inequalities would also help level and equalize the global playing field (e.g., Foroohar 2022; Gerstle 2022). The alienation of so many countries from contemporary international organizations and what currently go for the "rules" is illustrated by the number of UN delegations representing a majority of the world's population that abstained on a motion in the United Nations' General Assembly condemning the Russian invasion of Ukraine in 2022 (French 2022). Besides improving consistent access by all countries to global institutions, another good initiative would be in encouraging greater international coordination in targeting official corruption, tax evasion, and restricting the massive money laundering afflicting the world mentioned at the outset in the preface (see Michel 2021; Dezenski 2021).

Finally, the emerging problems facing the world, from climate change and biodiversity to pandemics and financial stability, require cooperative and coordinated responses across geographic scales rather than just competitive ones (Brilliant 2021; Carter 2021; Dalby 2021; Goldin 2021; Sun 2021). That was the burden of the arguments in chapters 7 and 9. Here again national states and local governments are hardly redundant but their relative functionality is in question. The answer is not necessarily some sort of global federalism but consistent attention to the ways in which a range of organizations, inter- and nongovernmental, can respond to and enforce rules and regulations that can prepare the world better for the material changes that are present and under way (e.g., Abbott and Faude 2021; Agnew 2002; Abrahamsen and Williams 2009; Perlman 2020; Zürn 2018; Grigorescu 2020; Herold et al. 2021; Barnett et al. 2022). A healthy global geopolitics recognizes the limits of dividing up purposes and policies entirely on a rigidly territorialized basis. The contemporary challenge of managing the negative fallout from the 2020–2021 global pandemic in terms of increasing price inflation and growth gaps between rich and poor countries is an excellent example of a problem that cannot be addressed solely on a country-by-country basis (Douglas and Barnett 2022; Wheatley 2022; James 2022).

Looking backward to the era of the Cold War or to that of late nineteenth- and early twentieth-century inter-imperial rivalry for inspiration as to the future is to ignore that the groundwork for more effective global governance has already begun in all sorts of ways that I have labeled hidden geopolitics. Always thinking that "capturing" this or that state for a more equitable and better-managed world will then change that world has turned out to be a hollow promise. Perhaps it is events like the 2007–2008 financial crisis and the pandemic of 2020–2021 that bring into focus the fact that the world today requires a different response from those of the past. There can be no singular national-geopolitical victors in a world of hidden geopolitics at the planetary scale.

References

Abbott, K. W. and Faude, B. 2021. Choosing low-cost institutions in global governance, *International Theory*, 13: 397–426.

Ablavsky, G. 2019. Empire states: The coming of dual federalism, *Yale Law Journal*, 128: 1792–1865.

Abrahamsen, R. and Williams, M. C. 2009. Security beyond the state: Global security assemblages in international politics, *International Political Sociology*, 3: 1–17.

Abrahamsen, R. et al. 2020. Confronting the international political sociology of the New Right, *International Political Sociology*, 14, 1: 94–107.

Acemoglu, D. 2021a. The dangers of decoupling, *Project Syndicate*, 22 July.

———. 2021b. The supply chain mess, *Project Syndicate*, 2 December.

Acemoglu, D. and Robinson, J. A. 2012. *Why Nations Fail: The Origins of Power, Prosperity and Poverty*. New York: Crown.

———. 2019. *The Narrow Corridor: States, Societies, and the Fate of Liberty*. New York: Penguin.

Acer, E. and Byrne, O. 2017. How the Illegal Immigration Reform and Immigrant Responsibility Act of 1996 has undermined US refugee protection obligations and wasted government resources, *Journal on Migration and Human Security*, 5, 2: 356–78.

Acharya, A. and Buzan, B. 2017. Why is there no non-western international relations theory? Ten years on, *International Relations of the Asia-Pacific*, 17, 3: 341–70.

Adamson, F. and Tsourapas, G. 2019. Migration diplomacy in world politics, *International Studies Perspectives*, 20, 2: 113–28.

Adler-Nissen, R. and Gammeltoft-Hansen, T. 2008. Epilogue: Three layers of a contested concept, in R. Adler-Nissen and T. Gammeltoft-Hansen (eds.), *Sovereignty Games: Instrumentalizing State Sovereignty in Europe and Beyond*. New York: Palgrave Macmillan.

AEI. 2018. Many large US firms sell, hire, and invest more overseas than in the US and they have to think globally not domestically to survive, *Carpe Diem*, Washington, DC: American Enterprise Institute, 13 June.

Agnew, J. 1987. *The United States in the World Economy*. Cambridge: Cambridge University Press.

———. 1994. The territorial trap: The geographical assumptions of international relations theory, *Review of International Political Economy*, 1, 1: 53–80.

———. 1999. North America and the wider world, in F. W. Boal and S. A. Royle (eds.), *North America: A Geographical Mosaic*. London: Arnold.

———. 2002. The limits of federalism in transnational democracy: Beyond the hegemony of the US model, in J. Anderson (ed.), *Transnational Democracy: Political Spaces and Border Crossings*. London: Routledge.

———. 2003. *Geopolitics: Re-Visioning World Politics*, 2nd ed. London: Routledge.

———. 2005. *Hegemony: The New Shape of Global Power*. Philadelphia: Temple University Press.

———. 2007a. Know-where: Geographies of knowledge of world politics, *International Political Sociology*, 1, 2: 138–48.

———. 2007b. No borders, no nations: Making Greece in Macedonia, *Annals of the Association of American Geographers*, 97, 2: 398–422.

———. 2008. Borders on the mind: Re-framing border thinking, *Ethics and Global Politics*, 1, 4: 175–91.

———. 2009. The geopolitics of European freedom and security, in C. Rumford (ed.), *Sage Handbook of European Studies*. London: Sage, 295–311.

———. 2010. Deus Vult: The geopolitics of the Catholic Church, *Geopolitics*, 15, 1: 39–61.

———. 2013. The "new regionalism" and the politics of the regional question, in J. Loughlin et al. (eds.), *Routledge Handbook of Regionalism and Federalism*. London: Routledge, 130–39.

———. 2014. By words alone shall we know: Is the history of ideas enough to understand the world to which our concepts refer?, *Dialogues in Human Geography*, 4, 3: 311–19.

———. 2016. Continuity, discontinuity and contingency, in T. Basaran et al. (eds.), *International Political Sociology: Transversal Lines*. London: Routledge.

———. 2017a. Enduring Russian messianism before and beyond the Russian Revolution, *Geopolitics*, 22: 679–83.

———. 2017b. Too many Scotlands? Place, the SNP and the future of nationalist mobilization, *Scottish Geographical Journal*, 134, 1–2: 5–33.

———. 2018. *Globalization and Sovereignty: Beyond the Territorial Trap*. Lanham, MD: Rowman & Littlefield.

———. 2019a. Low geopolitics and "realtà effettuale," *Rivista Geografica Italiana*, 126, 4: 198–203.

———. 2019b. Taking back control? The myth of territorial sovereignty and the Brexit fiasco, *Territory, Politics, Governance*, 8, 2: 259–72.

———. 2020a. Geoeconomics and the state, in S. Moisio et al. (eds.), *Handbook on the Changing Geographies of the State*. Cheltenham, England: Edward Elgar.

———. 2020b. Soli al mondo: The recourse to "sovereigntism" in contemporary Italian populism, *California Italian Studies*, online.

Agnew, J. and Corbridge, S. 1995. *Mastering Space*. London: Routledge.

Agnew, J. and Mantegna, A. 2018. Territorial politics and economic development, in K. Detterbeck and E. Hepburn (eds.), *Handbook of Territorial Politics*. Cheltenham: Edward Elgar, 306–18.

Agnew, J. and Shin, M. 2019. *Mapping Populism: Taking Politics to the People*. Lanham, MD: Rowman & Littlefield.

Alden, E. 2017. Is border enforcement effective? What we know and what it means, *Journal of Migration and Human Security*, 5, 2: 481–90.

Allen, J. 2003. *Lost Geographies of Power*. Oxford: Blackwell.

———. 2009. Three spaces of power: Territory, networks, plus a topological twist in the tale of domination and authority, *Journal of Power*, 2, 2: 197–212.

———. 2020. Power's quiet reach and why it should exercise us, *Space and Polity*, 24, 3: 408–13.

Allison, G. 2017. *Destined for War: Can America and China Escape the Thucydides Trap?* Boston: Houghton Mifflin.

Almond, G. and Verba, S. 1963. *The Civic Culture: Political Attitudes and Democracy in Five Nations*. Princeton: Princeton University Press.

American Immigration Council. 2016. How the United States Immigration System Works. https://www.americanimmigrationcouncil.org/research/how-united-states-immigration-system-works/

Amighetti, S. and Nuti, A. 2016. A nation's right to exclude and the colonies, *Political Theory*, 44, 4: 541–66.

Anderlini, J. 2021. Jack Ma personifies the contradiction of China's ideology, *Financial Times*, 1 March.

Anderson, B. 1983. *Imagined Communities: Reflections on the Origins and Spread of Nationalism*. London: Verso.

Anderson, J. L. 2021. Is the President of Honduras a narco-trafficker?, *New Yorker*, 8 November.

Andrews, N. and Collins, E. 2022. GOP lawmakers embrace Trump agenda, with or without Trump, *Wall Street Journal*, 3 April.

Appelbaum, B. 2021. Trump wanted to punish China. We're still paying for it, *New York Times*, 24 November.

Ashworth, L. M. 2013. Mapping a new world: Geography and the interwar study of international relations. *International Studies Quarterly*, 57, 1: 138–49.

Atkins, R. 2011. Germany and the Eurozone: Marked by the miracle, *Financial Times*, 20 September.

Auld, G. 2014. *Constructing Private Governance: The Rise and Evolution of Forest, Coffee, and Fisheries Certification*. New Haven: Yale University Press.

Axilrod, S. H. 2009. *Inside the Fed: Monetary Policy and its Management, Martin through Greenspan and Bernanke*. Cambridge, MA: MIT Press.

Baccini, L. and Weymouth, S. 2021. Gone for good: Deindustrialization, white voter backlash, and US presidential voting, *American Political Science Review*, 115, 2: 550–67.

Bagaran, T. et al. (eds.) 2016. *International Political Sociology: Transversal Lines*. London; Routledge.

Baker, D. R. and Court, E. 2020. States sidestep Trump to buy millions of virus tests, *Bloomberg*, 4 August.

Baker, P. 2020. Trump proceeds with post-impeachment purge amid pandemic, *New York Times*, 4 April.

Baldwin, R. 2016. *The Great Convergence: Information Technology and the New Globalization*. Cambridge, MA: Harvard University Press.

Bâli, A. and Rana, A. 2018. Constitutionalism and the American imperial imagination, *University of Chicago Law Review*, 85, 2: 257–92.

Balkin, J. M. and Siegel, R. B. (eds.) 2009. *The Constitution in 2020*. New York: Oxford University Press.

Bandler, J. et al. 2020. Inside the fall of the CDC, *ProPublica*, 15 October.

Barkan, J. 2013. *Corporate Sovereignty: Law and Government under Capitalism*. Minneapolis: University of Minnesota Press.

Barnett, M. N. et al. (eds.) 2022. *Global Governance in a World of Change*. Cambridge: Cambridge University Press.

Barron, D. J. and Frug, G. 2006. Defensive localism, *University of Virginia Journal of Law and Politics*, 21: 261–91.

Bartley, T. 2018. *Rules without Rights: Land, Labor, and Private Authority in the Global Economy*. New York: Oxford University Press.

Bassett, M. T. and Linos, N. 2020. Trump gave up on fighting the virus. Now we're paying for his laziness, *Washington Post*, 14 July.

Batalova, J. and Alperin, E. 2018. Immigrants in the US states with the fastest-growing foreign-born populations, *Migration Policy Institute*, 10 July. https://www.migrationpolicy.org/article/immigrants-us-states-fastest-growing-foreign-born-populations

Beaubien, J. 2020. Americans are dying in the pandemic at rates much higher than in other countries, NPR Radio, 13 October.

Beck, U. 2013. *German Europe*. Cambridge: Polity.

Beer, F. A. and Hariman, R. (eds.) 1996. *Post-Realism: The Rhetorical Turn in International Relations*. East Lansing, MI: Michigan State University Press.

Beer, F. A. and de Landtsheer, C. (eds.) 2004. *Metaphorical World Politics: Rhetorics of Democracy, War and Globalization*. East Lansing, MI: Michigan State University Press.

Beinart, P. 2021. The vacuous phrase at the core of Biden's foreign policy, *New York Times*, 22 June.

Beirich, H. 2018. Trump again chooses anti-immigrant hate group staffer for immigration job, Southern Poverty Law Center, 25 May. https://www.splcenter.org/news/2018/05/25/trump-again-chooses-anti-immigrant-hate-group-staffer-immigration-job

Béland, D. and Lecours, A. 2021. Nationalism and the politics of austerity: Comparing Catalonia, Scotland, and Québec, *National Identities*, 23, 1: 41–57.

Bennett, D. 1995. *The Party of Fear: The American Far Right from Nativism to the Militia Movement*. Chapel Hill: University of North Carolina Press.

Bergen, P. 2019. *Trump and His Generals: The Cost of Chaos*. New York: Penguin.

Bialasiewicz, L. and Minca, C. 2005. Old Europe, new Europe: For a geopolitics of translation, *Area*, 37, 4: 365–72.

Bigo, D. 2011. Pierre Bourdieu and international relations: Power of practices, practices of power, *International Political Sociology*, 5, 3: 225–58.

———. 2016. International political sociology: Rethinking the international through dynamics of power, in T. Basaran et al. (eds.), *International Political Sociology: Transversal Lines*. London: Routledge.

Binici, M. et al. 2018. Are credit rating agencies discredited?, BIS Working Paper No. 704, Basel: Bank for International Settlements.

Blackwill, R. D. and Harris, J. M. 2016. *War by Other Means: Geoeconomics and Statecraft*. Cambridge, MA: Harvard University Press.

Blanchard, E. M. 2013. Constituting China: The role of metaphor in the discourses of early Sino-American relations, *Journal of International Relations and Development*, 16, 2: 177–205.

Blanchette, J. 2021. Xi's gamble: The race to consolidate power and stave off disaster, *Foreign Affairs*, 100, 4 (July/August): 10–19.

Blitzer, J. 2018a. The link between America's lax gun laws and the violence that fuels immigration, *New Yorker*, 22 March.

———. 2018b. Will anyone in the Trump administration ever be held accountable for the zero-tolerance policy?, *New Yorker*, 22 August.

Bloomberg. 2021. China moves forward on credit rating rules as defaults climb, Bloomberg News, 27 March.

Blotcky, A. D. 2021. Donald Trump's "slow-motion coup" is becoming a runaway train, *Salon*, 27 October.

Blouet, B. 2001. *Geopolitics and Globalization in the Twentieth Century*. London: Reaktion.

Blow, C. M. 2018. White extinction anxiety, *New York Times*, 24 June.

Blyth, M. 2013. *Austerity: The History of a Dangerous Idea*. New York: Oxford University Press.

Bolter, J. 2021. It is too simple to call 2021 a record year for migration at the US-Mexico border, *Commentaries*: October, Washington, DC: Migration Policy Institute.

Bordo, M. and James, H. 2013. The European crisis in the context of the history of previous financial crises, Special Conference Paper, Bank of Greece Conference, 23–25 May.

Bradford, A. 2020. *The Brussels Effect: How the European Union Rules the World*. New York: Oxford University Press.

Brake, B. and Katzenstein, P. J. 2013. Lost in translation? Nonstate actors and the transnational movement of procedural law, *International Organization*, 67, 4: 725–57.

Branch, J. 2010. "Colonial reflection" and territoriality: The peripheral origins of sovereign statehood, *European Journal of International Relations*, 18, 2: 277–97.

Briant, P. 2012. *Alexandre des Lumières: Fragments d'histoire europèene*. Paris: Gallimard.

Brigety II, R. E. 2021. The fractured power: How to overcome tribalism, *Foreign Affairs*, March/April.

Brilliant, L. 2021. To fight the global Covid-19 pandemic, we need a global game plan, *Wall Street Journal*, 13 December.

Brousseau, E. et al. (eds.) 2012. *Reflexive Governance for Global Public Goods*. Cambridge, MA: MIT Press.

Brown, W. 2019. *In the Ruins of Neoliberalism: The Rise of Antidemocratic Politics in the West*. New York: Columbia University Press.

Broz, J. L. et al. 2021. Populism in place: The economic geography of the globalization backlash, *International Organization*, 75, 2, 464-94.

Brzezinski, Z. 1997. *The Grand Chessboard: American Primacy and its Geostrategic Imperatives*. New York: Basic.

———. 2006. *The Choice: Global Domination or Global Leadership*. New York: Basic.

Buchanan, B. 2020. *The Hacker and the State: Cyber Attacks and the New Normal of Geopolitics*. Cambridge, MA: Harvard University Press.

Buck, T. 2015. The reel-life struggles of Spain's footloose millennials, *Financial Times*, 16 April.

Budowsky, B. 2021. Chief Justice Roberts warns the Court, the bar and the country, *The Hill*, 14 December.

Bulkeley, H. and Schroeder, H. 2012. Beyond state/non-state divides: Global cities and the governing of climate change, *European Journal of International Relations*, 18, 4: 743–66.

Bulmer, S. 2014. Germany and the Eurozone crisis: Between hegemony and domestic politics. *West European Politics*, 37, 6: 1244–63.

Bump, P. 2018. Most immigrants are in the US legally, something most Americans don't know, *Washington Post*, 28 June.

———. 2020. The circumstances are wildly different; Trump's response is the same, *Washington Post*, 5 April.

Burgis, T. 2015. *The Looting Machine: Warlords, Oligarchs, Corporations, Smugglers, and the Theft of Africa's Wealth*. New York: Public Affairs.

Burton, K. 2021. A country divided: Why England's North-South divide is getting worse, *Geographical Magazine*, May.

Büthe, T. and Mattli, W. 2011. *The New Global Rulers: The Privatization of Regulation in the World Economy*. Princeton, NJ: Princeton University Press.

Buxbaum, H. 2006. Transnational regulatory litigation, *Virginia Journal of International Law* 46, 2: 251–317.

Byun, J. et al. 2021. The geopolitical consequences of Covid-19: Assessing hawkish mass opinion in China, *Political Science Quarterly*, 136: 641–65.

Cachia, J. C. 2021. The Europeanization of the Covid-19 pandemic and the EU's solidarity with Italy, *Contemporary Italian Politics*, 13, 1: 81–104.

Callahan, W. A. 2010. *China: The Pessoptimist Nation*. Oxford: Oxford University Press.

———. 2011. Introduction: Tradition, modernity, and foreign policy in China, in W. A. Callahan and E. Barabantseva (eds.), *China Orders the World: Normative Soft Power and Foreign Policy*. Baltimore: Johns Hopkins University Press.

———. 2015. History, tradition and the China dream: Socialist modernization in the world of great harmony, *Journal of Contemporary China*, 24, 96: 983–1001.

Cammack, P. 2003. The mother of all governments: The World Bank's matrix for global governance, in S. Hughes and R. Wilkinson (eds.), *Global Governance*. London: Routledge.

Campbell, C. 2022. China's embrace of Putin is looking more and more costly, *Time*, 1 April.

Campbell, D. 1992. *Writing Security: US Foreign Policy and the Politics of Identity*. Minneapolis: University of Minnesota Press.

Carlson, A. 2011. Moving beyond sovereignty? A brief consideration of recent changes in China's approach to international order and the emergence of the *tianxia* concept, *Journal of Contemporary China*, 20, 68: 89–102.

Carney, R. W. 2018. *Authoritarian Capitalism: Sovereign Wealth Funds and State-Owned Enterprises in East Asia and Beyond*. Cambridge: Cambridge University Press.

Carter, Z. D. 2021. The real problem with globalization: International crises demand international solutions, *Atlantic*, 19 June.

Cerny P. G. 1995. Globalization and the changing logic of collective action, *International Organization*, 49, 4: 618–38.

———. 2010. The competition state today: From raison d'État to raison du Monde, *Policy Studies*, 31, 1: 5–21.

Chait, J. 2022. Trump, Putin, and the paradox of propaganda, *The National Interest*, 10 April.

Chalfant, M. 2021. Trump haunts Biden vaccine mandate in courts, *The Hill*, 5 December.

Chazen Institute. 2019. The real cost of Trump's trade war, Research Brief, New York: Columbia Business School.

Che, C. 2022. How a book about America's history foretold China's future, *New Yorker*, 21 March.

Cheek, T. 2006. Xi Jilin and the thought work of China's public intellectuals, *China Quarterly*, 186, 186: 401–20.

Cheng, J. 2021. China's Xi lays out vision for a world without a single dominant power, *Wall Street Journal*, 20 April.

Chilton, P. and Lakoff, G. 1995. Foreign policy by metaphor, in C. Schäffner and A. L. Wenden (eds.), *Language and Peace*. Aldershot: Dartmouth.

Chishti, M. and Meissner, D. M. 2021. America's border dilemma, *Foreign Affairs*, 23 November.

Christensen, T. J. 2021a. There will not be a new Cold War: The limits of US-Chinese competition, *Foreign Affairs*, 24 March.

———. 2021b. A modern tragedy? COVID-19 and US-China relations, Policy Brief, Brookings Institution, May.

Clover, C. 1999. Dreams of the Eurasian heartland, *Foreign Affairs*, 78, 2: 9–13.

Coates, D. 2000. *Models of Capitalism: Growth and Stagnation in the Modern Era*. Cambridge: Polity.

Cocco, F. and Ivanova, P. 2022. Ukraine war threatens to deepen Russia's demographic crisis, *Financial Times*, 3 April.

Cochrane, E. 2021. Senate votes to scrap Biden vaccine mandate as Republicans eye 2022, *New York Times*, 8 December.

Coen, D. and Thatcher, M. 2005. The new governance of markets and non-majoritarian regulators, *Governance*, 18, 3: 329–46.

Cohen, M. 2020. White House delivers mixed explanations on Trump's vow to slow down testing, *Politico*, 22 June.

Cohen, S. S. and DeLong, J. B. 2016. *Concrete Economics: The Hamilton Approach to Growth and Policy*. Cambridge, MA: Harvard Business Review.

Coleman, M. 2011. Colonial war: Carl Schmitt's deterriorialization of enmity, in S. Legg (ed.), *Spatiality, Sovereignty and Carl Schmitt: Geographies of the Nomos*. London: Routledge, 127–42.

Coll, S. and Entous, A. 2021. The secret history of the US diplomatic failure in Afghanistan, *New Yorker*, 10 December.

Collins, C. 2021. *The Wealth Hoarders: How Billionaires Pay Millions to Hide Trillions*. Cambridge: Polity.

Cooban, A. 2022. BlackRock says Russia's war is the end of globalization, CNN Business, 24 March.

Cook, N. and Diamond, D. 2020. "A Darwinian approach to federalism:" States confront new reality under Trump, *Politico*, 31 March.

Cooley, A. and Nexon, D. 2020. *Exit from Hegemony: The Unraveling of the American Global Order*. New York: Oxford University Press.

Cooley, A. and Spruyt, H. 2009. *Contracting States: Sovereign Transfers in International Relations*. Princeton, NJ: Princeton University Press.

Connery, C. 1994. Pacific Rim discourse: The U.S. global imaginary in the late Cold War years, *boundary 2*, 21, 1: 30–56.

Council on Foreign Relations. 2015. The credit rating controversy, Backgrounder, Washington, DC: Council on Foreign Relations.

Cowen, D. 2014. *The Deadly Life of Logistics: Mapping Violence in Global Trade*. Minneapolis: University of Minnesota Press.

Coy, P. 2021. Can we trust what's happening to money?, *New York Times*, 10 December.

Creswell, J. et al. 2011. Behind S&P's downgrade, a committee that acts in private, *New York Times*, 8 August.

Crouch, C. 2011. *The Strange Non-Death of Neoliberalism*. Cambridge: Polity.

Csomós, G. and Derudder, B. 2012. European cities as command and control centres, 2006–11, GaWC Research Bulletin 402, 12 July.

Cumings, B. 1998. Rimspeak; or, the discourse of the "Pacific Rim," in A. Dirlik (ed.), *What Is in a Rim?: Critical Perspectives on the Pacific Region Idea*, 2nd ed. Lanham, MD: Rowman & Littlefield.

Dainotto, R. 2000. A South with a view: Europe and its other. *Nepantla: Views from South*, 1, 2: 375–90.

———. 2007. *Europe (In Theory)*. Durham, NC: Duke University Press.

Dalby, S. 2021. Unsustainable borders: Globalization in a climate-disrupted world, *Borders in Globalization Review*, 2, 2: 26–37.

Dalrymple, W. 2019. *The Anarchy: The East India Company, Corporate Violence, and the Pillage of an Empire*. London: Bloomsbury.

Davies, H. 2022. Will Western sanctions change the global financial system? *Project Syndicate*, 28 April.

Davis, J. H. and Shear, M. D. 2018. How Trump came to enforce a practice of separating migrant families, *New York Times*, 16 June.

Deaton, A. 2020. America's compromised state, *Project Syndicate*, 17 July.

Delong, J. B. 2021. Xi's historic mistake, *Project Syndicate*, 2 June.

Dempsey, H. et al. 2022. Can the EU wean itself off Russian gas?, *Financial Times*, 18 April.

Der Derian, J. and Shapiro, M. (eds.) 1989. *International/Intertextual Relations: Postmodern Readings of World Politics*. Lexington, MA: Lexington Books.

Desai, M. 2002. *Marx's Revenge: The Resurgence of Capitalism and the Death of Statist Socialism*. London: Verso.

Deudney, D. H. 1995. The Philadelphian system: Sovereignty, arms control, and balance of power in the American states-union, circa 1787–1861, *International Organization*, 49, 2: 191–228.

———. 2000. Geopolitics as theory: Historical security materialism, *European Journal of International Relations*, 6, 1: 77–107.

Devega, C. 2018. Trump's border violence is sick entertainment for his fans and they love it, *Salon*, 29 November.

Devine, P. 2021. Changing identities in Northern Ireland, *ARK: Research Update*, 138: March.

Dezenski, E. 2021. An international anti-corruption court is needed to deter kleptocrats, *Financial Times*, 21 June.

Dickerson, C. 2018. Who tracks migrant children who enter the US alone? Don't ask us, 4 agencies say, *New York Times*, 16 August.

Dizard, J. 2015. The future of Greek financial negotiations is ancient history, *Financial Times*, 17 April.

Djankov, S. et al. 2021. The United States has been disengaging from the global economy, Washington, DC: Peterson Institute for International Economics, 19 April.

Dobrokhotov, L. 2021. Dopo la botta, la Russia è di nuovo sé stessa, *Limes: Rivista Italiana di Geopolitica*, 6: 49–58.

Dodson, S. 2003. Vectoral federalism, *Georgia State University Law Review*, 20: 393–458.

Dolan, F. 1994. *Allegories of America: Narratives-Metaphysics-Politics*. Ithaca, NY: Cornell University Press.

Domonoske, C. and Gonzales, R. 2018. What we know: Family separation and "zero tolerance" at the border, NPR National, 19 June. https://www.npr.org/2018/06/19/621065383/

Donato, K. M. and Massey, D. S. 2016. Twenty-first century globalization and illegal migration, *Annals of the American Academy of Political and Social Science*, 666, 1: 7–26.

Doshi, R. 2021. *The Long Game: China's Grand Strategy to Displace American Order*. New York: Oxford University Press.

Douglas, J. and Barnett, A. 2022. How Covid-19 has widened the gap between rich and poor countries, *Wall Street Journal*, 14 January.

Drake, B. S. and Gibson, E. 2018. Vanishing protection: Access to asylum at the border, *CUNY Law Review*, 21: 91–142.

Drezner, D. 2020. Promises made, promises broken: Will it matter?, *Washington Post*, 14 April.

Drulák, P. 2006. Motion, container and equilibrium: Metaphors in the discourse about European integration. *European Journal of International Relations*, 12, 4: 499–531.

Duara, P. 1995. *Rescuing History from the Nation: Questioning Narratives of Modern China*. Chicago: University of Chicago Press.

———. 2015. *The Crisis of Global Modernity*. Cambridge: Cambridge University Press.

Du Mez, K. K. 2020. *Jesus and John Wayne: How White Evangelicals Corrupted their Faith and Fractured a Nation*. New York: Liveright.

Dutkiewicz, P. et al. (eds.) 2021. *Hegemony and World Order: Reimagining Power in Global Politics*. London: Routledge.

Earle, C. 2003. *The American Way: A Geographical History of Crisis and Recovery*. Lanham, MD: Rowman & Littlefield.

Earle, E. M. 1926. Problems of Eastern and Southeastern Europe. *Proceedings of the Academy of Political Science in the City of New York*, 12, 1: 265–68.

Eberstadt, N. 2019. With great demographics comes great power, *Foreign Affairs*, July/August.

Eckes Jr., A. E. and Zeiler, T. W. 2003. *Globalization and the American Century*. New York: Cambridge University Press.

Economist. 1960. The white Africans-advice and consent, October 15: 215–16.

———. 2014. Germany's flagging economy: Build some bridges and roads, Mrs Merkel. The German government should invest money in infrastructure, not worry about balancing its budget, 18 October.

———. 2015. The force assaulting the Euro: Europe's ageing population poses a long-term threat to monetary union, 6 June.

———. 2018. "When good men do nothing": America's immigration system is broken, 30 June.

———. 2020a. America's backwards coronavirus strategy, 22 July.

———. 2020b. Why the bond market might keep America's next president awake at night, 4 November.

———. 2021a. Down to the wire, 3 April.

———. 2021b. Will the dollar stay dominant? Digital money may pose a new threat to dollar hegemony, 8 May.

———. 2021c. India's national government looks increasingly hapless, 8 May.

———. 2021d. What could a new system for taxing multinationals look like?, 15 May.

———. 2021e. The new geopolitics of global business, 5 June.

———. 2021f. What's the Japanese for QAnon? Social media are turbocharging the export of America's political culture, 12 June.

———. 2021g. Decoupling is the last thing on business leaders' minds, 27 November.

———. 2022. Russia's attempt to sanction-proof its economy has been in vain, 2 March.

Economy, E. 2021. China's inconvenient truth: Official triumphalism conceals societal fragmentation, *Foreign Affairs*, 28 May.

Edelman, A. 2020. Trump: Government shouldn't rescue states and cities struggling under pandemic, NBC News, 27 April.

Edling, M. M. 2003. *A Revolution in Favor of Government: Origins of the US Constitution and the Making of the American State*. New York: Oxford University Press.

Edsall, T. B. 2021a. There's an exodus from the "Star Cities," and I have good news and bad news, *New York Times*, 12 May.

———. 2021b. How to tell when your country is past the point of no return, *New York Times*, 15 December.

Eggen, D. 2011. Standard and Poor's, others lobby government while rating its credit, *Washington Post*, 10 August.

Eichengreen, B. 2011. *Exorbitant Privilege: The Rise and Fall of the Dollar and the Future of the International Monetary System*. New York: Oxford University Press.

———. 2014. The Eurozone crisis: The theory of optimum currency areas bites back, Notenstein Academy White Paper Series, March.

Eilstrup-Sangiovanni, M. and Sharman, J. 2021. Enforcers beyond borders: Transnational NGOs and the enforcement of international law, *Perspectives on Politics*, 19, 1: 131–47.

Elden, S. 2011. Reading Schmitt geopolitically: Nomos, territory and Grossraum, in S. Legg (ed.), *Spatiality, Sovereignty and Carl Schmitt: Geographies of the Nomos*. London: Routledge, 91–105.

Ellis, M. and Wright, R. 1998. The balkanization metaphor in the analysis of U.S. immigration. *Annals of the Association of American Geographers*, 88, 4: 686–98.

Erman, E. and Uhlin, A. (eds.) 2010. *Legitimacy beyond the State? Re-examining the Democratic Credentials of Transnational Actors*. Basingstoke, UK: Palgrave Macmillan.

Ernst, J. and Malkin, E. 2018. Honduran President's brother, arrested in Miami, is charged with drug trafficking, *New York Times*, 26 November.

Esarey, A. and Qiang, X. 2008. Political expression in the Chinese blogosphere: Below the radar, *Asian Survey*, 48, 5: 752–72.

European CEO. 2020. New players are finally disrupting the credit rating sector, *European CEO*, 6 May.

Fan, R. (ed.) 2011. *The Renaissance of Confucianism in Contemporary China*. Dordrecht, Netherlands: Springer.

Fazal, T. M. 2022. The return of conquest? Why the future of global order hinges on Ukraine, *Foreign Affairs*, May/June.

Feld, L. P., Köhler, E. A. and Nientiedt, D. 2015. Ordoliberalism, pragmatism and the Eurozone crisis: How the German tradition shaped economic policy in Europe, CESifo Working Paper No. 5368, May.

Ferguson, N. 2003. Empire or hegemony?, *Foreign Affairs*, 82, 2: 151–64.

Fernandes, B. et al. 2021. US state-level interventions related to COVID-19 vaccine mandates, *Journal of the American Medical Association*, 327, 2: 178–9.

Fettweis, C. 2003. Revisiting Mackinder and Angell: The obsolescence of Great Power geopolitics, *Comparative Strategy*, 22: 109–29.

Financial Times. 2021. How to deal with a problem like Karlsruhe, Editorial Board, *Financial Times*, 29 March.
Firebaugh, G. 2003. *The New Geography of Global Income Inequality*. Cambridge, MA: Harvard University Press.
Fisher, C. A. 1962. Southeast Asia: The Balkans of the Orient?, *Geography*, 47, 4: 347–67.
Fisher, M. and Taub, A. 2018. Trump wants to make it hard to get asylum. Other countries feel the same, *New York Times*, 2 November.
Fitzmaurice, A. 2014. *Sovereignty, Property and Empire, 1500–2000*. Cambridge: Cambridge University Press.
Foot, R. and Goh, E. 2019. The international relations of East Asia: A new research prospectus, *International Studies Review*, 21, 3: 398–423.
Foroohar, R. 2021. Bitcoin's rise reflects America's decline, *Financial Times*, 14 February.
———. 2022. It's time for a new Bretton Woods, *Financial Times*, 17 April.
Foucault, M. 2010. *Security, Territory, Population*. London: Picador.
Foucher, M. 2007. *L'obsession des frontières*. Paris: Perrin.
Fouquin, M. and Hugot, J. 2016. *Two Centuries of Bilateral Trade: 1827–2014*. Paris: CEPII.
Frank, D. 2018. *The Long Honduran Night: Resistance, Terror and the United States in the Aftermath of the Coup*. Chicago: Haymarket.
Frank, T. 2008. *The Wrecking Crew: How Conservatives Ruined Government, Enriched Themselves, and Beggared the Nation*. New York: Holt.
Fraser, N. 2013. "A triple movement?" Parsing the politics of crisis after Polanyi, *New Left Review*, 81, 81: 119–32.
Fratzscher, M. 2014. *Die Deutschland-Illusion: Warum wir unsere Wirtschaft überschätzen und Europa brauchen*. Munich: Carl Hanser Verlag.
French, H. W. 2022. Why the world isn't really united against Russia. Global institutions have long relegated much of the world to second-class status, *Foreign Policy*, 19 April.
Friedberg, A. L. 2011. *A Contest for Supremacy: China, America, and the Struggle for Mastery in Asia*. New York: Norton.
Friedman, T. 2000. *The Lexus and the Olive Tree*. New York: Anchor.
———. 2005. *The World Is Flat: A Brief History of the Twenty-First Century*. New York: Farrar, Straus and Giroux.
Frug, G. 2001. A legal history of cities, in N. Blomley et al. (eds.), *The Legal Geo-graphies Reader*. Oxford: Blackwell.
Frye, T. 2021. *Weak Strongman: The Limits of Power in Putin's Russia*. Princeton, NJ: Princeton University Press.
Gabriel, T. and Lerer, L. 2020. Who are the voters behind Trump's higher approval rating?, *New York Times*, 31 March.
Ganesh, J. 2020. US Republicans must make peace with the state, *Financial Times*, 21 October.
———. 2021a. The US is too changed since the Cold War to repeat it, *Financial Times*, 13 April.
———. 2021b. Republicans win too often to ever change, *Financial Times*, 28 April.
———. 2021c. The US is not responsible for China's rise, *Financial Times*, 15 December.
Gapper, J. 2015. Deutsche Bank is still stuck in the middle of global finance, *Financial Times*, June 7.
Garcia, M. C. 2006. *Seeking Refuge: Central American Migration to Mexico, the United States, and Canada*. Berkeley: University of California Press.
Garde, P. 2004. *Le discours balkanique. Des mots et des hommes*. Paris: Fayard.
Gardels, N. 2020. The withering away of the state: Americans are complicit with their own demise, *Noema*, 14 August.
———. 2021. Planetary politics when the nation-state falters, *Noema*, 3 September.
Gardner, D. 2012a. Spain-style devolution can be part of a crisis solution. *Financial Times*, 17 May.

———. 2012b. Spain: Autonomy under fire, *Financial Times*, 16 August.

Garrett, A. D. 2008. The corporation as sovereign, *Maine Law Review*, 60, 1: 130–64.

Garrett, G. and Rodden, J. 2003. Globalization and fiscal decentralization, in M. Kahler and D. A. Lake (eds.), *Governance in a Global Economy: Political Authority in Transition*. Princeton: Princeton University Press.

Genschel, P. and Seelkopf, L. 2015. The competition state: The modern state in a global economy, in J. D. Stephens et al. (eds.), *The Oxford Handbook of the Transformations of the State*. Oxford: Oxford University Press.

Germann, J. 2014. German "grand strategy" and the rise of neoliberalism, *International Studies Quarterly*, 58, 4: 706–16.

Gerson, M. 2020. The dangerous conservative campaign against expertise, *Washington Post*, 9 April.

Gerstle, G. 2022. *The Rise and Fall of the Neoliberal Order: America and the World in the Free Market Era*. New York: Oxford University Press.

Giavazzi, F. 2015. Greeks chose poverty, let them have their way, *Financial Times*, 9 June.

Giles, C. 2015. How to deal with a problem child like Greece, *Financial Times*, 19 April.

Gilli, A. and Gilli, M. 2019. Why China has not caught up yet: Military-technological superiority and the limits of imitation, reverse engineering, and cyber espionage, *International Security*, 43, 3: 141–89.

Glasser, S. B. 2020. A President unequal to the moment, *New Yorker*, 12 March.

———. 2021. What does national security even mean any more, after January 6th and the pandemic?, *New Yorker*, 4 March.

Glenny, M. 2021. The Colonial Pipeline cyber attack is a warning of worse to come, *Financial Times*, 14 May.

Gerstle, G. 2015. *Liberty and Coercion: The Paradox of American Government from the Founding to the Present*. Princeton, NJ: Princeton University Press.

Gessen, M. 2018. How the media normalizes Trump's anti-immigrant rhetoric, *New Yorker*, 25 October.

Gibney, M. J. 2015. Refugees and justice between states, *European Journal of Political Theory*, 14, 4: 448–63.

Goettlich, K. 2018. The rise of linear borders in world politics, *European Journal of International Relations*, 25, 1: 203–28.

Goldin, I. 2021. *Rescue: From Global Crisis to a Better World*. London: Sceptre.

Goldstein, A. 2020. China's grand strategy under Xi Jinping: Reassurance, reform, and resistance, *International Security*, 45, 1: 164–201.

Goldstone, L. 2021. The Supreme Court's worship of originalism is destroying judicial review, *Slate*, 9 December.

Goldthau, A. and Hughes, L. 2021. Saudi on the Rhine? Explaining the emergence of private governance in the global oil market, *Review of International Political Economy*, 28, 5: 1410–32.

Goodman, J. D. 2021. Helicopters and high-speed chases: Inside Texas' push to arrest migrants, *New York Times*, 11 December.

Gorman, C. S. 2017. Redefining refugees: Interpretive control and the bordering work of legal categorization in US asylum law, *Political Geography*, 58: 36–45.

Gowa, J. 1983. *Closing the Gold Window: Domestic Politics and the End of Bretton Woods*. Ithaca, NY: Cornell University Press.

Graff, G. M. 2021. After 9/11, the US got almost everything wrong: A mission to rid the world of "terror" and "evil" led America in tragic directions, *Atlantic*, 8 September.

Grahl, J. 2001. Globalized finance: The challenge to the Euro, *New Left Review*, 8: 23–47.

Gramlich, J. and Scheller, A. 2021. What's happening at the US-Mexico border in 7 charts, Pew Research Center, 9 November.

Gramm, P. and Toomey, P. 2021. Trump's protectionist failure, *Wall Street Journal*, 2 March.

Greene, M. 2022. King dollar is in no danger of losing its financial crown, *Financial Times*, 13 April.

Greer, S. 2010. Territorial politics in hard times: The welfare state under pressure in Germany, Spain, and the United Kingdom, *Environment and Planning C Government and Policy*, 28, 3: 405–19.

Gregory, D. 1994. *Geographical Imaginations*. Oxford: Blackwell.

Grigorescu, A. 2020. *The Ebb and Flow of Global Governance: Intergovernmentalism versus Nongovernmentalism in World Politics*. Cambridge: Cambridge University Press.

Guay, T. 2000. Local government and global politics: The implications of Massachusetts' "Burma Law," *Political Science Quarterly*, 115, 3: 353–76.

Guénard, F. 2022. "The tragedy has never left us." On the war in Ukraine: Interview with Bruno Cabanes, *La Vie des Idées*, 18 April.

Guilhot, N. 2008. The realist gambit: Postwar American political science and the birth of IR theory, *International Political Sociology*, 2: 281–304.

Guriev, S. and Treisman, D. 2022. *Spin Dictators: The Changing Face of Tyranny in the 21st Century*. Princeton, NJ: Princeton University Press.

Guzzini, S. (ed.) 2012. *The Return of Geopolitics in Europe? Social Mechanisms and Foreign Policy Identity Crisis*. Cambridge: Cambridge University Press.

Haffajee, R. L. and Mello, M. M. 2020. Thinking globally, acting locally—The US response to Covid-19, *New England Journal of Medicine*, 2 April.

Haffert, L. et al. 2021. Misremembering Weimar: Hyperinflation, the Great Depression, and German collective economic memory, *Economics and Politics*, online first.

Hakelberg, L. and Rixen, T. 2021. Is neoliberalism still spreading? The impact of international cooperation on capital taxation, *Review of International Political Economy*, 28, 5: 1142–68.

Hale, T. 2015. The rule of law in the global economy: Explaining intergovernmental backing for private commercial tribunals, *European Journal of International Relations*, 21, 3: 483–512.

Hale, T. et al. 2021. Wall Street's new love affair with China, *Financial Times*, 28 May.

Hall, B. et al. 2020. Europe's regional leaders chafe at curbs from above as second wave hits, *Financial Times*, 25 October.

Hall, P. A. 2014. Varieties of capitalism and the Euro crisis, *West European Politics*, 37, 6: 1223–43.

Hall, P. A. and Soskice, D. 2001. *Varieties of Capitalism: The Institutional Foundations of Comparative Advantage.* Oxford: Oxford University Press.

Halper, S. and Clarke, J. 2007. *The Silence of the Rational Center: Why American Foreign Policy Is Failing.* New York: Basic.

Halperin, S. and Palan, R. (eds.) 2015. *Legacies of Empire: Imperial Roots of the Contemporary Global Order*. Cambridge: Cambridge University Press.

Hameiri, S. and Jones, L. 2015. Rising powers and state transformation: The case of China, *European Journal of International Relations*, 22: 72–98.

Hamilton, A. et al. 2014 [1788]. *The Federalist Papers*. Mineola, NY: Dover.

Hamilton, P. E. 2021. *Made in Hong Kong: Transpacific Networks and a New History of Globalization.* New York: Columbia University Press.

Harter, P. 2012. The white elephants that dragged Spain into the red, *BBC News Magazine*, 26 July.

Hartz, L. 1955. *The Liberal Tradition in America*. New York: Harcourt Brace.

Harvey, D. 2011. *The Enigma of Capital and the Crises of Capitalism*. London: Profile.

Hass, R. 2021. China is not ten feet tall: How alarmism undermines American strategy, *Foreign Affairs*, 3 March.

Hawkes, T. 1977. *Structuralism and Semiotics*. Berkeley: University of California Press.

Hayton, B. 2020. *The Invention of China*. New Haven: Yale University Press.

Heilmann, S. 2011. Policy-making through experimentation: The formation of a distinctive policy process, in S. Heilmann and E. J. Perry (eds.), *Mao's Invisible Hand: The Political Foundations of Adaptive Governance in China*. Cambridge, MA: Harvard University Press.

Heiss, M. A. 2002. The evolution of the imperial idea and US national identity, *Diplomatic History*, 26, 4: 511–40.

Henderson, A. 2010. Why regions matter: Sub-state polities in comparative perspective, *Regional and Federal Studies*, 20, 4–5: 439–45.

Herold, J. et al. 2021. Why national ministries consider the policy advice of international bureaucracies: Survey evidence from 106 countries, *International Studies Quarterly*, online first.

Herrera, J. 2018. A memo reveals how the Trump administration built a family separation policy while denying the policy existed, *Pacific Standard*, 25 September.

Heuman, A. N. and González, A. 2018. Trump's essentialist border rhetoric: Racial identities and dangerous liminalities, *Journal of Intercultural Communication*, 47: 326–42.

Heyer, K. E. 2018. Internalized borders: Immigration ethics in the age of Trump, *Theological Studies*, 79, 1: 146–64.

Hibbing, J. R. 2020. *The Securitarian Personality: What Really Motivates Trump's Base and Why It Matters for the Post-Trump Era*. New York: Oxford University Press.

Higgins, M. 2021. Biden and the border security-industrial complex, *New York Review of Books*, 2 March.

Hille, K. 2022. Russia's invasion of Ukraine sparks fierce debate in China, *Financial Times*, 23 March.

Hillebrand, R. 2015. Germany and its Eurozone crisis policy: The impact of the country's ordoliberal heritage, *German Politics and Society*, 33, 1: 6–24.

Himmelstein, D. U. and Woolhandler, S. 2016. Public health's falling share of US health spending, *American Journal of Public Health*, 106, 1: 56–57.

Hirschman, A. O. 1991. *The Rhetoric of Reaction: Perversity, Futility, Jeopardy*. Cambridge, MA: Harvard University Press.

Ho, B. T. E. 2016. About face—The relational dimension in Chinese IR discourse, *Journal of Contemporary China*, 25, 98: 307–20.

Hoffmann, A. 2021. The transnational and the international: From critique of statism to transversal lines, *Cambridge Review of International Affairs*, online first.

Hofstadter, R. 2008. *The Paranoid Style in American Politics*, rev. ed. New York: Vintage.

Hollinger, P. 2021. Russian satellite debris is a wake-up call for emerging space industry, *Financial Times*, 16 November.

Holpuch, A. 2021. Missouri withheld data showing effectiveness of mask mandates, *New York Times*, 2 December.

Holsti, K. J. 1991. *Peace and War: Armed Conflicts and International Order, 1648–1989*. New York: Cambridge University Press.

Hopewell, K. 2016. *Breaking the WTO: How Emerging Powers Disrupted the Neoliberal Project*. Stanford, CA: Stanford University Press.

Horton, R. 2020. *The COVID-19 Catastrophe: What's Gone Wrong and How to Stop It Happening Again*. Cambridge, UK: Polity.

Howland, D. and White, L. (eds.) 2009. *The State of Sovereignty: Territories, Laws, Populations*. Bloomington, IN: Indiana University Press.

Hsu, A. 2021. As NYC sets broad vaccine mandate for workers, federal vaccine rules remain blocked, NPR, 7 December.

Huang, Y. and Levy, J. 2021. The shrinking Chinese state, *Foreign Policy*, 10 March.

Hughes, C. 2011. Reclassifying Chinese nationalism: The geopolitik turn, *Journal of Contemporary China*, 20, 71: 601–20.

Hurd, E. S. 2018. The border president, *Boston Review*, 28 June.

Ignatius, A. 2021. "Americans don't know how capitalist China is," *Harvard Business Review*, May/June: 61–63.

Ignatius, D. 2021. Putin barrels toward invading Ukraine, encouraged by Trump, *Washington Post*, 9 December.

Inayatullah, N. and Rupert, M. 1994. Hobbes, Smith, and the problem of mixed ontologies in neorealist IPE, in S. J. Rosow, N. Inayatullah, and M. Rupert (eds.), *The Global Economy as Political Space*. Boulder, CO: Lynne Rienner.

Ince, O. U. 2014. Primitive accumulation, new enclosures, and global land grabs: A theoretical intervention, *Rural Sociology*, 79, 1: 104–31.

Ingham, G. 1984. *Capitalism Divided? The City and Industry in British Social Development*. London: Palgrave Macmillan.

Innerarity, D. 2016. *Governance in the New Global Disorder: Politics for a Post-Sovereign Society*. New York: Columbia University Press.

Irwin, D. A. 2020. Trade truths will outlast Trump, *Wall Street Journal*, 19 November.

Jackson, M. 2002. *The Politics of Storytelling: Violence, Transgression and Intersubjectivity*. Copenhagen: Museum Tusculanum.

Jackson, R. H. 1993. *Quasi-States: Sovereignty, International Relations and the Third World*. Cambridge: Cambridge University Press.

Jacoby, W. 2014. The politics of the Eurozone crisis: Two puzzles behind the German consensus, *German Politics and Society*, 32, 2: 70–85.

Jakobson, L. and Manuel, R. 2016. How are foreign-policy decisions made in China?, *Asia and the Pacific Policy Studies*, 3, 1: 101–10.

James, H. 2021a. Globalization's coming golden age, *Foreign Affairs*, May/June: 10–19.

———. 2021b. A little geopolitics is a dangerous thing, *Project Syndicate*, 29 June.

———. 2022. Inflation may pave the way to a new era of globalisation, *Financial Times*, 4 April.

Jameson, F. 1991. *Postmodernism, or, The Cultural Logic of Late Capitalism*. Durham, NC: Duke University Press.

Jentleson, B. W. 2021. Be wary of China threat inflation, *Foreign Policy*, 30 July.

Jesné, F. 2004. Les frontières balkaniques: Frontières européenes ou frontière de l'Europe?, in G. Pécout (ed.), *Penser les frontières de l'Europe du XIXe au XXIe siècle*. Paris: PUF.

Jessop, B. 2010. The "return" of the national state in the current crisis of the world market, *Capital and Class*, 34, 1: 38–43.

———. 2012. The world market, variegated capitalism, and the crisis of European integration, in P. Nousios et al. (eds.), *Globalisation and European Integration: Critical Approaches to Regional Order and International Relations*. London: Routledge, 91–111.

———. 2016. Territory, politics, governance and multispatial metagovernance, *Territory, Politics, Governance*, 4, 1: 8–32.

Jiang Rong (Lu Jiamin). 2008. *Lang tuteng* [*Wolf Totem*], Wuhan: Changjiang wenyi chubanshe, 2004. Translated into English as *Wolf Totem*. London: Penguin.

John, A. 2020. From "birther" to "Obamagate" to "treason." Trump fueled his political career with unfounded theories against Obama. Here are a few falsehoods, *Los Angeles Times*, 29 June.

Johnson, S. and Ustenko, O. 2022. Russia is finished as a major energy power, *Project Syndicate*, 31 March.

Jones, H. 2021. Britain told to "go into battle" for the City of London, Reuters, 20 May.

Jones, L. and Hameiri, S. 2021a. COVID-19 and the failure of the neoliberal regulatory state, *Review of International Political Economy*, online first.

———. 2021b. *Fractured China: How State Transformation Is Shaping China's Rise*. Cambridge: Cambridge University Press.

Jones, S. et al. 2022. "A serious failure": Scale of Russia's military blunders becomes clear, *Financial Times*, 11 March.

Jozuka, E. 2019. How Honda survived a trade war with the US and won over Americans, CNN Business, 26 June.

Kaelberer, M. 2005. Deutschmark nationalism and Europeanized identity: Exploring identity aspects of Germany's adoption of the Euro, *German Politics*, 14, 3: 283–96.

Kahler, M. 1993. International relations: Still an American social science?, in L. B. Miller and M. J. Smith (eds.), *Ideas and Ideals: Essays on Politics in Honor of Stanley Hoffmann*. Boulder, CO: Westview Press.

Kahler, M. and Walter, B. F. (eds.) 2006. *Territoriality and Conflict in an Era of Globalization*. New York: Cambridge University Press.

Kaplan, R. D. 2010. The geography of Chinese power: How far can Beijing reach on land and sea?, *Foreign Affairs*, 89, 7: 22–41.

Katsikas, D. 2010. Non-state authority and global governance, *Review of International Studies*, 36, 1: 113–35.

Keane, J. 2003. *Global Civil Society?* Cambridge: Cambridge University Press.

Kearns, G. 2009. *Geopolitics and Empire: The Legacy of Halford Mackinder*. Oxford: Oxford University Press.

Keith, R. C. 2009. *China from the Inside Out: Fitting the People's Republic into the World*. London: Pluto.

Kennedy, D. 2007. Essay and reflection: On the American empire from a British imperial perspective, *International History Review*, 29, 1: 83–108.

Kennedy, D. W. 2008. The mystery of global governance, *Ohio Northern University Law Review*, 34: 827–60.

Kennedy, P. 1986. *The Rise and Fall of the Great Powers*. New York: Basic.

Kennedy, S. 2008. China's emerging credit rating industry: The official foundations of private authority, *China Quarterly*, 193, 193: 65–83.

Kerwin, D. 2018. From IIRIRA to Trump: Connecting the dots to the current US immigration policy crisis, *Journal on Migration and Human Security*, 6, 3: 192–204.

———. 2021. Real needs, not fictitious crises account for the situation at US-Mexican border, Center for Migration Studies, Briefing, 3 March.

Ketcham, R. ed. 1986. *The Anti-Federalist Papers and the Constitutional Convention Debates*. New York: New American Library.

Kettl, D. F. 2020. *The Divided States of America: Why Federalism Doesn't Work*. Princeton, NJ: Princeton University Press.

Khan, S. W. 2021. Wolf Warriors killed China's grand strategy, *Foreign Policy*, 28 May.

Khanna, P. and Srinivasan, B. S. 2021. Great Protocol Politics: The 21st century doesn't belong to China, the United States, or Silicon Valley. It belongs to the internet, *Foreign Policy*, 11 December.

Khazan, O. 2020. The most American COVID-19 failure yet: Contact tracing works almost everywhere else. Why not here?, *Atlantic*, 31 August.

Khong, Y. F. 1992. *Analogies at War: Korea, Munich, Dien Bien Phu, and the Vietnam Decisions of 1965*. Princeton, NJ: Princeton University Press.

Kilgore, E. 2020. Red America may blame Blue America for coronavirus, *New York Magazine*, 20 March.

Kim, H. J. 2016. Will IR theory with Chinese characteristics be a powerful alternative?, *Chinese Journal of International Politics*, 9, 1: 59–79.

King, C. 2020. How a Great Power falls apart: Decline is invisible from the inside, *Foreign Affairs*, 30 June.

King, S. D. 2017. *Grave New World: The End of Globalization, The Return of History*. New Haven, CT: Yale University Press.

Kirshner, J. 2014. *American Power After the Financial Crisis*. Ithaca, NY: Cornell University Press.

———. 2021. Gone but not forgotten: Trump's long shadow and the end of American credibility, *Foreign Affairs*, March/April.

Kline, H. F. et al. 2018. *Latin American Politics and Development*. London: Routledge.

Knight, P. (ed.) 2002. *Conspiracy Nation: The Politics of Paranoia in Postwar America*. New York: New York University Press.

Knox, P. et al. 2015. *The Geography of the World Economy*, 5th ed. London: Routledge.

Kolko, J. 2020. Yes, rich cities are getting richer. But that's not the whole story, *New York Times*, 19 February.

Kopper, A. and Peragovics, T. 2019. Overcoming the poverty of Western historical analogies: Alternative analogies for making sense of the South China Sea conflict, *European Journal of International Relations*, 25, 2: 360–82.

Koskenniemi, M. 2011. What use for sovereignty today?, *Asian Journal of International Law*, 1, 1: 61–70.

———. 2017. Sovereignty, property, and empire: Early modern English contexts, *Theoretical Inquiries in Law*, 18, 2: 355–89.

Krasner, S. D. 1999. *Sovereignty: Organized Hypocrisy*. Princeton, NJ: Princeton University Press.

Krastev, I. 2022. Putin lives in historic analogies and metaphors, *Spiegel International*, 17 March.

Krauze, L. 2021. Biden must stop the "iron river" of US weapons devastating Mexico, *Washington Post*, 10 March.

Kreitner, R. 2020. *Break It Up*. New York: Little Brown.

Kripendorff, E. 1989. The dominance of American approaches to international relations, in H. C. Dyer and L. Mangasarian (eds.), *The Study of International Relations*. London: Macmillan.

Krishnan, V. 2021. How to end vaccine apartheid, *Foreign Policy*, 9 November.

Kristensen, P. M. 2015. Revisiting the "American social science"—Mapping the geography of international relations, *International Studies Perspectives*, 16, 3: 246–69.

Kristensen, P. M. and Nielsen, R. 2013. Constructing a Chinese international relations theory: A sociological approach to intellectual innovation, *International Political Sociology*, 7, 1: 19–40.

Kristof, N. 2020. America and the virus: "A colossal failure of leadership," *New York Times*, 22 October.

Kundnani, H. 2015. *The Paradox of German Power*. New York: Oxford University Press.

Kuper, S. 2021. Why the US is becoming more European, *Financial Times*, 20 May.

Kynge, J. 2021. US-China investment flows belie geopolitical tensions, *Financial Times*, 3 February.

Labrosse, D. 2022. H-Diplo Roundtable XXIII-29 on Hamilton, *Made in Hong Kong*, 14 March.

Lake, D. A. 2021. The organizational ecology of global governance, *European Journal of International Relations*, 27, 2: 345–68.

Lake, D. A. and O'Mahony, A. 2006. Territory and war: State size and patterns of interstate conflict, in M. Kahler and B. F. Walter (eds.), *Territoriality and Conflict in an Era of Globalization*. New York: Cambridge University Press.

Lakoff, G. and Johnson, M. 1980. *Metaphors We Live By*. Chicago: University of Chicago Press.

Lamb, C. 2021. Chronicle of a defeat foretold: Why America failed in Afghanistan, *Foreign Affairs*, July/August.

Lane, C. 2021. For world peace, this is the most threatening "ism," *Washington Post*, 14 December.

Larkins, J. 2010. *From Hierarchy to Anarchy: Territory and Politics before Westphalia*. New York: Palgrave Macmillan.

Larrabee, F. S. 1990–1991. Long memories and short fuses: Change and instability in the Balkans, *International Security*, 15, 3: 58–91.

Larson, D. W. 2020. Can China change the international system? The role of moral leadership, *Chinese Journal of International Politics*, 13, 2: 163–86.

LA Times Editorial 2020. Pretending not to see coronavirus cases won't make them go away, *Los Angeles Times*, 25 June.

Latour, B. 2016. *Onus orbis terrarum*: About a possible shift in the definition of sovereignty, *Millennium*, 44, 3: 305–20.

Lavelle, K. C. 2013. *Money and Banks in the American Political System*. New York: Cambridge University Press.

Lavergne, R. P. 1983. *The Political Economy of US Tariffs: An Empirical Analysis*. Ottawa: North-South Institute.

Lebor, A. 2013. *Tower of Basel: The Shadowy History of the Secret Bank that Runs the World.* New York: Public Affairs.

Lee, C. K. and Zhang, Y. 2013. The power of instability: Unraveling the microfoundations of bargained authoritarianism in China, *American Journal of Sociology*, 118, 6: 1475–1508.

Legg, S. (ed.) 2011. *Spatiality, Sovereignty and Carl Schmitt: Geographies of the Nomos*. London: Routledge.

Leonard, M. 2008. *What Does China Think?* London: Public Affairs.

Leoni, Z. 2021. *American Grand Strategy from Obama to Trump: Imperialism after Bush and China's Hegemonic Challenge*. London: Palgrave Macmillan.

Lerner, A. M. et al. 2020. Preventing the spread of SARS-CoV-2 with masks and other "low tech" interventions, *Journal of the American Medical Association*, 324, 19: 1935–36.

Levy, J. 2021. The hybrid workplace probably won't last, *Boston Globe*, 9 May.

Lieberthal, K. and Oksenberg, M. 1988. *Policy Making in China: Leaders, Structures, and Processes.* Princeton, NJ: Princeton University Press.

Lim, D. 2020. Coronavirus testing hits dramatic slowdown in US, *Politico*, 14 April.

Lim, E. T. 2014. *The Lovers Quarrel: The Two Foundings and American Political Development*. New York: Oxford University Press.

Lim, K. F. 2019. *On Shifting Foundations: State Rescaling, Policy Experimentation, and Economic Restructuring in Post-1949 China*. Oxford: Wiley-Blackwell.

Lind, D. 2018. Trump keeps making it harder for people to seek asylum legally. It's legal to seek asylum at an official border crossing. But border agents are blocking people from getting that far, *Vox*, 5 June. https://www.vox.com/policy-and-politics/2018/6/5/17428640/border-families-asylum-illegal

Linthicum, K. 2018. Trump says Mexico's violence is a threat to the US. Here are three ways the US helps drive that violence, *Los Angeles Times*, 1 August.

Lipton, E. et al. 2020. He could have seen what was coming: Behind Trump's failure on the virus, *New York Times*, 11 April.

Liste, P. 2016. Colliding geographies: Space at work in global governance, *Journal of International Relations and Development*, 19, 2: 199–221.

Liu M. 2010. *Zhongguo meng: Hou Meigou shidai de da guo siwei yu zhanlue dingwei* [*China Dream: Great Power Considerations and Fixing Strategy in the Post-American Era*]. Beijing: Zhongguo youyi chubanshe.

Livesey, F. 2017. *From Global to Local: The Making of Things and the End of Globalization*. New York: Vintage.

Livni, E. 2021. For rules in technology, the challenge is to balance code and law, *New York Times*, 23 November.

Louis, M. 2018. The social diplomacy of multinational corporations, *La Vie des Idées*, 9 October.

Luce, E. 2021. Afghanistan and the tragic verdict on post-9/11 America, *Financial Times*, 17 August.

Luke, T. W. 2021. *The Travails of Trumpification*. New York: Telos.

Lukes, S. 2000. Different cultures, different rationalities?, *History of the Human Sciences*, 131, 1: 5–18.

Luoma-Aho, M. 2002. Body of Europe and malignant nationalism: A pathology of the Balkans in European security discourse, *Geopolitics*, 7, 3: 117–42.

Lusk, M. et al. 2012. Social justice in the US-Mexico border region, in M. Lusk et al. (eds.), *Social Justice in the US-Mexico Border Region*. Dordrecht: Springer, 3–40.

Lussault, M. 2017. *Hyper-Lieux: Les nouvelles géographies de la mondialisation.* Paris: Seuil.

Lynch, D. 2009. Chinese thinking on the future of international relations: Realism as the *Ti*, rationalism as the *Yong*?, *China Quarterly*, 197, 3: 87–107.

Lynch, J. M. 1999. *Negotiating the Constitution: The Earliest Debates over Original Intent.* Ithaca, NY: Cornell University Press.

MacFarquhar, R. 2015. China: The superpower of Mr. Xi, *New York Review of Books*, 15 August.

Madrigal, A. C. and Meyer, R. 2020. A dire warning from COVID-19 test providers, *Atlantic*, 30 June.

Mance, H. 2021. Inside Scotland's pandemic: Has it made independence more likely?, *Financial Times*, 21 April.

Manela, E. 2020. International society as a historical subject, *Diplomatic History*, 44, 2: 184–209.

Mann, M. 1984. The autonomous power of the state, *European Journal of Sociology*, 25: 185–213.

———. 1997. Has globalization ended the rise and rise of the nation-state?, *Review of International Political Economy*, 4, 3: 472–96.

Manson, K. 2021. Has America had enough of war?, *Financial Times*, 6 May.

Marazzi, C. 2011. *The Violence of Financial Capitalism*. Cambridge, MA: Semiotext(e).

Massey, D. S. et al. 2016. Why border enforcement backfired, *American Journal of Sociology*, 121, 5: 1557–1600.

Maswood, S. J. 2021. Origins and consequences of economic globalization: Moving beyond a flawed orthodoxy, *European Journal of International Relations*, 27, 2: 428–49.

Mavelli, L. 2018. Citizenship for sale and the neoliberal political economy of belonging, *International Studies Quarterly*, 62, 3: 482–93.

Maxwell, A. and Shields, T. 2019. *The Long Southern Strategy: How Chasing White Voters in the South Changed American Politics*. New York: Oxford University Press.

May, C. 2015. *Global Corporations and Global Governance*. London: Routledge.

Mazzucato, M. 2013. *The Entrepreneurial State: Debunking Public vs. Private Sector Myths.* London: Anthem.

McCormick, M. and Murphy, H. 2021. Hackers target US infrastructure after digitisation on the cheap, *Financial Times*, 21 May.

McCoy, A. W. 2018. These 5 academics have brought us to the brink of geopolitical disaster, *Washington Post*, 3 December.

McGann, J. G. 2012. *Chinese Think Tanks, Policy Advice and Global Governance*, Indiana University Research Center for Chinese Politics and Business, Working Paper Number 21.

McGinty, J. C. 2018a. The changing face of illegal border crossing, *Wall Street Journal*, 13 July.

———. 2018b. Asylum requests have reached a new high, *Wall Street Journal*, 8–9 December.

McGregor, R. 2019. *Xi Jinping: The Backlash.* London: Penguin.

McKay, S. 2021. Pro-Union non-unionists, *London Review of Books*, 4 March.

———. 2022. In Portadown, *London Review of Books*, 10 March.

McMorrow, R. 2021. Xi calls for new world order in attack on US global leadership, *Financial Times*, 21 April.

Mearsheimer, J. 2006. China's unpeaceful rise, *Current History*, April: 160–62.

Meek, J. 2021. Who holds the welding rod? Our turbine futures, *London Review of Books*, 15 July.

Mellow, N. 2008. *The State of Disunion: Regional Sources of Modern American Partisanship.* Baltimore: Johns Hopkins University Press.

Michel, C. 2021. *American Kleptocracy: How the US Created the World's Greatest Money Laundering Scheme in History*. New York: St. Martin's.

Michel, C. and Massaro, P. 2021. The US Midwest is foreign oligarchs' new playground, *Foreign Policy*, 3 June.

Michta, A. A. 2021. Russia and China's dangerous decline: The risk of war arises not because they're strong but because they foresee their advantages slipping away, *Wall Street Journal*, 14 December.

Micklethwait, J. and Wooldridge, A. 2022. Putin and Xi exposed the great illusion of capitalism, *Bloomberg*, 23 March.

Milanovic, B. 2018. *Global Inequality: A New Approach for the Age of Globalization*. Cambridge, MA: Harvard University Press.

Miller, E. H. 2015. *Nut Country: Right-Wing Dallas and the Birth of the Southern Strategy*. Chicago: University of Chicago Press.

Millhiser I. 2021. The enormous advantage that the Electoral College gives Republicans, in one chart, *Vox*, 11 January.

Ming, W. 2012. Introduction: Chinese traditions in international relations, *Journal of Chinese Political Science*, 17, 2: 105–9.

Minian, A. R. 2018. America didn't always lock up immigrants, *New York Times*, 1 December.

Miroff, N. 2018. Border arrest data suggest that Trump's push to split families had little deterrent effect, *Washington Post*, 10 August.

Miroff, N. and Sacchetti, M. 2021. Family groups crossing border in soaring numbers point to next phase of crisis, *Washington Post*, 28 March.

Miroff, N. et al. 2018. Trump administration weighs new family-separation effort at border, *Washington Post*, 12 October.

Mirowski, P. 2013. *Never Let a Serious Crisis Go to Waste: How Neoliberalism Survived the Financial Meltdown*. London: Verso.

Mishra, P. 2020. Flailing states: Anglo-America loses its grip, *London Review of Books*, 16 July.

Mittal, V. 2022. How the Ukrainian military strategy stalled the Russian offensive, *Forbes*, 27 March.

Mitter, R. and Johnson, E. 2021. What the West gets wrong about China, *Harvard Business Review*, May/June: 42–48.

Molteni, M. 2021. "Just stupid stuff": Logistics and lack of testing stymied finding the Omicron variant in the US, *STAT*, 2 December.

Montes, J. and Caldwell, A. A. 2021. Men looking for work drive surge in illegal crossings at the US border, *Wall Street Journal*, 24 March.

Monti, M. 2021. An ambitious agenda is needed for the post-Covid "normal," *Financial Times*, 16 March.

Moon, E. 2018. Research tells us that immigration does not lead to higher crime rates, *Pacific Standard*, 22 August.

Morefield, J. 2005. States are not people: Harold Laski on unsettling sovereignty, rediscovering democracy, *Political Research Quarterly*, 58, 4: 659–69.

Morgan, G. and Whitley, R. (eds.) 2012. *Capitalisms and Capitalism in the Twenty-First Century*. Oxford: Oxford University Press.

Mortenson, J. D. and Bagley, N. 2020. There's no historical justification for one of the most dangerous ideas in American law, *Atlantic*, 26 May.

Mossaad, N. and Baugh, R. 2018. Refugees and asylees: 2016, Annual Flow Report, Department of Homeland Security, Office of Immigration Statistics, January.

Mulder, N. 2022. *The Economic Weapon: The Rise of Sanctions as a Tool of War*. New Haven, CT: Yale University Press.

Münchau, W. 2014. The wacky economics of Germany's parallel universe, *Financial Times*, 17 November.

Muro, M. et al. 2020. Biden-voting counties equal 70% of the US economy. What does this mean for the nation's political-economic divide?, Brookings Institution, 10 November.

Murphy, A. B. 2008. Rethinking multi-level governance in a changing European Union: Why metageography and territoriality matter, *GeoJournal*, 72, 1: 7–18.

Murphy, D. D. 2004. *The Structure of Regulatory Competition: Corporations and Public Policies in a Global Economy*. New York: Cambridge University Press.

Murphy, M. C. and Evershed, J. 2021. Contesting sovereignty and borders: Northern Ireland, devolution and the Union, *Territory, Politics, Governance*, online first.

Murray, J. 2017. Interlock globally, act domestically: Corporate political unity in the 21st century, *American Journal of Sociology*, 122, 6: 1617–63.

Murtha, A. 2009. Fragmented authoritarianism 2.0: Political pluralization in the Chinese policy process, *China Quarterly*, 200: 995–1012.

Narea, N. 2021. Migrants are heading north because Central America never recovered from last year's hurricanes, *Vox*, 22 March.

Narins, T. P. and Agnew, J. 2020. Missing from the map: Chinese exceptionalism, sovereignty regimes, and the Belt Road initiative, *Geopolitics*, 25, 4: 809–37.

Nau, H. R. and Ollapally, D. (eds.) 2012. *Worldviews of Aspiring Powers: Domestic Foreign Policy Debates in China, India, Iran, Japan, and Russia*. New York: Oxford University Press.

Nevins, J. 2001. *Operation Gatekeeper: The Rise of the "Illegal Alien" and the Remaking of the US-Mexico Boundary*. London: Routledge.

Nexon, D. H. 2021. Against Great Power competition, *Foreign Affairs*, 16 February.

Ngai, M.M 2014. *Impossible Subjects: Illegal Aliens and the Making of Modern America*. Princeton, NJ: Princeton University Press.

Nolan, P. 2012. *Is China Buying the World*? Cambridge: Polity.

NY Times. Russonello, G. 2020. On politics: Trump pledges to halt immigration, *New York Times*, 21 April.

———. Bosman, J. et al. 2021. Covid deaths in the US surpass 800,000, *New York Times*, 15 December.

Nye, J. S. 2021. With China, a "Cold War" analogy is lazy and dangerous, *New York Times*, 2 November.

Obermayer, B. and Obermaier, F. 2016. *The Panama Papers*. London: One World.

O'Callaghan, P. 2012. Collective memory in law and policy: The problem of the sovereign debt crisis, *Legal Studies*, 32, 4: 642–60.

OECD 2016. *Regions at a Glance, 2016*. Paris: OECD.

Offner, A. C. 2019. *Sorting Out the Mixed Economy: The Rise and Fall of Welfare and Developmental States in the Americas*. Princeton, NJ: Princeton University Press.

O'Hara, K. and Hall, W. 2018. *Four Internets: The Geopolitics of Digital Governance*. Waterloo, Canada: Centre for International Governance Innovation.

Okwudire, C. and Madhyastha, H. V. 2021. Distributed manufacturing for and by the masses, *Science*, 372, 6540: 341–2.

O'Reilly, M. W. 2018. Border blame game: Trump doesn't want credit for his cruelty, *Commonweal*, 6 July.

Ormsby, E. A. 2017. The refugee crisis as a civil liberties crisis, *Columbia Law Review*, 117, 5: 1191–1229.

Osipovich, A. 2022. Putin acknowledges impact of sanctions on Russian economy, *Wall Street Journal*, 16 March.

O'Sullivan, M. 2019. *The Levelling: What's Next After Globalization?* New York: Public Affairs.

O'Toole, M. 2021. The key to Northern Ireland's future lies in retaining its young talent, *Financial Times*, 5 May.

Ó Tuathail, G. 1996. *Critical Geopolitics*. Minneapolis: University of Minnesota Press.

Ó Tuathail, G. and Agnew, J. 1992. Geopolitics and discourse: Practical geopolitical reasoning in American foreign policy, *Political Geography Quarterly*, 11, 2: 190–204.

Packer, G. 2020. We are living in a failed state: The coronavirus didn't break America. It revealed what was already broken, *Atlantic*, June.

Pagden, A. 2021. *The Pursuit of Europe: A History*. Oxford: Oxford University Press.

Painter, J. 2006. Prosaic geographies of stateness, *Political Geography*, 25, 7: 752–74.

Palmer, D. 2021. US trade deficit soars to 14-year high in November, *Politico*, 7 January.

Pan, C. 2009. What is Chinese about Chinese businesses? Locating the "Rise of China" in global production networks, *Journal of Contemporary China*, 18, 58: 7–25.

———. 2012. *Knowledge, Desire and Power in Global Politics: Western Representations of China's Rise*. Cheltenham: Elgar.

Pan, S-Y. and. Lo, J. T-Y. 2015. Re-Conceptualizing China's rise as a global power: A neo-tributary perspective, *Pacific Review*, 30, 1: 10.

Paris, R. 2020. The right to dominate: How old ideas about sovereignty pose new challenges for world order, *International Organization*, 74, 3: 453–89.

Parker, A. and Rucker, P. 2020. How Trump's attempts to win the daily news cycle feed a chaotic coronavirus response, *Washington Post*, 4 April.

Parkinson, J. and Hinshaw, D. 2021. Leaking hull, hazardous cargo: Aboard a stranded ship no one would help, *Wall Street Journal*, 10 December.

Patomäki, H. 2010. Cosmological sources of critical cosmopolitanism, *Review of International Studies*, 36, 1: 181–200.

Patrick, S. M. 2021. The international order isn't ready for the climate crisis, *Foreign Affairs*, November/December: 166–76.

Patterson, P. H. 2003. On the edge of reason: The boundaries of Balkanism in Slovenian, Austrian, and Italian discourse, *Slavic Review*, 62, 1: 110–41.

Paul, D. 2002. Re-scaling IPE: Subnational states and the regulation of the global political economy, *Review of International Political Economy*, 9, 3: 465–89.

Payne, S. 2021. *Broken Heartlands: A Journey through Labour's Lost England*. London: Macmillan.

Peel, P. 2018. The populist theory of the state in early American political thought, *Political Research Quarterly*, 71, 1: 115–26.

Pells, R. 1997. *Not Like Us: How Europeans Have Loved, Hated, and Transformed American Culture Since World War II*. New York: Basic.

Peltier, E. 2021. Belgian port city grapples with a flood of cocaine, *New York Times*, 4 December.

Perdue, P. C. 2021. A singular entity: Classical China, *London Review of Books*, 20 May.

Perez, S. 2022. Former Honduras President to be extradited to the US on drug-trafficking charges, *Wall Street Journal*, 28 March.

Perlman, R. L. 2020. The domestic impact of international standards, *International Studies Quarterly*, 64, 3: 600–608.

Perlroth, N. 2021. *This Is How They Tell Me the World Ends: The Cyberweapons Arms Race*. London: Bloomsbury.

Perlstein, R. 2008. *Nixonland: The Rise of a President and the Fracturing of America*. New York: Scribner.

Phillips, A. and Sharman, J. C. 2020. *Outsourcing Empire: How Company-States Made the Modern World*. Princeton, NJ: Princeton University Press.

Pidd, H. 2019. Half of job growth to be limited to London, inequality inquiry finds, *Guardian*, 29 May.

Piketty, T. 2013. *Le capital au xxi siècle*. Paris: Seuil.

Piller, C. 2020. Official inaction, *Science*, 370, 6512: 24–29.

Pinker, S. 2007. *The Stuff of Thought: Language as a Window into Human Nature*. New York: Viking.

Piris, J. C. 2011. *The Future of Europe: Towards a Two-Speed EU?* Cambridge: Cambridge University Press.

Pisani-Ferry, J. 2021. The end of globalization as we know it, *Project Syndicate*, 28 June.

Pistor, K. 2019. *The Code of Capital: How the Law Creates Wealth and Inequality.* Princeton, NJ: Princeton University Press.

Polito, V. and Wickens, M. 2014. How the Euro crisis evolved and how to avoid another: EMU, fiscal policy and credit ratings, *Journal of Macroeconomics*, 39, 2: 364–74.

Pomerantsev, P. 2022. What Putin's Nazi talk reveals about his plans for Ukraine, *Time*, 4 March.

Porter, D. 2001. *Ideographia: The Chinese Cipher in Early Modern Europe*. Stanford: Stanford University Press.

Posen, A. S. 2021. The price of nostalgia: America's self-defeating economic retreat, *Foreign Affairs*, May/June: 28–43.

Potts, S. 2020. Law as geopolitics: Judicial territory, transnational economic governance, and American power, *Annals of the American Association of Geographers*, 110, 4: 1192–1207.

Qin Y. 2011a. Development of international relations theory in China: Progress through debates, *International Relations of the Asia-Pacific*, 11, 2: 231–57.

———. 2011b. The possibility and inevitability of a Chinese school of international relations, in W. A. Callahan and E. Barabantseva (eds.), *China Orders the World: Normative Soft Power and Foreign Policy*. Baltimore: Johns Hopkins University Press.

Quinn, S. L. 2019. *American Bonds: How Credit Markets Shaped a Nation*. Princeton, NJ: Princeton University Press.

Rachman, G. 2021a. A second Cold War is tracking the first, *Financial Times*, 29 March.

———. 2021b. China is still a long way from being a superpower, *Financial Times*, 19 July.

Reich, R. 2021. The US's greatest danger isn't China. It's much closer to home, *Guardian*, 20 June.

Reinhart, C. M. and Rogoff, K. S. 2009. *This Time Is Different: Eight Centuries of Financial Folly*. Princeton: Princeton University Press.

Restrepo, D. 2021. Central Americans are fleeing bad governments, *Foreign Affairs*, 5 March.

Ricolfi, L. 2010. *Il sacco del nord. Saggio sulla giustizia territoriale.* Milan: Guerini.

Rid, T. 2019. *Active Measures: The Secret History of Disinformation and Political Warfare*. New York: Farrar, Straus and Giroux.

Riley, D. 2017. American Brumaire?, *New Left Review*, 103: 21–32.

Ritter, G. A. 2011. *The Price of German Unity: Reunification and the Crisis of the Welfare State.* Oxford: Oxford University Press.

Rizzo, S. 2018. Trump's false claim that Obama had the same family separation policy, *Washington Post*, 27 November.

Roberts, A. 2010. *The Logic of Discipline: Global Capitalism and the Architecture of Government.* Oxford: Oxford University Press.

Roberts, A. and Lamp, N. 2021. *Six Faces of Globalization: Who Wins, Who Loses, and Why it Matters*. Cambridge, MA: Harvard University Press.

Roberts, D. 2020. *The Myth of Chinese Capitalism: The Worker, the Factory, and the Future of the World.* New York: St. Martin's Press.

Robertson, R. 1994. Globalisation or glocalisation?, *Journal of International Communication*, 1, 1: 33–52.

Robin, C. 2004. *Fear: The History of a Political Idea*. New York: Oxford University Press.

Robinson, W. I. 2018. *Into the Tempest: Essays on the New Global Capitalism*. Chicago: Haymarket.

Rodden, J. 2019. *Why Cities Lose: The Deep Roots of the Urban-Rural Political Divide*. London: Hachette.

Rodrik, D. 2013. Who needs the nation-state?, *Economic Geography*, 89, 1: 1–18.

Rolf, S. 2020. *China's Uneven and Combined Development*. London: Palgrave Macmillan.

Rolf, S. and Agnew, J. 2016. Sovereignty regimes in the South China Sea: Assessing contemporary Sino-US relations, *Eurasian Geography and Economics*, 57, 2: 249–73.

Rosen, D. H. 2021. China's economic reckoning: The price of failed reforms, *Foreign Affairs*, July/August: 20–29.

Rosenberg, E. S. 1983. *Spreading the American Dream: American Economic and Cultural Expansion, 1890–1945*. New York: Hill and Wang.

Rosenthal, L. 2020. *Empire of Resentment: Populism's Toxic Embrace of Nationalism*. New York: New.

Roshwald, A. 2007. Between balkanization and banalization: Dilemmas of ethnocultural diversity, *Ethnopolitics*, 6, 3: 365–78.

Rostow, W. W. 1961. *The Stages of Economic Growth: A Non-Communist Manifesto*. New York: Cambridge University Press.

Rozelle, S. and Hell, N. 2020. *Invisible China: How the Urban-Rural Divide Threatens China's Rise*. Chicago: University of Chicago Press.

Rozman, G. 2012. Invocations of Chinese traditions in international relations, *Journal of Chinese Political Science*, 17, 2: 111–24.

Rubin, J. 2018. Trump is in full retreat. Now we can see it was a self-made crisis all along, *Washington Post*, 26 June.

Rucker, P. and Costa, R. 2020. Commander of confusion: Trump sows uncertainty and seeks to cast blame in coronavirus crisis, *Washington Post*, 2 April.

Rucker, P. and Leonnig, C. 2020. *A Very Stable Genius: Donald J. Trump's Testing of America*. New York: Penguin.

Sakellaropoulos, S. 2007. Towards a declining state? The rise of the headquarters state, *Science and Society*, 71, 1: 7–34.

Sandbu, M. 2019. More than a third of foreign investment is multinationals dodging tax, *Financial Times*, 8 September.

———. 2021. Shortages what shortages? Global markets are delivering, *Financial Times*, 14 December.

Sapiro, G. (ed.) 2009. *L'espace intellectuel en Europe. De la formation des États-nations à la mondialisation XIX–XXI siècles*. Paris: La Découverte.

Sassen, S. 2006. *Territory, Authority, Rights: From Medieval to Global Assemblages*. Princeton, NJ: Princeton University Press.

Sayer, D. 1992. A notable administration: English state formation and the rise of capitalism, *American Journal of Sociology*, 97, 5: 1382–1415.

Schapiro, R. A. 2005–2006. Toward a theory of interactive federalism, *Iowa Law Review*, 91: 243–317.

———. 2009. *Polyphonic Federalism: Toward a Protection of Fundamental Rights*. Chicago: University of Chicago Press.

Schmitt, C. 2003 [1950]. *The Nomos of the Earth in the International Law of the Jus Publicum Europaeum*. New York: Telos.

Schrader, S. 2019. *Badges without Borders: How Global Counterinsurgency Transformed American Policing*. Berkeley: University of California Press.

Schuck, P. H. 2014. *Why Government Fails So Often: And How It Can Do Better*. Princeton: Princeton University Press.

Schuman, M. 2020. *Superpower Interrupted: The Chinese History of the World*. New York: Public Affairs.

Schwartz, M. 2020. William Barr's long crusade for theocracy, *New York Times Magazine*, 7 June: 20–25, 42–45.

Scott, A. J. 1998. *Regions and the World Economy*. Oxford: Oxford University Press.

———. (ed.) 2001. *Global City-Regions: Trends, Theory, Policy*. Oxford: Oxford University Press.

Segreto, L. and Wubs, B. 2014. Resistance of the defeated: German and Italian big business and the American antitrust policy, 1945–1957, *Enterprise and Society*, 15, 2: 307–36.

Selee, A. 2018. *Vanishing Frontiers: The Forces Driving the United States and Mexico Together*. New York: Public Affairs.

Sellers, C. 1991. *The Market Revolution: Jacksonian America, 1815–1846*. New York: Oxford University Press.

Serwer, A. 2018. Trump's caravan hysteria led to this, *Atlantic*, 28 October.

———. 2021. *The Cruelty Is the Point: The Past, Present, and Future of Trump's America*. New York: One World.

Shapin, S. 1998. Placing the view from nowhere: Historical and sociological problems in the location of science, *Transactions of the Institute of British Geographers*, 23, 1: 5–12.

Shapiro, M. 1989. Representing world politics: The sport/war intertext, in J. Der Derian and M. Shapiro (eds.), *International/Intertextual Relations: Postmodern Readings of World Politics*. Lexington, MA: Lexington Books.

———. 1997. *Violent Cartographies: Mapping Cultures of War*. Minneapolis: University of Minnesota Press.

Sharma, R. 2021. The idea that the state has been shrinking for forty years is a myth, *Financial Times*, 25 April.

Sharman, J. 2012. Canaries in the coal mine: Tax havens, the decline of the West and the rise of the Rest, *New Political Economy*, 14, 4: 493–513.

———. 2017. *The Despot's Guide to Wealth Management*. Ithaca, NY: Cornell University Press.

Shaub Jr., W. M. 2020. Ransacking the republic, *New York Review of Books*, 2 July.

Shaxson, N. 2011. *Treasure Islands: Uncovering the Damage of Offshore Banking and Tax Havens*. New York: Palgrave Macmillan.

Sheng, Y. 2010. *Economic Openness and Territorial Politics in China*. Cambridge: Cambridge University Press.

Silver, B. J. and Arrighi, G. 2003. Polanyi's "double movement": The belles époques of British and U.S. hegemony compared, *Politics and Society*, 31, 2: 325–55.

Simmons, B. A. et al. 2018. The global diffusion of law: Transnational crime and the case of human trafficking, *International Organization*, 72, 2: 249–81.

Sinclair, T. J. 2005. *The New Masters of Capital: American Bond Rating Agencies and the Politics of Creditworthiness*. Ithaca, NY: Cornell University Press.

Sinn, H-W. 2014. *The Euro Trap: On Bursting Bubbles, Budgets, and Beliefs*. Oxford: Oxford University Press.

Skidelsky, R. 2021. The case against economic sanctions, *Project Syndicate*, 19 October.

Skowronek, S. et al. 2021. *Phantoms of a Beleaguered Republic: The Deep State and the Unitary Executive*. New York: Oxford University Press.

Slater, D. 1999. Situating geopolitical representations: Inside/outside and the power of imperial interventions, in D. Massey, J. Allen, and P. Sarre (eds.), *Human Geography Today*. Cambridge: Polity.

Slaughter, A-M. 2018. *The Chessboard and the Web*. New Haven, CT: Yale University Press.

Slobodian, Q. 2018. *Globalists: The End of Empire and the Birth of Neoliberalism*. Cambridge, MA: Harvard University Press.

Smil, V. 2010. *Prime Movers of Globalization: The History and Impact of Diesel Engines and Gas Turbines*. Cambridge, MA: MIT Press.

Smith, H. and Burrows, R. 2021. Software, sovereignty and the post-neoliberal politics of exit, *Theory, Culture & Society*, 38, 6: 143–66.

Smith, M. R. and Choi, C. 2021. Vaccine rollout conforms public health officials' warnings, AP, 10 January.

Smith, R. M. and King, D. 2021. White protectionism in America, *Perspectives on Politics*, 19, 2: 460–78.

Sokol, D. 2007. Globalization of law firms: A survey of the literature and a research agenda for further study, *Indiana Journal of Global Legal Studies*, 14, 5: 5–28.

Solingen, E. 2021. The uncertain future of global supply chains, IGCC, UC San Diego: Interviews, 8 September. igcc.ucsd.edu

Solis, M. 2018. Trump brands migrant caravan a "disgrace," orders homeland security officials to turn away immigrants at border, *Newsweek*, 23 April.

Sorokin, V. 2014. Let the past collapse on time! The vicious nature and archaic underpinnings of the Russian state, *New Yorker*, 8 May.

Spiegel, P. 2022. The Ukraine crisis' new F-word: Finlandisation, *Financial Times*, 11 February.

Spiegelberger, W. 2021. *Even Thieves Need a Safe: Why the Putin Regime Causes, Deplores, and Yet Relies on Capital Flight for its Survival*. Philadelphia: Foreign Policy Research Institute.

Steil, B. and Della Rocca, B. 2021. Unalloyed failure: The lessons of Trump's disastrous steel tariffs, *Foreign Affairs*, 7 May.

Stein, J. 2010. *Pivotal Decade: How the United States Traded Factories for Finance in the Seventies*. New Haven: Yale University Press.

Steinhauer, J. and Goodnough, A. 2020. Contact tracing is failing in many states. Here's why, *New York Times*, 31 July.

Stenslie, S. 2014. Questioning the reality of China's grand strategy, *China: An International Journal*, 12, 2: 161–78.

Stephens, P. 2012. Downgrade the rating agencies, *Financial Times*, 19 January.

Stern, P. J. 2011. *The Company-State: Corporate Sovereignty and the Early Modern Foundations of the British Empire in India*. New York: Oxford University Press.

Stevenson, T. 2021. Miner conflicts: Why wars are fought over strategic interests, not mere minerals, *Times Literary Supplement*, 14 May.

Stillman, S. 2018. The five-year-old who was detained at the border and persuaded to sign away her rights, *New Yorker*, 11 October.

Stoller, M. 2019. *Goliath: The 100-Year Struggle between Monopoly Power and Democracy*. New York: Simon and Schuster.

Stark, J. 2015. The historical and cultural differences that divide Europe's union, *Financial Times*, 11 February.

Streeck, W. 2015. The strikes sweeping Germany are here to stay, *Guardian*, 22 May.

———. 2017. The return of the repressed, *New Left Review*, 104: 5–18.

Streeck, W. and Yamamura, K. (eds.) 2001. *The Origins of Nonliberal Capitalism: Germany and Japan in Comparison*. Ithaca, NY: Cornell University Press.

Studemann, F. 2020. Even Germany's localism is questioned in the pandemic, *Financial Times*, 22 October.

Sun, L. H. 2021. Two years into this pandemic, the world is dangerously unprepared for the next one, report says, *Washington Post*, 8 December.

Sweet, A. S. 2004. Islands of transnational governance, in C. K. Ansell and G. Di Palma (eds.), *Restructuring Territoriality: Europe and the United States Compared*. Cambridge: Cambridge University Press.

Tam, K. and Caldwell, A. A. 2018. The immigration issue in eight charts, *Wall Street Journal*, 21 June.

Tam, P-W. 2021. One family's global quest for vaccination, *New York Times*, 11 April.

Tan, Y. 2021. How the WTO changed China: The mixed legacy of economic engagement, *Foreign Affairs*, March/April.

Taylor, A. 2022. Researchers are asking why some countries were better prepared for Covid: One surprising answer: Trust, *Washington Post*, 1 February.

Taylor, P. J. 2004. *World City Network: A Global Urban Analysis*. London: Routledge.

———. 2013. *Extraordinary Cities: Millennia of Moral Syndromes, World-Systems and City/State Relations*. Cheltenham: Edward Elgar.

Tett, G. 2021. What the US failed to understand about Afghanistan, *Financial Times*, 21 April.
Tharoor, I. 2021. Biden's border "crisis" has little to do with the border, *Washington Post*, 30 March.
Thornhill, J. 2018. How to fix Facebook, *Financial Times*, 6 August.
Tjalve, V. S. (ed.) 2020. *Geopolitical Amnesia: The Rise of the Right and the Crisis of Liberal Memory*. Montreal: McGill-Queen's University Press.
Todorov, T. 2010. *The Fear of Barbarians*. Chicago: University of Chicago Press.
Todorova, M. 1997. *Imagining the Balkans*. New York: Oxford University Press.
Tóibin, C. 2021. Ireland's bloody line of division, *Financial Times*, 30 March.
Tooze, A. 2012. Germany's unsustainable growth: Austerity now, stagnation later, *Foreign Affairs*, 95, September/October: 23–30.
Torres, R. M. 2018. A crisis of rights and responsibilities: Feminist geopolitical perspectives on Latin American refugees and migrants, *Gender, Place and Culture*, 25: 13–36.
Traub, J. 2021. The United States keeps doing what it can't, *Foreign Policy*, 20 August.
Treisman, D. S. 2007. *The Architecture of Government: Rethinking Political Decentralization*. Cambridge: Cambridge University Press.
Trubek, D. et al. 1994. Global restructuring and the law: Studies of the internationalization of the legal fields and the creation of transnational arenas, *Case Western Reserve Law Review*, 44, 2: 407–98.
Trubowitz, P. and Burgoon, B. 2022. The retreat of the West, *Perspectives on Politics*, 20, 1: 102–22.
Tseng-Putterman, M. 2018. A century of US intervention created the immigration crisis, *Medium*. https://medium.com/s/story/timeline-us-intervention-central-america-created-the-immigration-crisis/
Turner, F. J. 1896. The problem of the West, *Atlantic Monthly*, 78, 1896: 289.
Twain, M. 1894. *Tom Sawyer Abroad*. New York: Charles L. Webster.
Ullman, H. K. 2018. *Anatomy of Failure: Why America Loses Every War It Starts*. Annapolis, MD: Naval Institute Press.
Unger, C. 2021. *American Kompromat: How the KGB Cultivated Donald Trump*. New York: Dutton.
UNHCR 2019. *Global Trends: Forced Displacement in 2019*. Geneva: UNHCR.
UUSC. 2018. *A Cautionary Tale: The US Follows Hungary's Dangerous Path to Dismantling Asylum*. Cambridge, MA: Unitarian Universalist Service Committee.
Van Creveld, M. 1999. *The Rise and Decline of the State*. Cambridge: Cambridge University Press.
Van Hulten, A. 2012. Remapping the fiscal state after the global financial crisis, *Economic Geography*, 88, 3: 231–53.
Vergerio, C. 2021. Beyond the nation-state, *Boston Review*, 27 May.
Verkuil, P. R. 2007. *Outsourcing Sovereignty: Why Privatization of Governmental Functions Threatens Democracy and What We Can Do About It*. Cambridge: Cambridge University Press.
Vogl, F. 2022. *The Enablers: How the West supports Kleptocrats and Corruption—Endangering Our Democracy*. Lanham, MD: Rowman & Littlefield.
Wagstyl, S. 2015. Germans' unhealthy obsession with a Greek "Stinkefinger," *Financial Times*, 20 March.
Waldmeir, P. 2020. Trump's support rallies round his flag in the Midwest, *Financial Times*, 7 April.
———. 2021. Infrastructure investment: Michigan, a tale of US neglect, *Financial Times*, 14 March.
Walker, R. B. J. 2010. *After the Globe, Before the World*. London: Routledge.
Wallerstein, I. et al. 2013. *Uncertain Worlds: World-Systems Analysis in Changing Times*. Boulder, CO: Paradigm.

Wang, F-L. 2017. *The China Order: Centralia, World Empire, and the Nature of Chinese Power.* Albany, NY: SUNY Press.

Wang, H. 2011. *The Politics of Imagining Asia.* Cambridge, MA: Harvard University Press.

———. 2014. *China from Empire to Nation-State.* Cambridge, MA: Harvard University Press.

Wang Y. 2007. Between science and art: Questionable international relations theories, *Japanese Journal of Political Science*, 8, 2, 192–210.

Wang, Y-K. 2022. The Ukraine war and China's second strategic opportunity, *H-Diplo Essay 427*, 31 March.

Warren, R. 2021. In 2019, the US undocumented population continued a decade-long decline and the foreign-born population neared zero growth, *Journal on Migration and Human Security*, 9, 1: 1–13.

Warren, R. and Kerwin, D. 2017. The 2,000 mile wall in search of a purpose: Since 2007 visa overstays have outnumbered undocumented border crossers by a half million, *Journal on Migration and Human Security*, 5, 1: 1–8.

Watling, J. 2022. Friendly fire blunders, confusion, low morale: Why Russia's army has stalled, *Guardian*, 2 April.

Webber, J. 2018. Tensions rise as migrants rush the US-Mexico border fence, *Financial Times*, 25 November.

Weber, I. 2021. *How China Escaped Shock Therapy: The Market Reform Debate*. London: Routledge.

Weber, R. H. 2021. *Internet Governance at the Point of No Return*. Zurich: EIZ.

Wedel, J. R. 2004. Blurring the state-private divide: Flex organizations and the decline of accountability, in M. Spoor (ed.), *Globalisation, Poverty and Conflict*. Dordrecht, Netherlands: Kluwer, 217–35.

Wehner, P. 2020. The party of the aggrieved, *Atlantic*, 21 April.

Weiner, M. 1971. The Macedonian syndrome: An historical model of international relations and political development, *World Politics*, 23, 4: 665–83.

Weiner, R. 2020. Trump administration's approach to testing is chaotic and unhelpful, states say, *Washington Post*, 9 July.

Weiner, R. and Helderman, R. 2020. States are wrestling on their own with how to expand testing, with little guidance from the Trump administration, *Washington Post*, 10 June.

Welch, C. B. 2003. Colonial violence and the rhetoric of evasion: Tocqueville on Algeria, *Political Theory*, 31, 2, 235–64.

Wellings, B. 2020. Brexit, nationalism, and disintegration in the European Union and the United Kingdom, *Journal of Contemporary European Studies*, 29, 3: 322–34.

Wertheim, S. 2021. Delusions of dominance: Biden can't restore American primacy—and shouldn't try, *Foreign Affairs*, 25 January.

Wheare, K. C. 1963. *Federal Government*, 4th ed. London: Oxford University Press.

Wheatley, J. 2022. Poorest countries face $11bn surge in debt repayments, *Financial Times*, 17 January.

Whelan, R. 2018. Why are people fleeing Central America? A new breed of gangs is taking over, *Wall Street Journal*, 2 November.

White, J. 2022. The de-institutionalisation of power beyond the state, *European Journal of International Relations*, 28, 1: 187–208.

Whitney, M. 2011. The hidden state financial crisis, *Wall Street Journal*, 18 May.

Williams, P. J. 2018. Bad blood, *Times Literary Supplement*, 17 July.

Wimmer, A. 2004. Introduction: Facing ethnic conflicts, in A. Wimmer et al. (eds.), *Facing Ethnic Conflicts: Toward a New Realism*. Lanham, MD: Rowman & Littlefield.

Wimmer, A. and Min, B. 2006. From empire to nation-state: Explaining wars in the modern world, 1816–2001, *American Sociological Review*, 71, 6: 867–97.

Wimmer, A. et al. (eds.) 2004. *Facing Ethnic Conflicts: Toward a New Realism*. Lanham, MD: Rowman & Littlefield.

Winecoff, W. K. 2020. "The persistent myth of lost hegemony" revisited: Structural power as a complex network phenomenon, *European Journal of International Relations*, 26, S1: 209–52.

Winkler, A. 2018. *We the Corporations: How American Businesses Won Their Civil Rights*. New York: Liveright.

Wintour, P. 2022. Putin thought Ukraine was a missile to NATO. It may be a boomerang, *Guardian*, 15 April.

Witt, J. F. 2020. *American Contagions: Epidemics and the Law from Smallpox to COVID-19*. New Haven: Yale University Press.

Witte, G. et al. 2021. In the shadow of its exceptionalism, America fails to invest in the basics, *Washington Post*, 13 March.

Wodtke, G. T. 2016. Social class and income inequality in the United States: Ownership, authority, and personal income distribution from 1980 to 2010, *American Journal of Sociology*, 121, 5: 1375–1415.

Wolf, E. 1982. *Europe and the People Without History*. Berkeley: University of California Press.

Wolf, M. 2015. Divorce Greece in haste, repent at leisure, *Financial Times*, 17 June.

———. 2021a. Containing China is not a feasible option, *Financial Times*, 2 February.

———. 2021b. The economic recovery masks a global divide, *Financial Times*, 21 April.

———. 2021c. How can we share our divided world?, *Financial Times*, 2 November.

Wolff, L. 1994. *Inventing Eastern Europe: The Map of Civilization on the Mind of the Enlightenment*. Stanford, CA: Stanford University Press.

Wong, A. 2021. How not to win allies and influence geopolitics, *Foreign Affairs*, May/June: 44–53.

Wong, C. H. 2021. Is China's Communist Party still communist?, *Wall Street Journal*, 30 June.

Wong, C. H. and Zhai, K. 2021. How Xi Jinping is rewriting China's history to put himself at the center, *Wall Street Journal*, 17 November.

Wood, D. 2021. Pro-Trump counties now have far higher COVID death rates. Misinformation is to blame, NPR, 5 December.

Wood, E. M. 2003. *Empire of Capital*. London: Verso.

Wood, T. 2022. The Ukrainian matrix, *New Left Review*, 133/134: 41–64.

Woodley, D. 2015. *Globalization and Capitalist Geopolitics: Sovereignty and State Power in a Multipolar World*. London: Routledge.

Woodside, A. 1998. The Asia-Pacific idea as a mobilization myth, in A. Dirlik (ed.), *What Is in a Rim?: Critical Perspectives on the Pacific Region Idea*, 2nd ed. Lanham, MD: Rowman & Littlefield.

———. 2006. *Lost Modernities: China, Vietnam, Korea, and the Hazards of World History*. Cambridge, MA: Harvard University Press.

Woon, C. Y. 2018. China's contingencies: Critical geopolitics, Chinese exceptionalism and the uses of history, *Geopolitics*, 23, 1: 67–95.

Wright, T. and Campbell, K. 2020. The coronavirus is exposing the limits of populism, *Atlantic*, 4 March.

Wyatt, E. 2011. S.E.C. faults credit raters, but doesn't name them, *New York Times*, 30 September.

Xu, Y. and Bahgat, G. (eds.) 2011. *The Political Economy of Sovereign Wealth Funds*. New York: Palgrave Macmillan.

Yan X. 2011. Xunzi's thoughts on international politics and their implications, in W. A. Callahan and E. Barabantseva (eds.), *China Orders the World: Normative Soft Power and Foreign Policy*. Baltimore: Johns Hopkins University Press.

———. 2014. From keeping a low profile to striving for achievement, *Chinese Journal of International Politics*, 7, 2: 153–84.

———. 2018. Trump can't start a Cold War with China, even if he wants to, *Washington Post*, February 6.

Yates, J. and Murphy, C. N. 2019. *Engineering Rules: Global Standard Setting since 1880.* Baltimore: Johns Hopkins University Press.

Ye, M. 2015. China and Competing Cooperation in Asia-Pacific: TPP, RCEP, and the New Silk Road, *Asian Security*, 11, 3, 206–24.

Ye, Z. and Long, Q. 2013. *Huaxia zhuyi* [*China-ism: The Grand Wisdom of the 500-Years China System*]. Beijing: Renmin.

Zacarés, J. M. 2021. Euphoria of the rentier?, *New Left Review*, 129: 47–68.

Zafesova, A. 2022. Le madri dei soldati, *La Stampa*, 10 March.

Zakaria, F. 2021. Xi's China can't seem to stop scoring own goals, *Washington Post*, 27 May.

———. 2022. Russia is the last multinational empire, fighting to keep its colonies, *Washington Post*, 31 March.

Zarrow, P. 2012. *After Empire: The Conceptual Transformation of the Chinese State, 1885–1924*. Stanford: Stanford University Press.

Zhang, F. 2015. Confucian foreign policy traditions in Chinese history, *Chinese Journal of International Politics*, 8, 2: 197–218.

Zhang, Q. 2016. Bureaucratic politics and Chinese foreign policy-making, *Chinese Journal of International Politics*, 9, 4: 435–58.

Zhang, Y. and Kristensen, P. M. 2017. The curious case of "schools" of IR: From the sociology to the geopolitics of knowledge, *Chinese Journal of International Politics*, 10, 4: 429–54.

Zhao T. 2005. *Tianxia tixi: Shijie zhidu zhexue daolun* [*The Tianxia System: An Introduction to the Philosophy of a World Institution*]. Nanjing: Jiangsu jiaoyu chubanshe.

———. 2011. Rethinking empire from the Chinese concept "All-under-Heaven" (Tianxia, 天下), in W. A. Callahan and E. Barabantseva (eds.), *China Orders the World: Normative Soft Power and Foreign Policy.* Baltimore: Johns Hopkins University Press.

———. 2018. Trump sees the world as a battlefield. This Chinese view offers an alternative, *Washington Post*, February 7.

Zhu, X. 2009. The influence of think tanks in the Chinese policy process: Different ways and mechanisms, *Asian Survey*, 49, 2: 333–57.

Zielonka, J. 2014. *Is the EU Doomed?* Cambridge: Polity.

Žižek, S. 2005. Against human rights, *New Left Review*, 34: 115–31.

Zucman, G. 2015. *The Hidden Wealth of Nations: The Scourge of Tax Havens*. Chicago: University of Chicago Press.

Zürn, M. 2018. *A Theory of Global Governance: Authority, Legitimacy, and Contestation.* Oxford: Oxford University Press.

Index

Page numbers in italics indicate figures.

Afghanistan, 5–6, 45, 67, 166
agglomeration economies, 34, 108–9, 114
Agnew, John, 11
Albania and Albanians, 64, 68
Alexander the Great, 7–8
Amazon, 9, 14
antitrust policies, 9, 17, 126, 158
Apple, 1, 18
Arendt, Hannah, 166
Armenia, 66
Asia, 66, 80, 116; Asia-Pacific region, 97; East Asia, 12, 90, 99, 109; South Asia, 25; Southeast Asia, 52, 58, 67, 68, 98, 166
asylees, 72, 73, 75, 81, 86
asylum seekers, 72, 73, 79, 81, 83, 87
atavism, 4, 57, 61–62, 65
Australia, 77, 117, 127, 133
Austrian Empire, 64
autarky, 16, 24, 25–26, 28, 32
Axilrod, Stephen, 143

balance-of-payment deficits, 29, 48
balance-of-power regimes, 27, 99
Balkans and balkanization, 58, 61, 84; describing and defining, 57, 67–68; Balkan analogies, 62, 63–66; Macedonian syndrome and, 60, 69–70
Bank for International Settlements, 37
bank-held debt, 152, *153*
Bannon, Steve, 128, 130
Barr, William, 122–23
Basel Committee on Banking Supervision, 144
Beers, David, 143
Belgium, *153*
Biden, Joe, 73, 129, 168
Bild (periodical), 150
Bitcoin, 14
Blouet, Brian, 24
bonds, 32, 125, 141, 152, 155; credit rating-agencies and, 35, 139–40; foreign investment in, 101, 130; regional government bonds, 37, 117; sovereign bonds, 21, 108, 109–10, 138, 140, 145–46, 151; US federal bonds, downgrade of, 142–43
Border Patrol (US), 80, 85
Bradford, Anu, 20
Brazil, 30, 33
Bretton Woods: Bretton Woods Agreement, 29, 45; Bretton Woods currency system, 13, 48; Bretton Woods Era, 139
Brexit, 1, 32, 116, 118–19, 168
Britain, 24, 33, 42, 64, 107, 110, *115*, 126, *154*, *161*; British banks, 36, 109; British colonial system, 11, 49; British-dominated globalism, disruption of, 27,

28; British Empire, 43, 51; as a dominant power, 9, 75; EU, leaving, 1, 32, 116, 118–19, 168; in Eurozone crisis, 152, 153, 157; as first international state, 12; hegemony, commitment to, 44; London, tension with rest of UK, 113–14; national spending, 111, 160; neoliberalism, turning to, 159; pandemic response, 125
British East India Company, 18
Brzezinski, Zbigniew, 58
Buchanan, Pat, 86
Bulgaria, 64
Burma Law, 125
Bush, George W., 45, 46, 59, 69, 83
Büthe, Tim, 36, 144

Callahan, William, 90, 91, 96
Canada, 32, 50, 77, 116, 143
Carlson, Allen, 100
Cayman Islands, 33, 36
Centers for Disease Control and Prevention (CDC), 122, 134
Central America, 60, 76, 84, 88; migration from, 73, 75, 80, 81–82, 85; as unequal border partner with US, 74, 78
Chamberlain, Neville, 56, 59
Chambers, John, 143
China, 18, 29, 33, 109, 154, 160, *161*, 167; 1949 Revolution, 101, 102; 2008 financial crisis, responding to, 151, 153; Chinese exceptionalism, 91, 98, 99; credit-rating industry of, 141, 146; devolution in, 116, 117; globalization, economic accommodation under, 26, 30; hidden geopolitics of, 95–96; international relations narratives, 91–92, 94, 101–4; Marxist-Leninist thought in, 100, 103; One-Belt-One-Road infrastructure, 15, 90, 98; pandemic response, 90, 106, 124, 129, 166; rise of, 12, 13, 14, 16, 21, 32, 42, 89, 100, 104; rivalry with world powers, 11, 93; Taiwan, territorial dispute with, 3; US-China relations, 2, 19, 45, 52, 56, 128, 135; US dollar, Chinese currency pegged to, 48; world politics, Chinese narratives on, 96–100
China Dream (Liu), 99
Chinese Exclusion Act (1882), 85, 94
Clinton, Bill, 68, 70
Clinton, Hillary, 86, 130
Cold War, 2, 25, 34, 53, 55, 65, 101, 169; American hegemony after end of, 43, 45; containment strategies and, 28, 56, 63; geopolitical order before and after, 4, 11, 46, 77; globalization as associated with, 12, 13; trade and investment during, 24
colonialism, 5, 8, 9, 12, 43, 47, 63, 80; British colonial system, 11, 49; colonial history as incapacitating, 23, 33–34; European colonial empires, 8, 27, 52; postcolonial approaches, 34, 95, 98; settler-colonial societies, 76, 77
Colonial Pipeline ransomware attack, 6
Concert of Europe-British Geopolitical Order, 11
Confucianism, 92, 96, 98, 99, 100, 103
Congress of Vienna, 11
consociationalism, 119
containment, 24, 28, 63, 64, 101, 127
Corbridge, Stuart, 11
COVID-19 pandemic, 1, 11, 90, 106, *107*, 116, 119, 140, 169; blame for pandemic, 103, 166; Eurozone responses, 149, 162–63; US response to, 13, 19, 21, 41, 120, 122–24, 125, 133, 134, 136; vaccine nationalism in relation to, 16–17
Cowen, Deborah, 30
credit rating agencies (CRAs), 7, 37, 112; Big Three agencies, 35, 37, 111, 138, 140–45, 165; privatized authority of, 13, *36*, 146–47; sovereign debt, as rating, 21, 110, 139, 140–41
creeping liberalization, 159–60
Croatia, 64, 150
Cuba, 50, 53, 79
Cumings, Bruce, 98

Davies, Howard, 116
debt, public, 109, 152–53
Deutsche Bank, 109, 156
devolution, 108, 111, 113, 116–19, 124–25
Dizard, John, 150
Dodd-Frank Act, 143
Dolar, Mladen, 66
domesticating the exotic, 60
Draghi, Mario, 157
Drug Enforcement Administration (DEA), 78
"Dutch disease," 57, 114

Economist (periodical), 68, 123
Ellis, Mark, 62
El Salvador, 78, 79
ethnic conflict, 57, 66, 67
Eurasia, xi, 42, 58

European Central Bank (ECB), 150, 151, 162; bank-held debt owed to, 152, *153*; credit-rating agencies, affected by, 35–36; German model, policy paradigm derived from, 154, 156, 157
Europe and the People Without History (Wolf), 94
European Union (EU), 11, 15, 21, 34, 36, 48, 117; Britain as leaving, 1, 32, 116, 118–19, 168; Brussels effect and, 20; German policy model, 148–49; as a supranational authority, 13, 19, 25, 33; transnational organizations, stance toward, 35
Eurozone crisis, 21, 36, 109, 139, 148, 165; analyzing the Eurozone crisis, 152–56; credit rating agencies and, 35, 138, 146; Germany, role in, 150–51, 152–53, 157–59, 160–61; popular accounts of, 149–51; territorial mismatch thesis, applying to, 162–63
exchange rate, 2, 25, 29–30, 36
expropriation of land, 38, 54, 147

far-right politics, 85
federalism, 41, 113; anti-federalism, 121–22, 124, 131–33, 134, 135–36; breakdown and dysfunction of, 14, 33; dualism *vs.* polyphony in federal governance, 124–27; fashion for federalism, 116–17
Federalist Society, 123, 131
Federal Reserve, 29, 48
Federal Trade Commission (FTC), 36, 144
financial crisis (2007-2008), 13, 14, 19, 35, 107, 111, 117, 122, 165, 169; austerity measures as a response to, 112, 118; credit-rating agencies, role in, 38, 138, *142*, 146; empirical trends enhanced by, 113; geography of the crisis, 108–10; global financial system shakeup during, 119; highly rated products, implosion of, 141; neoliberal capitalism as triggering, 149; rich countries most affected by, 106; roots of crisis, flawed assumptions of, 154–56; subprime mortgage crisis, as brought on by, 30, 152; territorial regulation of financial products during, 127. *See also* Eurozone crisis
Financial Times (periodical), 142, 150
Finland, 63
Finlandization, 57, 61
fiscal decentralization, 117
Fisher, Charles, 68
Fitch Ratings, 35, 138, 141, 143
Fordism, 45
Forest Stewardship Council (FSC), *36*, 144
Fox News, 86
France, 9, 34, 63, 64, 92, 126, 141, 160, *161*; AAA rating, downgrade of, 139, 143; dirigiste model of capitalism, 156; in Eurozone economy, 152–53
Freud, Sigmund, 66
Friedman, Thomas, 31
Frug, Gerald, 126
futility thesis, 62

Ganesh, Janen, 131
Garrett, Geoffrey, 117
General Agreement on Tariffs and Trade (GATT), 28–29
geographical analogies, 56–57, 58–63. *See also* Balkans and balkanization
geography of power, 3, 42, 55
Geopolitical Order of Inter-Imperial Rivalry, 11
geopolitics: describing and defining, 3–7; classical geopolitics, 23, 24, 41–42, 90; Cold War geopolitical order, 11, 46; conventional geopolitics, 7, 38, 43, 102, 138; credit rating agencies, geopolitical consequences from, 145–46; critical geopolitics, 60–61; first geopolitical order in nineteenth century, 12; geopolitics of development, 23, 26, 31–34; geopolitics of globalization, 17–20, 23, 26, 27–31; geopolitics of global regulation, 23, 34–37; globalization *vs.* geopolitics, 24–27. *See also* global geopolitics; hidden geopolitics
geopolitik posture, 92, 96, 99
Germany, 11, 60, 84, 99, 109, 114, 116, 118, 163; as a dominant power, 9, 25, 27; Eurozone crisis and, 150–51, 152–53, 157–59, 160–61; German model of fiscal practice, 148–49, 154–56, 157, 159, 162, 163; Nazi regime, 25, 59, 96, 157; pandemic response, 124, 127, 133
Giavazzi, Francesco, 150
Giles, Chris, 150
global geopolitics, 13, 34, 55, 75, 77, 169; Big Three credit-rating agencies and, 138, 145; China's rise within, 21, 42; geographical labels, acting on, 57–58; Global Geopolitical Order, 11, 17, 46–48
Google, 1, 6, 9, 67–68, 69

governmentality, 17
Gramsci, Antonio, 7
Great Depression, 158
Great Powers, 10, 42, 56, 58, 93, 102; China as a Great Power, 89, 96; domination, as pursuing, 4, 7; Great Power politics, 3, 70; hegemony developing from values of, 49, 55; invasions and interventions by, 9, 166; near abroad, foreign policy focus on, 57; United States as a Great Power, 40, 42, 55
Greece, 64, 149, 156; ancient Greece, 42, 65; in Eurozone crisis, 152, 153–54, 155; national economy of, 148, 150
gross domestic product (GDP), 27, 110, 140, 152–53, 154, *161*, 168
Grossräumen (regional spheres), 25
Guatemala, 53, 78, 84
Guzzini, Stefano, 4–5

Haitian refugees, 73, 79, 81
Hall, Peter A., 156
Hamilton, Alexander, 50, 121, 131
Hay, John, 94
Hegel, Georg Wilhelm, 63, 65
hegemony, 7, 12, 90, 104, 140; China, hegemonic succession of, 89; empire *vs.* hegemony, 43–45; hegemonic stability theory, 100; regional hegemons, 11, 25, 26; US hegemony, 46, 48, 49–55, 75, 77
hidden geopolitics, 3, 6, 20, 114, 119; China's hidden geopolitics, 95–96; consequences for, 37–38; features of, 167–69; hidden geopolitics as not new, 7–17; non-state actors, role in, 138, 146–47; pandemic as exposing to view, 121; tragedy of the nation-state and, 166
high geopolitics, 35, 138
Hirschman, Albert O., 62
Hitler, Adolf, 56, 59
Hobbes, Thomas, 7
Honduras, 78–79, 81, 84
Hong Kong, 32, 103, 109
HSBC (Hongkong and Shanghai Banking Corporation Limited), 1, 109
Hughes, Christopher, 99
Hungary, 84, 130, 168
Hussein, Saddam, 59

Illegal Immigration Reform and Immigrant Responsibility Act (IIRIRA), 79
immigration, 69, 79, 84, 113, 125, 135, 167; balkanization analogy, applying to US immigration, 62; globalization crisis and, 10, 16; immigration lawyers, lack of access to, 80; Muslim migrant ban, 82, 83; US immigration debate, 85–87; US immigration practice, change in, 72–75
Immigration Act (1924), 85
Immigration and Customs Agents (ICE), 83
India, 33, 66, 67, 92, 130, 168
industrial bourgeoisie, 51, 160
Ingraham, Laura, 86
An Inquiry into the Nature and Causes of the Wealth of Nations (Smith), 50
inter-imperial rivalry, 2, 28, 35, 39; epoch of, 4, 11, 16, 24, 42; geopolitics as displacing, 23, 56, 169; in second political order, 11, 12
International Accounting Standards Board (IASB), *36*, 144
International Electrotechnical Commission (IEC), *36*, 144
International Labour Organization (ILO), 17, *36*
International Monetary Fund (IMF), 13, 17, *36*, 144, 168; bank-held debt and money owed to, 152; credit-rating agencies and, 35, 138; German political leaders, concordance with, 148
international relations theory (IR theory), 92, 93, 95–96, 100, 102, 104
Iran, 53, 68, 69
Iraq, 28, 56, 67, 68, 69, 166
Iraq War, 43, 59–60
Ireland, 33, 57, 63, 114, 116, 119, 152, 153, 155
irredentism, 57, 67
Italy, 27, 116, 117, 126, 156, 158; in Eurozone economy, 152, *153*, 155, 162; exports as a percent of GDP, *161*; national populism in, 15

Jameson, Fredric, 68
Japan, 27, 48, 99, 153, *154*, *161*; car production of, 30, 45; in inter-imperial rivalry, 11, 12; as a world power, 9, 32, 52, 96, 167
Jefferson, Thomas, 50
Jessop, B., 156
Judicial Watch, 86
junk rating, 139
just-in-time (JIT) system, 30

Kashmir, 67
Katsikas, Dimitrios, 145
Kennedy, David, 20
Kennedy, John F., 55
Keynes, John Maynard, 50
Keynesianism, 132, 157, 159
Kissinger, Henry, 4
Kolomoisky, Ihor, viii, ix
Korematsu decision (1944), 83
Krasner, Stephen D., 9
Kyoto Protocol, *36*, 144

Lamp, Nicolas, x–xi
land-and-sea geopolitics, 6
land- *vs.* sea-powers, 41–43, 55
Larrabee, F. S., 67
League of Nations, 76
Lex Mercatoria system, 114
Long Depression, 52
low geopolitics, 26–27, 35

Ma, Jack, 102
Macedonian syndrome, 57, 60, 61, 66–68, 69–70
MacFarquhar, Roderick, 103
Machiavelli, Niccolò, 7
Mackinder, Halford, 38
macroeconomics, 106, 108
Madison, James, 49–50, 131
Malaysia, 32, 33
Mann, Michael, 127
Mao Zedong, 103
Mariel Boatlift, 79
marketplace society, 45, 51, 140; describing and defining, 40; American exceptionalism and, 75; globalization as an outcome of, 49, 53, 76
Marx and Marxism, 40, 61, 103
Mattli, Walter, 36, 144
Maxwell, Angie, 132
McCoy, Alfred W., 4, 5
Mexico, 2, 33, 75; refugee panic of 2018 and, 80–82, 84, 86; Trump antagonism towards Mexicans, 128, 131; US-Mexico border, 21, 72–75, 78–80, 87–88, 125
Microsoft, 14, *36*, 144
Miller, Stephen, 83
Min, Brian, 67
Modi, Narendra, 130, 168
Montesquieu, 7–8, 65
Moody, John, 140
Moody's Investors Service, 35, 141, 142, 143
mortgage-backed securities, 109, 140, 143
multitier governance, 117, 120, 124, 125–26, 133
Münchau, Wolfgang, 163
Munich syndrome, 56
Myanmar, 125

narcotics trafficking, 79
national-populism, 15, 113; anti-government sentiment and, 21; "left behind" regions as attracted to, 168; Trump and, 121, 124, 127–31, 134, 136
nation-statehood, 10, 47, 64, 78; Afghanistan as a nation-state, 5–6; Balkans model, 65–66, 69; tragedy of the nation-state, 166
Nazism, 4, 25, 60, 96, 150, 157, 158
neoliberalism, 18, 110, 132, 156, 163; Keynesianism, turning away from, 159; low corporate tax rates, favoring, 146; neoliberal capitalism, 90, 148, 149
Netherlands, 33, 75, 116, *153*
New Deal, 12, 50, 113, 119, 122
Nicaragua, 53, 78
Nixon, Richard, 4, 29, 48, 132
The Nomos of the Earth (Schmitt), 25
non-majoritarian regulators (NMRs), 17
North American Free Trade Agreement (NAFTA), 19, 33
North Atlantic Treaty Organization (NATO), 16, 68
Northern Ireland, 118–19
North Korea, xii, 32

Obama, Barack, 128, 134
oligarchs, viii, 56
open borders, 19, 53, 76–77, 82
Open Door policy, 94
Orbán, Viktor, 130, 168
Ordnungspolitik (ordering policies), 149; describing and defining, 157–59; Eurozone management, as narrative guiding, 148, 162–63; variegated capitalism, limits of *Ordnungspolitik* under, 159–61
ordoliberalism, 157–58, 160
Orientalism, 92, 96, 98, 100
Ottoman Empire, 64–65, 66

Pacific Rim, 92, 96, 97–98
Perdiendo el Norte (film), 150
Philadelphian system of government, 121

Pinker, Steven, 59
polyphony, 125, 127, 133, 136, 163
Poor, Henry, 140
Portugal, 42, 43, 152
Principles of Peaceful Coexistence, 103–4
Putin, Vladimir, 16, 60, 130, 168

Qin Yaqing, 100

Raumhoheit (spatial supremacy), 25
Reagan, Ronald, 131, 132
refugee panic of 2018, 75, 80–85, 86–87, 88
Ritter, Gerhard A., 159
Roberts, Alasdair, 37
Roberts, Anthea, x–xi
Rodden, Jonathan, 117
Rostow, Walt W., 55
Rousseau, Jean-Jacques, 65
Rozman, Gilbert, 100
Russia, 18, 26, 44, 56, 92, 130, 168; as a dominant power, 9, 11, 25, 166; Russian Empire, 64, 65; Ukraine, invasions of, 16, 28, 57, 60, 101, 166, 169. *See also* Soviet Union

Sakellaropoulos, Spyros, 144
Sarkozy, Nicolas, 143
Schapiro, Robert A., 125–26, 133
Schmitt, Carl, 25–26, 38
Scotland, 33, 62, 118
Securities and Exchange Commission (SEC), 36, 143, 146
Serbia, 64, 68, 70
Sessions, Jeff, 83, 84
Shaxson, Nicholas, 116
Shields, Todd, 132
Shklovsky, Viktor, 61
Singapore, 32, 33, 109
sinicization, 100, 151
Slovenia, 64
Smith, Adam, 40, 50
social-market economy, 158, 159–60
social media, 7, 9, 20, 87
South Korea, 26, 32, 33
sovereign debt, 109, 138, 139, 140–41, 152
sovereignty, 8–10, 32, 144–45
Soviet Union, 11, 12, 55, 56, 60; autarky within territory of, 28, 32; Cold War with US, 34, 53, 101; collapse of, 33, 68; Communist Party and, 90, 103
Spain, 34, 126, 150; devolution of powers in, 116; in Eurozone crisis, 152, 153, 155; hegemony and, 43, 75
Spanish-American War, 44, 76
spatiale Bereich (spatial sphere of influence), 25
Staatslehre (theory of the state), 95
stagflation, 159
Standard and Poor's (S&P), 35, 138, 139, 141, 142, 143
Stark, Jürgen, 150
subprime mortgages, 30, 108, 109, 143, 152
Suez Canal container blockage, 6
supply-side stimulus, 132
Swann, Nikola, 143
Switzerland, 33, 57, 117, 152

Taiwan, 3, 30, 99
tax havens, 14, 26, 33, 36, 110, 116, 140
territorialized geopolitics, 7, 20
territorial mismatch thesis, 149
tianxia (all-under-heaven) concept, 98–99
Tjalve, Vibeke S., 5
Tom Sawyer Abroad (Twain), 112–13
transnational organizations, 35, 144, 146
Treisman, Daniel S., 117
Trump, Donald, 1, 13, 31, 88, 132, 168; child-separation policy, 72, 75, 83–84, 134; immigration as central to political campaign, 82, 86; as a national-populist, 124, 127–31; pandemic response, 14, 90, 120–21, 124, 129, 133–35, 136; refugees, viewing as a threat, 72–73, 75, 84–85; rhetorical dictatorial style, 122–23; withdrawal of administration from wider world, 14, 18–19
Turkey, 18, 58, 66
Turner, Frederick Jackson, 52, 76
Twain, Mark, 112–13

Ukraine, 16, 28, 57, 60, 101, 129, 169
unitary executive theory, 123
United States, 33, 35, 92, 111, 113, *151*, 165; balance of power, disrupting, 27–28; Cold War and, 2, 12, 13, 24, 77, 101; credit agencies and, 139–40, 141, 146; decline on economic and military fronts, 91; as a dominant power, 9, 11; economic globalization, as enabling, 23, 26, 38–39, 102; employment and income in, 107, 112, 114; Eurozone crisis and, 151, 152,

154, 157; exceptionalism concept, 49, 50, 75, 100, 126; hegemony of, 43–45, 46–48, 49–55, 140; home field advantage of businesses, 6, 15; immigration debate, 85–87; land- *vs.* sea-powers, perspective of, 41–43; legal norms, international modeling of, 30–31; Monroe Doctrine, 25, 76; pandemic response, 13, 19, 21, 41, 120, 122–24, 125, 133, 134, 136, 166; refugee panic of 2018, 80–85; S&P downgrade of long-term debt, 139, 141; subprime mortgage debacle, 108, 109, 152; territorial economy of, 167–68; US-China relations, 2, 19, 45, 52, 56, 98, 101, 104, 128, 135; US dollar, 10, 13, 29–30, 48, 139, 140; US International Relations theory, 94, 95, 100, 101; US-Mexico border, 21, 72–75, 78–80, 87–88, 125; world trade, providing main currency for, 29–30. *See also* federalism; Trump, Donald

Universal Declaration of Human Rights (1951), 79

variegated capitalism, 148, 156, 159–61, 162

Varoufakis, Yanis, 150

Vietnam War, 28, 30, 60

Voltaire, 7–8

Wang Yiwei, 100

War on Drugs, 78

Wedel, Janine, 35

Weiner, Myron, 66–67

Westphalia, 25, 100; Peace of Westphalia, 93; Treaty of Westphalia, 24–25; Westphalian sovereignty, 9, 103

white populism, 13, 75, 86, 128, 132

Wilson, Woodrow, 78

Wimmer, Andreas, 67

Wolf, Eric, 94

Wolf, Martin, 154

Wolff, Larry, 65

Wolf Totem (film), 99

Wood, Ellen, 46

World Bank, 35, *36*, 168

World Health Organization (WHO), 135, 138, 168

World Trade Organization (WTO), 13, 16, 17, 20, 138, 168

World War I, 4, 64, 66, 76, 113

World War II, 2, 28, 43, 55, 56, 60, 76, 107, 113, 150, 158

Wright, Richard, 62

Xi Jinping, 101, 102, 103, 104

Xunzi, 99, 100

Yan Xuetong, 99, 100, 103–4

Yugoslavia, 64, 65, 68, 118

zero-sum conflicts, 93, 102, 166

zero-tolerance policy, 83, 84

Zhou Tingyang, 99, 103–4

Žižek, Slavoj, 66

About the Author

John Agnew is Distinguished Professor of Geography at the University of California, Los Angeles. A native of Cumbria in England, he has taught at a number of US, Canadian, and European universities. A Fellow of the British Academy, in 2019 he received the Vautrin Lud Prize, the highest academic award for the field of geography, and in 2022 he was elected to the American Academy of Arts & Sciences. As well as being the founding editor of *Territory, Politics, Governance*, he is on numerous editorial boards including the *Review of International Political Economy*, *International Political Sociology*, and the *European Journal of International Relations*. For 2008–2009 he was president of the American Association of Geographers and he is currently president of the Regional Studies Association. He is the author of numerous books including *Hegemony: The New Shape of Global Power* (2005), *Globalization and Sovereignty: Beyond the Territorial Trap* (2017), and *Mapping Populism: Taking Politics to the People* (with M. Shin 2019).